TO
WORK
AND
TO
WED

TO WORK AND TO WED

FEMALE EMPLOYMENT, FEMINISM, AND THE GREAT DEPRESSION

LOIS SCHARF

Contributions in Women's Studies, Number 15

GREENWOOD PRESS
WESTPORT, CONNECTICUT · LONDON, ENGLAND

Library of Congress Cataloging in Publication Data

Scharf, Lois.
   To work and to wed.

   (Contributions in women's studies ; no. 15
ISSN 0147-104X)
   Bibliography: p.
   Includes index.
   1. Wives—Employment—United States—History.
2. Feminism—United States—History. 3. Sex
discrimination in employment—United States—
History. 4. Women—Employment—United States—
History. 5. Sex discrimination against women—
United States—History. I. Title. II. Series.
HD6095.S3   331.4'3'0973   79-52325
ISBN 0-313-21445-X

Library of Congress Catalog Card Number: 79-52325
ISBN: 0-313-21445-X
ISSN: 0147-104X

First published in 1980

Greenwood Press
A division of Congressional Information Service, Inc.
51 Riverside Avenue, Westport, Connecticut 06880

Printed in the United States of America

10 9 8 7 6 5 4 3 2 1

Contents

Preface

Few events in this nation's history have left a greater imprint on the private psyche or have had more influence on the direction of public policy than the Great Depression of the 1930s. Sociologists at the time explored the effects of unemployment and deprivation on workers and their families; historians since have examined the political, economic, and intellectual developments that marked the period; popular writers then and now have tried to describe the social landscape and convey some sense of the Depression's impact on those who lived through those incredible years. While I have no personal recollection of the Depression decade, for years, my parents and their contemporaries have tried to fill this gap in my experience and memory. Occasionally, they have even implied that my lack of personal knowledge somehow constituted a shortcoming somewhat akin to a character flaw. This attempt to research and re-create an aspect of life during the 1930s is an historical inquiry to which I bring a hint of compensation for some ill-defined guilt at having come of age after the economic tide had turned.

This singular fascination with the Depression would not have been translated into scholarship nor would the specific subject of this book have been selected were it not for a more recent development of major historical significance—the contempory woman's movement. Resumption of graduate studies, discovery of the missing dimension of the female experience from historical accounts, and the emergence of a feminist perspective occurred because of the ideological support of the new feminism and the intellectual stimulation of a flourishing sisterhood of scholars.

Every historian knows that the final monograph involves more than the selection of topic, whatever the circumstances. The acknowledgments that accompany publications are much more than academic rituals. Obligations are real and debts of gratitude deserve recounting. The staffs of the Schlesinger Library, Archives of Labor History, Library of Congress, and the National Archives were all extremely helpful. The librarians of the Government and Social Studies Division of the Cleveland Public Library searched for every volume requested and answered every question asked no matter how I must have taxed their patience. David D. Van Tassel first brought some order out of the murky chaos of my research and writing. My friends Susan Becker and Winnie Bolin researched neighboring fields and allowed me to benefit from their rich discoveries. Marian Morton, Donna Van Raaphorst, Mary Kay Howard, and Marion Siney encouraged, read, discussed, and critiqued. Marlene Carlson not only can type but can untangle convoluted sentences as well. And finally, to Victor, Gary, Laura, and David—who have not always completely understood the basic issues with which this study deals or the personal conflicts involved in its writing—a special expression of gratitude, just the same, because I love them very much.

L.S.

Introduction

With the winter of 1931 approaching, Chicago's commissioner of public welfare drove from Grant and Lincoln parks to the Chicago lakefront to verify reports that hundreds of homeless, unemployed women were sleeping in these public areas at night.[1] She learned about some of the more desperate situations in which jobless women found themselves during that bleak period. Not all women workers fared so badly. Even during periods of extreme dislocation, the event's impact on people vary; their behavior and reactions differ. This study attempts to describe some of the diverse experiences of women workers, especially married women, during the 1930s, and to assess the Depression's effect on patterns of female employment. The investigation began not with any knowledge of the extent of female unemployment like that uncovered by the Chicago official, but rather with two morsels of information: first, that women's status in professional occupations slipped during the 1930s; second, that working wives encountered widespread discrimination. These were the starting points from which to range, both topically and chronologically, over the variegated terrain of women's work.

The entrance of married women into the work place marked an important shift in the social and demographic composition of the female labor force. Like the changing female occupational structure, this development dated from the closing years of the nineteenth century. While recent surveys of working women have corrected an unfortunate oversight in U.S. social and economic history, most studies focus either on earlier nineteenth-century New England mill girls or on turn-of-the-century immigrant women laborers. This book begins with an overview of the economic forces, institutional needs and technological developments that stimulated the growth of new white-collar occupations which in turn attracted new categories of women into areas of gainful employment.

Married women were among the new "types" assuming economic roles outside their homes, and their gradual emergence as a factor in the work force during the early twentieth century leads to an examination of feminist ideology and rhetoric as well as to actual occupational trends. The central role assigned to work in the writings of Charlotte Perkins Gilman is well known to students of women's history, but the modified, more widely articulated subject of jobs for wives, which captured public attention during the 1920s, is less familiar. The individuals who advocated employment for married women did not constitute an organized movement with a consistent ideological focus, but their arguments contained positive features stressing the importance of female self-fulfillment and the need for elevated status. The debate that ensued over women's roles challenges the historical consensus that feminist consciousness dissipated in the aftermath of the suffrage victory because no comparable issue engaged widespread attention, because a younger generation of women was only interested in new-found moral and behavioral freedoms, or because social reformers and committed feminists preoccupied themselves with internecine struggles.[2]

The position of marriage and career advocates of the 1920s takes on special significance when the women who fulfilled their expectations, working wives, aroused public hostility and encountered employment constraints during the Depression. The leadership of a number of women's organizations—some of whom were bitter foes over a number of issues, especially the efficacy of protective legislation for working women—then united in defense of the workers under attack. But, over the course of the decade, the vocal defenders of married women workers and of working women generally discarded the more positive features of the earlier rationale. They surrendered to expedient arguments that may have corresponded more closely to actual economic structures and familial values but which undermined their feminist anxiety over women's economic status and right to gainful employment.

The deleterious effect of Depression-related pressure on feminist consciousness was duplicated in the sphere of women's occupational achievements. This latter development raises questions of periodization referable to women's history. As the study of women within conventionally conceived time spans attains greater sophistication, it becomes increasingly clear that the traditional characteristics of an era and generalizations about its impact on people are not always applicable to women.[3] The Depression decade is one clearly defined period, and, in broad terms, many working men and women shared economic disruption, deprivation, and even despair. The distinctions in experience between the sexes were differences between short-term occurrence and long-term impact. When prosperity returned, the occupational (and related educational) levels attained by women around 1930 had dissipated and were not recovered.[4] The present study suggests how and why these developments may have occurred as well as how working women and their concerned, well-meaning vocational advisors reacted to economic and emotional adversity and insecurity, possibly contributing to deteriorating status. New Deal programs for women, be they beneficial or discriminatory, are also examined in this context since some programs were temporary and limited to the 1930s while others were lasting in their effects.

In addition, periodization involves the problem of distinguishing between those developments that were specifically related to the Depression decade and trends that predated and continued, which were accelerated or slowed by events of the 1930s. Changes in the female labor force, changes in the economic functions and material aspirations of the American family, and the ebb and flow of feminism and its relationship to women's employment—were and are continuous processes. Recurring themes such as heightened anxiety over the stability of the family and practices such as discrimination against married women workers were clearly present during the last half of the 1920s, that is, before the onset of the economic collapse. In these instances, the Depression exacerbated or reinforced existing attitudes and policies.

Many of the developments described in this study derive from census data which itself presents a number of difficulties. Enumerative inaccuracies, changing definitions of occupational classifications, and even the concept of employment itself place limitations on attempts to trace more than just the broad outlines of change. Descriptions of major trends are all that is attempted here. More sophisticated analyses and correlations among the variables of ethnicity, age, and geography are not attempted. Only the latter can be qualified to the extent that changing patterns of female employment as well as shifting family functions and values are essentially urban phenomena. A look at women's work and the quality of life on the farm lie outside the boundaries of this study, although, as one would expect, the women thus ignored constitute an ever diminishing proportion of those employed during the time period under investigation.[5]

Inconsistencies in the categorizing of census data also apply to the classifications of marital status. Prior to 1920, enumerators combined divorced, widowed, and separated women with single females. After that date, single women were counted separately. In 1940 a distinction was made between married women living with and those separated from their husbands. For comparison purposes, the total number of women living with husbands in 1940 is used in conjunction with total married women in previous years since, unless otherwise noted, "married" implies family structure in its most traditional sense.

A variety of conventional literary materials have been used to examine issues that decennial statistics do not address. No study of women workers can stray far from an examination of the complex constellation of values and attitudes that has swirled around the issue of female employment. As Robert Smuts has noted, it "involves two subjects which lie near the center of human emotions: work and the relationship between men and women."[6] From the late nineteenth century, social commentators reacted to increasing numbers of gainfully employed women with varied combinations of alarm, antagonism, and misconception. The "pin money" label emerged, embodying the supposition that young women worked only for extra luxuries. The catch phrase could be hurled at women by opponents to their employment, who believed that the public work place threatened assumed female physical, social, or moral attributes and that the desire for self-indulgent consumption was hardly a mitigating factor. Or the pin money theory could be used to justify the discrepancies in wage rates paid men and women since the latter, who supposedly worked only for "extras," needed less monetary compensation.

While reformers and advocates continuously stressed the economic need that underlay most female employment, the theory endured, while its more onerous implications became identified with the economic motivation of married women workers. Through the 1920s and increasingly during the Depression, defenders of working women, especially working wives, insisted that the earnings of women did not provide luxuries for themselves or their families but were the very means of individual and family survival. According to the apologists of working women, the women's "so-called pin money is often the family coupling pin, the only means of holding the family together."[7]

The distinction, however, between pin money and coupling pins was not always so clear. Social norms defining married women's roles remained inexorably static and contributed, in large measure, to the public hostility wives encountered when they worked during the 1930s. But even as the prescribed distribution of breadwinning and homemaking roles within the family persisted, other economic pressures and values were changing. During the depths of the Depression, the level of material wants and expectations of many American families indicated that coupling pins could be made of a variety of metals. The metal could even be expensive enough to require the gainful employment of a wife and mother, thereby creating conflicts and contradictions among familial functions, wants, and values. It is this counterpoint among the altering economic roles of women within the labor market and within their families, the traditional social attitudes toward women that resisted change, the potential mediating force of feminist ideology, and the ways in which these threads intersected during the 1930s, especially over the issue of married women workers, that provides the themes and underlying structure of this book.

TO
WORK
AND
TO
WED

chapter 1

Women's Work-Working Women, 1890-1920

The Chicago World's Fair of 1893 excited and astounded viewers. Among the exhibition's unique features was a separate building for the display of female achievements and the discussion of issues concerning the welfare and status of women. It was a response to what many Americans recognized, with varying degrees of approval or opposition, as the appearance of "a new woman" with greater education and interest in public affairs and occasionally with the ability and desire to earn her own living. She emerged during a decade when numerous political, economic, and cultural forces were unleashed, and if she did not actually toss her corset on the rubbish heap, numerous new activities indicated a decided loosening of the laces of constraint.[1]

Eighteen ninety was a banner year for the founding of several organizations that marked the new activism and broadening horizons of upper- and middle-class women. As the last decade of the nineteenth century opened, the splintered suffrage movement mended its schism and established the National American Women's Suffrage Association. With a narrow focus and a conservative ideology, and after thirty years of campaigns, parades, and intensive lobbying, enfranchisement was achieved. In 1890, sixty-one women's clubs responded to an invitation to a convention issued by Sorosis, a literary group in New York City, and the General Federation of Women's Clubs was born. Originally comprising groups primarily interested in sociability and the cultural improvement of their members, the federation soon admitted organizations also interested in social welfare and reform.[2]

The Consumers' League of New York City represented the new
social consciousness among some clubwomen. Founded in 1890 by
Josephine Shaw Lowell and quickly emulated in Philadelphia, Boston
and Chicago, the organization tried to arouse the sensibilities of American consumers to the abusive conditions to which working women
were exposed in the rapidly expanding American industrial economy.
First by selective buying, and then through legislation to regulate wages,
hours, and working conditions, the unified league helped focus attention on a large group of women whose lives were far removed from the
comfortable, leisure-class membership of literary societies, philanthropic
clubs, and reform organizations.[3]

The working women whose plight attracted the attention of the
Consumers' League were among the three million gainfully employed
females, sixteen years and older, counted by census enumerators in 1890.
Women in paid occcupations represented 16 percent of the total number
of women in that age group and accounted for 16.5 percent of the total
labor force. With the exception of immigrant wives in New England
and black married women in the South, working women in 1890 were
predominantly young, single, and relative newcomers to urban areas
from American farms and European towns and villages. Immigrants
sent the largest proportion of women into gainful occupations. Forty-
four percent of foreign-born women or native-born women of foreign
parentage were employed compared to only 10 percent of white, native-
born women of native-born parents and 23 percent of black women (in
nonagricultural jobs).[4]

The work these women performed was principally menial, unskilled,
or semi-skilled. Over 1.25 million, more than 40 percent of all working
women, were engaged in domestic and other personal service. An additional 20.3 percent were classified as mill and factory workers principally
in nondurable goods industries that manufactured textiles and garments
or processed food. Large numbers of women who were home laundresses
or seamstresses were not included in these figures, for the physical
separation of home from productive work was well established in the
popular imagination and in Census Bureau methodology. Less than 15
percent of working women were employed in professions or clerical
pursuits. The overwhelming majority of female participants in the
labor force was earning income at jobs where the function or product

was directly related to the kind of work women traditionally performed in the home.[5]

During the following thirty years, from 1890 to 1920, dramatic changes occurred in both the demographic profile and the occupational structure of the female labor force. By the time the Nineteenth Amendment was ratified, the ages, marital status, race, and nativity characteristics of working women had shifted perceptibly. While the National Consumers' League and reform-minded allies battled for protective legislation, increasingly large numbers of women found employment in occupations outside the scope of regulations that were concerned primarily with industrial conditions. Occupational redistribution began in the 1890s with growth in the established profession of teaching, the founding of the new professions of nursing, social work, and librarianship, and with the astonishingly rapid development of service jobs in the clerical and sales fields. Feminization of these areas also was quick and dramatic.

From the time of the public school reform movement during the second quarter of the nineteenth century, teaching had been the only occupation other than domestic service and factory work open to large numbers of young women. Prior to 1830, teaching was a male preserve, but the spread of the common school caused a greater demand than men could meet. Agriculture required their labor, and for those whose ambitions extended beyond the farm, trade and business enterprise provided more lucrative opportunities than did teaching. Educational reformers encouraged women's entrance into the field. They stressed women's supposed nurturing qualities and moral superiority along with the economies that resulted from young women's willingness to accept lower wage rates.[6]

Public schools and female teachers grew in numbers, but teacher training lagged behind. The normal school was conceived to meet the need for trained personnel, but not until after the Civil War, and particularly after 1890, were concerted efforts made to upgrade standards. By 1898, 167 normal schools had been established and integrated into state school systems, yet only Massachusetts required high school graduation as a condition for entrance. Students were, in effect, completing basic education, and because most courses of study lasted only two years, there was little time for extended training. Some progress resulted from establishing departments of education in colleges and universities, thereby applying higher entrance qualifications, and also from efforts to centralize control of standardized curriculum and certification requirements. By 1921, twenty-one states were granting all certificates within their jurisdictions, but training and scholarship expectations remained appallingly low. In 1907, only Indiana made high school graduation a prerequisite for certification, and fourteen years later less than a majority of states emulated this minimal criterion.[7]

While quantity of the demand for teachers prevailed over quality of the supply, female teachers continued to increase in numbers. From 1890 to 1920, the number of women employed as teachers doubled from approximately 238,000 to 584,000. During the same time period, the proportion of teachers who were female increased from 65.5 percent to 86 percent. Not only had public school teaching become feminized, but the field had also become the principal feminine profession. Two-thirds of all working women classified as professionals in 1920 were teachers.[8]

In spite of the lag in the development of professional standards, not all female teachers were poorly educated and trained. Teaching attracted large numbers of college-educated women. So many early graduates were concentrated in this field that the Association of Collegiate Alumnae (forerunner of the American Association of University Women [AAUW]) created a standing committee in 1910 to examine vocational opportunities outside teaching. They published a pamphlet detailing their findings, but their efforts were largely futile.[9] Surveys of employed women who had matriculated at colleges and universities revealed that more than two-thirds were engaged in public school teaching.[10] Studies also revealed that growing numbers of female graduates with advanced degrees were employed as teachers in institutions of higher education. But, like women in the public schools whose ranks thinned at the higher grade levels and in administrative positions, women teaching in colleges and universities were most numerous in the lower academic ranks.[11]

Although teaching remained the predominant pursuit of professional women, new service areas, which developed to meet the needs of an increasingly urbanized, impersonal society, also offered opportunities for professional employment. Nursing was one example. Distressed by their Civil War experiences and aware of schools founded by Florence Nightingale, American women led efforts to establish nursing schools to meet the needs of patient care in growing numbers of hospitals.

Efforts by female reformers in Boston brought about the founding of the Massachusetts General Hospital Training School for Nurses in the 1870s. The women revealed an additional motive: they admitted they were searching for new female-employing occupations.

By 1890, thirty-five schools, which had graduated 471 nurses, had been established, almost all of them under the control of hospitals. The number of schools increased to 432 during the following decade, but their graduates had hardly attained professional stature or public respect for their abilities, which often amounted to little more than keeping patients and wards clean. During the Spanish American War, the government turned to the Daughters of the American Revolution rather than the Nurses Associated Alumnae to provide needed nurses. Census enumerators counted over 11,000 trained nurses in their 1900 tabulation, but they included them with midwives and classified them under domestic service. The listing was not entirely unjustified. Nursing education meant, at most, two years of hospital ward work with little formal instruction. The graduate then was engaged in private duty nursing in patients' homes, which usually involved more housekeeping than medical care.

Efforts to control the disorganized growth of nursing schools, to improve and standardize training, and to gain state control of curriculum and licensure spurred the founding of the American Nursing Association (ANA) in 1911, and the National League of Nursing Education the following year. The efforts of the organizations to establish a thirty-six month course of study and a maximum work week of sixty-three hours met constant opposition from private hospitals. The institutions were more interested in providing student nurses with a minimum of training in exchange for a maximum of service. Schools of nursing, affiliated with university hospitals, helped to regularize standards of admission and study, but these schools suffered from a chronic lack of financial support. An independent survey and report completed in 1923, *Nursing and Nursing Education,* scored the lag in training and practice. The authors recommended that the positions of head nurse and director of the nursing school be separated, thus indicating the administrative tie between low-cost patient care and low-quality training.[12]

The persistent shortcomings of the nursing profession, however, failed to deter large numbers of women from entering the field. The number of trained nurses jumped from 11,119 in 1900, to 76,500 in

1910, when they were listed under professional occupations. And the 1910 figure almost doubled during the following decade. Nurses constituted 11 percent of all professional women in 1910; 14.5 percent in 1920. Unlike teaching, where men were a diminishing but still visible proportion of those employed, nurses were and have remained virtually all female.[13]

Whereas teaching had engaged women prior to the Civil War and nursing had always engaged women in their homes before its identification with a public institution, social work was a creation of industrial, urbanized society. As social dislocation undermined the ability of families and small-scale communities to meet the needs of their disadvantaged members, the charity organization movement developed to fill the vacuum. Begun in the 1880s, the movement quickly relinquished its concern over civic and community problems to settlement house workers and concentrated on the relief and rehabilitation of individual families. The transformation of the American Association for Organized Charity into the Family Welfare Association of America signaled this shift in method and philosophy.

This change in emphasis was accompanied by the need for better trained people to serve as links between the charitable organization and the charity recipient. Originally, the needs of individual families had been determined and the charity dispensed by friendly visitors, women who worked as volunteers. As agencies sought more sound, scientific theories and procedures of investigation, diagnosis, and treatment, formal training became necessary. As early as 1898, the New York School of Social Work gave short courses, and by 1910 it offered a two-year study program. The Chicago School of Civics and Philanthropy, affiliated with the University of Chicago, represented the first university sponsorship of social work education.[14]

As the character of social work emerged and the numbers of workers increased, organizations were founded. By 1921, the American Association of Social Workers, the American Association of Medical Social Workers, and the American Association of Professional Social Work were firmly established. The latter was particularly concerned with the curriculum in training programs and with the standards for membership in the organization. These programs remained varied, but they all emphasized casework approaches and practical field experience at the expense of generalized, theoretical education in the classroom. The close affiliation between educational institutions and local social agencies and the need of these agencies to secure the services of caseworkers worked at cross-purposes with the didactic needs of students. The similarity with the difficulties encountered by nursing educators was recognized in 1915 when Abraham Flexner, in delivering his critique of the developing field of social work, described the areas in which it failed to meet the criteria of a true profession. Social work, according to Flexner, existed in a twilight zone, as did the field of nursing.[15]

Whatever its professional shortcomings, the new vocational area received census recognition in 1910 when members were included in a new occupational classification: religious, charity, and welfare workers. In that year, almost 16,000 were counted, of whom about 9,000 or 56 percent, were women. Ten years later the number had more than doubled, and women comprised 66 percent of the total.[16] Although the profession was hardly so feminized as nursing, like the schoolteacher, the caseworker was identified in professional literature with a feminine pronoun.

Librarianship offered employment to only half the number of women listed as charity and welfare workers in 1920. Librarianship had struggled through the now familiar process of professionalization during the same period and quickly became identified as women's work. Dusting, preserving, and recopying "is work which suits a woman better than a man. . . . Women would not feel humiliated by serving, by playing in the library the part they play at home."[17] In rhetoric reminiscent of statements used in the recruitment of female teachers, Justin Winsor of the Boston Public Library, in an 1877 report, emphasized the social and economic advantages of having female librarians: "They soften our atmosphere, they lighten our labour, they are equal to our work, and for the money they cost they are infinitely better than equivalent salaries will produce of the other sex."[18]

A decade later, the establishment of the School of Library Economy at Columbia University, over the objections of faculty and trustees, represented a partial victory for formal training over haphazard apprenticeship. The number of schools grew, and in 1915 the Association of American Library Schools organized to standardize courses and criteria for accreditation. Those goals remained elusive. A critical report of 1923 recommended that there should be a full-time faculty chosen for ability, concentration on courses emphasizing professional rather than clerical content, and the establishment of a national examining board. The 13,500 women listed in the 1920 census as librarians (more than twice the number counted in 1910) had discovered a new area of employment. They represented 88 percent of all enumerated librarians, but this newly feminized field barely merited the professional status census compilers accorded it.[19]

By 1920, teaching, nursing, social work, and librarianship were still struggling to achieve true professional stature. Their associations and professionally conscious individuals worked diligently to upgrade the training, performance, and remuneration of the worker and to define the nature of their work. But attempts to improve the quality of the workers' performance constantly conflicted with the demand for growing numbers of workers necessary to meet new social needs at the lowest possible cost. The feminized professions all lacked lengthy periods of preparation and training, standardized examination or registration administered by public agencies, achievement of positions of responsibility in and to the community, and the earning of income commensurate with the quality of services performed.[20]

The traditionally male professions of medicine and law gained professional standards more readily. An increasing number of women entered these less conventional areas after 1890, but they faced difficulties in obtaining the required education and post-graduate training as well as in acquiring membership in the associations that legitimized their status once attained. Female doctors founded their own hospitals and schools, and women doctors and lawyers alike established their own societies to meet their professional and communal needs. But regardless of the difficulties encountered in upgrading new professions or entering non-traditional ones, almost one million women were employed in a variety of professional endeavors by 1920. The proportion of all working women engaged in these pursuits grew from 9.5 percent in 1890 to 13.3 percent thirty years later.[21]

The growth and feminization of professional activities were impressive but not nearly so dramatic as the increase in female employment in the white-collar clerical and sales fields. In the three decades following 1890, the number of women typists, stenographers, sales people, and others in related occupations grew from a little over 171,000 to almost two million, from 5.3 percent to 25.6 percent of all gainfully employed women. A propitious conjunction of forces contributed to the spectacular increase in both jobs and workers. A burgeoning demand for book-keepers, recordkeepers, and correspondents by a bureaucratized society and economy, a large number of young women with some high school education to meet the level of needed skills, and technological innova-tions in office equipment were all contributing factors. The typewriter had no history of association with either sex, but the female typist-stenographer was soon inseparable from the new machine. In 1890, 63.8 percent of the 33,400 workers classified as typist-stenographer were women; by 1920, 91.8 percent of 615,100. Female bookkeepers, accountants, and cashiers also grew in number and in proportion, but feminization in these areas was not so overwhelming (from 17 percent in 1890 to 49 percent thirty years later).[22]

Two other fields of employment offered new opportunities to women. By 1920, 350,000 women worked as salespersons in retail stores. An additional 175,000 were employed as telephone operators, an area that was 94 percent female. Although identified with other emerging white-collar jobs, the working conditions of saleswomen conformed more closely to patterns prevalent in industrial employment. Efforts to over-come low pay and long hours in retail stores had furnished the initial impetus for the founding of the New York Consumers' League. The social status of sales work, however, was higher than that of factory employment and so became an important element in the appeal of the emerging clerical occupations to hitherto nonworking segments of the female population.[23]

The social and demographic characteristics of female participants in the labor force changed along with occupational restructuring. Increas-ing vocational opportunities resulted in absolute growth in the numbers of working women within all race and nativity groups. The proportion of employed females to the total working population grew from 16.5 percent in 1890 to 20.2 percent in 1920. Native white women of native parentage accounted for the largest percentage of the growth. Native-born women of foreign parents and black women also increased slightly, but the proportion of working women who were foreign born declined. More revealing than changes in the racial and national origin character-istics of employed women were the types of occupations in which they were primarily engaged. In some areas there were decided shifts, while in others the background of the worker remained constant as the occupa-tion assumed a greater or lesser role in the total occupational picture.

Approximately 45 percent of all domestic servants were native-born whites of either native- or foreign-born parentage throughout the thirty-year period. At the same time, the proportion of foreign-born servants decreased and that of blacks grew. Within manufacturing categories— although disparities existed among different industries and locations— the social composition of industrially employed women remained fairly constant, with only a slight increase in the proportion of black women. Over 90 percent of professional and clerical workers were native born in 1920, as well as in 1890. Shifts within occupational classifications involved foreign-born and black women. Native-born white women maintained a constant level of participation in each major job category. But the relative importance of the job classes changed with decided growth in those white-collar fields in which native-born, better-educated, white females predominated. These were the women who entered the labor force in great numbers, taking advantage of the new vocational opportunities.[24]

Large-scale entrance of white, native-born women into gainful employment required an alteration in attitudes toward women's work outside the home. During the last quarter of the nineteenth century, fears concerning the consequences of female employment were widespread. In 1875, a physician, Azel Ames, warned of the dire physiological and moral consequences that would result if women joined their male relatives in the work force. Physical labor would cause irreparable damage to female reproductive organs; earnings would contradict woman's natural dependency upon a male provider; and social contact between the sexes would result in gross immorality, he warned.[25] These anxieties were not the special preserve of Victorian alarmists, however; they underlay the arguments in defense of protective legislation for working women at the state level, and gained national attention in the Brandeis defense of the Oregon ten-hour law argued before the Supreme Court in 1908. The court majority accepted the Brandeis-Goldmark thesis and ruled that hours of labor could be regulated because a woman needed physical protection for "a proper discharge of her maternal functions" and moral protection from "the greed as well as the passion of man."[26] As long as the potential mothers of the working class could be safeguarded from apparent harm and retired from the labor force upon marriage, reformers of the Consumers' League, along with their allies in the Women's Trade Union League (WTUL) and in settlement houses, sanctioned their employment.[27]

The growing number of young women moving into offices and retail stores received less attention from reformers than from social critics. At the turn of the century, Edward Bok, editor of the *Ladies' Home Journal*, insisted that women could not tolerate the pace of the business world and that there existed an alarming increase in the "tendency among business girls and women to nervous collapse."[28] But this railing did not prevail. The new white-collar opportunities were appealing to upwardly mobile newcomers to the city and to daughters of more comfortable families who had previously whiled away the years between school and marriage. The wages and status of clerical work exceeded those gained in domestic service or in factories. And when the clerical worker was invested with "womanly" attributes, expected to radiate the "office with sunshine and sympathetic interest," to inventory and arrange furniture for efficiency and attractiveness, thereby making the office as livable as the home, then office employment joined other occupations in which traditional female functions once performed at home moved into the public sphere. As specialized clerical work became feminized, precluding competition with men within an office hierarchy dominated by men, the office took on the overtones of traditional family structure and sexual division of labor, duplicating the characteristics of the female labor force along the entire occupational spectrum.[29]

Several innovations marked the growing popularity and acceptance of white-collar work for young women. Private business and commercial schools opened to provide training. The Katherine Gibbs schools were going concerns by 1911. Until commercial courses were added to the high school curriculum, enrollment in private enterprises grew from 91,500 in 1900 to 336,000 twenty years later.[30] A new literary genre, the advice manual for young women in search of an office job, appeared on the scene before the end of the nineteenth century, complete with instructions on dress, manners, training, attitudes toward work, and heavy doses of general moralizing.[31] Success testimonials followed. In 1905, *Woman's Home Companion* published the winning letters in its "How I Earned My Own Support" contest. The editors admitted they were astonished by the number of entries illustrating "heroic endeavor and splendid achievement." And that year, the same popular women's magazine initiated an advice column, "For the Girl Who Earns Her Own Living," to counteract the prevalent "pin money" argument, that women worked only for the sake of luxuries, as well as to provide counsel.[32]

Popular fiction reflected the growing acceptance and appeal of white-collar occupations for single, middle-class women and for those with middle-class aspirations. A sample of short stories in selected women's and mass circulation magazines found an increasing number of heroines who were working women, a proportion that conformed closely to census data. But the occupations of these fictional workers, who appeared in stories published in 1905 and 1915, were overwhelmingly professional and clerical. These occupations had apparently captured the imagination of middle-class readers.[33]

A growing acceptance of the gainful employment of young women evolved into a general expectation. The integration of vocational education into the schools and the appearance on the scene of a new semi-professional worker, the guidance counselor, reflected the trend. Vocational education for girls was often identified with instruction in sewing and cooking, especially after the founding of the American Home Economics Association in 1909, and after provisions for federal funding of this training in the Smith-Hughes Act of 1917. Commercial courses, however, were also initiated and gained in popularity. A government survey discovered that 14 percent of students in secondary schools were enrolled in home economics courses in 1922. That same year, 12.6 percent of students learned bookkeeping; 9 percent were enrolled in shorthand; and 13 percent were in typing courses, and all of these courses had been added to the curriculum after 1910.[34] Even home economics teachers noted the necessity of acquiring skills not associated with homemaking. One complained that a woman's "lack of equipment for breadwinning brings even more disastrous results than her lack of knowledge of the household arts."[35]

Proliferation of vocational guidance literature aided the counselor or the young woman embarked on a self-help program. Books were directed at girls at various educational levels, describing jobs that required diversified degrees of preparation and skill. Information on obtaining a job as a dressmaker was often combined with data on preparation for a career in law. Most books surveyed developing opportunities in advertising, journalism, and photography as well. Traditionally male professions often received attention. *Good Housekeeping* ran a series on "Your Daughter's Career" in which requirements and opportunities in medicine, law, and finance were examined at length. More often, the guidance literature emphasized those new fields that were quickly becoming female stereotyped vocations, with the implicit assumption that the reader was more interested in a short-term job than a lifelong commitment to a career.[36]

However, many women did take their new vocational pursuit seriously, and workers from a variety of white-collar and professional occupations sought organizational cohesion. Under the impetus of the wartime need to mobilize women of ability, the Young Women's Christian Association (YWCA) sponsored a conference of representatives from many local business and professional women's groups. With the YWCA's initial moral and financial support, the National Federation of Business and Professional Women's Clubs (BPW) was formed in 1919. Conscious of both new economic opportunities and enduring discriminatory impediments, the BPW hoped that its efforts would enable "young women of the future to come into the business and professional fields better able to cope with the conditions and with fewer handicaps to overcome than the women of today."[37] By 1920, the new organization boasted over 25,000 members. Although the leadership consisted of successful doctors, lawyers, and educators, whose interests often coincided with the specialized professional groups to which they also belonged, the general membership was predominantly composed of teachers and clerical workers, representative of the female, white-collar occupations that had expanded so dramatically during the previous decades.

Statistics confirmed what advice literature, popular fiction, and formal organizations indicated: The proportion of employed native-born white women of native parentage in the sixteen-to-twenty-four-year-old age group increased from 21 percent in 1900 to 31 percent twenty years later. Labor force participation by native-born white women in the same age category, whose parents had been born abroad, grew from 39 percent to 50 percent during those two decades. (No other age cohort experienced comparable increases.) At the same time, the percentage of working foreign-born and black women in that age bracket, while still at high levels, declined slightly. Growing demand for female workers drew largely from native-born women in general as well as from that particular age group representing the time period between school and marriage.[38]

With the exception of black females, the proportion of working women in the next age category, twenty-five to forty-four years old, was markedly lower than the younger group, as many women retired from the labor market upon marriage. But the percentage in this classification did grow over these years. This increase indicated a trend in the demographic characteristics of employed women as important in its nature and implications as the changing occupations and the altered attitudes toward the employment of young, native women. The growth represented increased employment of married women. From 1890 to 1920, the proportion of married women who worked rose from 3.3 percent to 7.3 percent, while the percentage of working women who were married grew from 12 percent to a little over 21 percent.[39]

The occupational distribution of married women workers differed from that of employed women in general. The proportion working as domestic servants, unskilled and semi-skilled factory operatives, and laundresses outside commercial laundries, exceeded the percentage in those categories for all women workers. The large number of gainfully employed blacks, who constituted one-third of all married women workers, accounts in large measure for the difference. However, in spite of the disproportionate numbers of married women at the lower end of the female occupational scale, their increased numbers were related to the developing white-collar occupations. Even if black women are included in total figures, the rate at which married women entered these new vocational fields was greater than increases for women workers in general.

Comparisons between the years 1910 and 1920 are especially illuminating because married women entered the labor force at a slower rate during that decade than during the previous one. Yet, whereas the number of women in clerical fields increased 140 percent during those ten years, working wives in clerical occupations grew at double that rate. The same disparities existed in transportation and communications (principally, telephone operators), where there was a 100 percent increase for all women but a 208 percent rise for married women; and in professional services, 38 percent growth for all women, 62 percent for married females. At the same time, single and married women entered industry at a much lower rate, 7 percent and 41 percent, respectively. The contrasts are somewhat less dramatic when one considers that the large percentage increases of working wives reflected, in part, the small absolute numbers with which computation began. In 1920, less than 10 percent of all married working women were engaged in clerical, trade, or professional occupations.[40]

The acceptance of gainful employment of women was predicated to a great extent on the belief that they would and should retire to the home after marriage. Vocational training and employment were encouraged when they allowed for premarital financial independence or enabled an unfortunate widow to provide for the support of herself and her children, but the notion of working wives undermined their socially valued contribution as mothers and homemakers. Work was permissible as a stopgap "between the subrogation of school and the independence of marriage," but all girls should be taught that childbearing, not gainful employment, was woman's prime duty; otherwise, young women would remain unaware of the "fatal racial consequences," warned one social alarmist.[41]

Even reformers joined conservative defenders of women's traditional roles in opposing employment of wives and mothers. As executive secretary of the National Consumers' League, Florence Kelley spent years of time and effort promoting protective legislation and blocking any programs that might have encouraged the employment of married women, such as day nurseries, charitably run kindergartens, or cash relief payments contingent upon women's accepting any available work. To Kelley, the lowered birth rate, infant mortality, and the presumed neglect of children born to married women who were gainfully employed were intolerable social costs.[42] This attention to the supposed effect of married women's employment on births reflected the contemporary concern with the diminishing birth rate in general. To many social critics, it was both cause and symptom of what was perceived as the growing instability and disintegration of the family as a viable institution. In the early years of the twentieth century, this alarm reached manic proportions. "Race-suicide" was blamed on the unwillingness or inability of white, middle-class, native American women to bear children. Reformers focused their attention on women in industry. But, for many social critics, the educated women from economically comfortable backgrounds were singled out for condemnation.[43]

The movement for higher education for women had met with ridicule and prophecies of dire consequences in the years following the Civil War. The exposure of women to the intellectual rigors of college training, according to Dr. Edward Clarke of Harvard, without special dispensations for their physiological needs, would result in diverting the blood supply from their reproductive organs to their brains. Disastrous effects on their ability to bear children could be expected.[44] Whatever the shortcomings of Clarke's analysis of female anatomy and physiology, reduced marriage and childbearing rates among the first generation of women graduates from colleges and universities led hand-wringers to assume some cause-and-effect relationship. Foreign-born women bore twice the number of offspring as native-born white women, and the birth rate of those who had graduated from college was lowest of all. This phenomenon was blamed, in large measure, on the perception that these educated women continued to work after marriage. "Married, they refuse to be mothers; mistresses of home, they refuse to be house-wives." All of which could only result in the "overthrow of the family, the destruction of humanity."[45]

Critics could foresee remedies for the assumed disruptive effects on marriage and family patterns attributed to higher education of women and employment of wives by somehow increasing and reinforcing the social value and prestige of the traditional female sphere of the home. They encountered direct attack from contemporary feminists, however, who were examining and criticizing family structure and the social and economic relationships among family members. Feminism questioned the division between home and work, on the one hand, and between marriage and a sexual division of labor, on the other. For guardians of the status quo, feminist attitudes toward work were especially trouble-some, for they lay at the basis of their analysis of women's inferior social position. To Charlotte Perkins Gilman, low female status stemmed entirely from women's economic dependence on their income-providing husbands. This relationship reduced the woman to a love object, com-pletely reliant upon her good looks and charm for economic support through marriage. This entangling web could be broken by work. Wheth-er married or single, women must be active labor force participants. Gilman carried her analysis a step forward with an incisive critique of the home, to which women were relegated, and of the functions per-formed within its confines. Inefficient, individualized household chores, she believed, must be rationalized and placed on a communal basis. Not only would homemaking become more efficient, but fewer domestic tasks would also free women for productive work outside the home. Community kitchens, laundries, and child nursery centers were inseparable from gainful employment with concomitant economic independence, enhanced self-esteem, and raised social status.[46]

Other feminists elaborated on Gilman's thesis. South African Olive Schreiner described women's existence in Western industrial societies as parasitic. The essence of the woman's movement was, she wrote, the attempt "to find new fields of labor as the old slip away from them," to regain their "share of honored and socially useful human toil" in order to stop the decline into enervating, inactive dependence upon their sex function and appeal. Like Gilman and contemporary Greenwich Village feminists, Schreiner developed an ideology in which socially and economically rewarded work was the pivot around which all other social reorganization revolved.[47]

Henrietta Rodman, a New York feminist teacher, addressed the problem of the double burden of housekeeping and wage earning. She hired an architect to design an apartment with kitchenless units and centralized areas for the preparation of meals, furnishing of laundry services, and the education of children complete with Montessori teachers. She envisioned collectivizing all domestic chores so that professional women could pursue careers without the distractions of household functions. The plans never materialized because of lack of support—financial and popular. Even contemporary apartment hotels without such auxiliary services were criticized for the same reason that Rodman's plans met with derision: they undermined the family.[48]

Defenders of the conventional family recognized the threat posed by the feminist critique. "Under the influence of this modern propaganda, advocating 'equal rights' to women to engage in men's work, the neglect of women's natural sphere of life—the domestic—becomes a virtue," complained one critic.[49] The feminist tenet of economic independence might appeal more to educated women than to those who labored in factories and for whom marriage provided an escape from undesirable working conditions, so it was absolutely essential that these ideas be discouraged at all costs. A sizable gap existed between the anxieties of opponents of working wives and the extent of married women's labor force participation, but the feminists had struck a responsive chord. Gilman's books went through many editions.

While serious critics of feminist social diagnosis and remedies were correct in their assessment of the middle-class bias and appeal of Gilman

and Rodman, they also reflected an awareness of the portents of change.[50] A handful of sociologists, economists, and educators, reflecting varied degrees of acceptance, approval, and encouragement of working wives, examined and described the motivating factors behind the trend and the possible benefits that might accrue. Sociologist J. E. Cutler diagnosed the problem of family instability as a sign of ineffective institutional functioning in a changing society. Necessary adjustments included "the entrance of women into wage-earning occupations and their participation once more into the support and maintenance of the family."[51] Economist Simon Patten stressed the income increments and the futility of distinguishing between the earnings that single and married women contributed to the family coffers. Female educators echoed many of the arguments of feminists on the value of productive labor.[52]

These advocates of the employment of married women were the forerunners of growing numbers of individuals who would elaborate upon their arguments and make the subject of combining careers and homes the dominant feminist issue of the 1920s. With the passage of the Nineteenth Amendment, women's preoccupation with political status and legal disabilities diminished. A new group of women, in generational terms, and a new focus, social and economic, would dominate the arena where women's place in American society was an issue of ongoing debate.[53] New professions and white-collar jobs for women provided the opportunities for gainful employment, devoid of the onus that had been attached to menial, unskilled labor. Single women with middle-class social origins or aspirations had gained acceptance as gainful employees. As a new decade opened, the stage was set for those who wished to extend the acceptance and expectation of work to married women as well.

chapter 2

Marriage and Careers:
Feminism in the 1920s

For close to half a century, attainment of female suffrage has been equated with social and economic progress for women as well as with their political gain. A few observers, who realized that equality for women remained elusive, believed the young, hedonistic flapper had replaced the committed feminist as the "new woman," and they bade "farewell to reform" with feelings that ranged from sorrowful acquiescence to bitter denunciation. But the flapper phenomenon has been pushed back a decade, and the female social reformers of the 1920s have been rediscovered and presented as an alternative image of womanhood. The most visible and vocal repository of feminism was the National Woman's Party, the elitist, radical, reconstructed wing of the suffrage movement, whose introduction of an equal rights amendment in 1923 encountered bitter opposition from the social reformers. To the extent that an organized women's movement waned after the passage of the Nineteenth Amendment, this internecine dispute, with the issue of protective legislation for working women at the core, has been held primarily accountable.[1]

American feminism after 1920 has been judged moribund because its redirected focus has been largely overlooked and its articulation was more often individual than collective. The problems and issues concerned with the status of women became increasingly economic rather than political and legal. Barnard professor of economics Emilie Hutchinson wrote that "economic opportunity is beginning to have the emphasis that education and suffrage have received." This was especially true with regard to gainful employment for married women. Selectively building on the ideological foundations laid by Charlotte Perkins Gilman, Olive Schreiner, and others who had recognized that women's position in society involved more than exclusion from the franchise, feminists of the 1920s advocated the possibility and desirability of women's combining marriage with income earning. These proponents of working wives had not figured prominently in the battle for the vote, nor were they actively involved with organizations concerned primarily with social reform. Their ranks consisted of native-born, well-educated professional women like academicians Lorine Pruette, Viva Booth, and Chase Going Woodhouse, psychiatrist Beatrice Hinkle, and writers and members of the editorial staffs of prominent periodicals like Alice Beal Parsons, Dorothy Bromley, Mary Ross, and Katherine Angell.[2]

Work and marriage advocates perceived themselves and their program as distinct from the feminists and feminism of the preceding generation. Dorothy Bromley contrasted the increasing numbers of younger women in their twenties and thirties who married, had children, and also worked from "the old school of fighting feminists who wore flat heels and had little feminine charm." She acknowledged accomplishments stemming from "their zealotry and their inartistic methods" but wanted none of these traits associated with a clearly defined "Feminism—New Style." Mary Ross differentiated growing numbers of working wives from feminist "propagandists," who extolled the need for self-expression through gainful employment.[3] But however they delineated, defined, or denied their feminism, proponents of working wives engaged in feminist activity. They advocated and rationalized new female functions, often for the purpose of elevating women's economic status, sometimes in order to raise women's sense of self-esteem. While either benefit or both were conceived within the framework of traditional marriage, inherent in their arguments were a reorientation of family life and a redefinition of sex roles to contribute to the enhancement of women's social position, and a positive model of a "new woman."[4]

Advocates of women who both worked and married found a large, if not always receptive, audience. The number of articles that appeared in mass circulation periodicals, women's magazines, literary publications, and the journals of women's organizations attests to extensive interest. The Woman's Press of the YWCA published a debater's manual at the request of the National Federation of Business and Professional women's Clubs (BPW) to help answer the increasingly common question,

"Shall I go on with my job after marriage?" Under the auspices of its Committee on the Economic and Legal Status of Women, the American Association of University Women (AAUW) undertook a study of various and possibly conflicting aspects of marriage, children, and work because "more and more college women are demanding that in some way they be enabled to marry and also to carry on the work for which they were prepared in college." *Woman Citizen,* voice of the National League of Women Voters (LWV), substituted a debate on the subject for a serial because "our mail keeps proving to us the constant interest in the pressing problem of a double job for women." But the issue was by no means confined to women who had obtained a higher education or belonged to women's organizations. Dorothy Dix, in her nationally syndicated advice column, informed her readers that the question that she was asked most often was,"Should a woman work outside of the home after marriage?"[5]

While the issue was often phrased as a question about which there was hesitation and debate, marriage and career feminists believed some alteration in women's traditional social and economic roles was necessary in order to counter the negative impact of industrialization and urbanization on their lives. Like a litany, they described and analyzed the effects of economic change on female roles and status. The family farm, they argued, had constituted a self-sufficient socioeconomic entity in which all members performed prescribed work and contributed individually to the economic well-being of the entire family. "The wife's duties were quite comparable in economic return with the husband's work," was a common refrain. But industrialization had taken many of the female functions out of the home and into the factory. Textile and garment manufacturing and much of food processing were removed from the hands of women. While many girls of working-class families followed these jobs into the factories, middle-class women, they insisted, were literally technologically unemployed. Feminists of the 1920s also identified, described, and attacked the ideology that had evolved during the nineteenth century that prescribed and justified the sexual division of labor resulting from the physical separation of home from productive work. Men worked in the public arena, earning the cash income to support the women and children who remained in the privatized home. Passive roles as child nurturers and homemakers superseded women's earlier functions as economic producers. Whether separate spheres of activity were justified on the basis of biological differences, inherent emotional traits, or on Scripture, economic dependency for women and financial burdens for men resulted. Feminists agreed with the diagnosis of parasitism made by Gilman and Schreiner earlier in the century, and they elaborated upon and popularized aspects of those analyses.[6]

Women's new nurturing functions, home and career proponents argued, were in no way compensatory for the old productive ones, either in terms of personal satisfaction or economic contribution. The new economic order was radically different not only in the nature of the modes of production and distribution but also in the methods of compensation and exchange. Work now earned money, and the value of work derived directly from the amount of money earned. The family obtained none of the goods and services formerly produced at home unless purchased with cash income. Pious platitudes about the moral superiority of women and the virtues with which they imbued their children and all mankind could not, according to new-style feminists, overcome the fact that women's contribution to their families within the urban home received no monetary reward. Viva Booth, editor of an excellent survey of women's roles, status, achievements, and problems, pointed to the cruel irony of glorifying wives and mothers as "priceless." In a money-oriented society, women and women's work had become severely devalued, essentially worthless.[7]

The descriptions of the negative ramifications of economic change on female status and the attack on the concept of separate spheres during the 1920s have the familiar ring of recent analyses of the impact of industrialization on urban work and living patterns. But the tone of the feminists of the 1920s was different. They discussed the passing of agrarian society and the undermining of women's productive functions with a sense of immediacy that implied personal memory. The women who once made the valued contributions to the family economy, thereby earning respect and elevated status as well as personal satisfaction, were often described as "our grandmothers." More than a hint of nostalgia and a feeling of personal loss permeated their analysis of the economic and psychological rewards that accrued to the rural housewife. They indicated the extent to which early nineteenth-century developments, creating, prescribing, and rationalizing a distinct sphere of activities for women, were just the beginning of an ongoing process that continued as the nation moved westward and from rural areas to towns and cities. Feminists during the 1920s remembered or experienced social and economic changes in addition to depicting and analyzing them.[8]

Changes in economic structure and sex role ideology were accompanied by dramatic alterations in demographic patterns, and those who advocated and explained employment for married women remembered and recognized these developments as well. "American women have more years of adult life than did their grandmothers, and fewer and healthier children. . . . Many a grandmother of the present young American generation spent eight or nine out of twenty adult years in bearing and nursing her children, while her granddaughter is spending perhaps three or four out of forty."[9] Smaller families were noted casually and approvingly by feminists, at least implicitly indicating a high degree of acceptance and approval of birth control methods and the degree to which family limitation had become integrated into upper and middle-class family life style. Feminists descriptions and implications were accurate. Americans had experienced a perceptible increase in life expectancy from the turn of the century, while the entire nineteenth century had been marked by a declining birth rate.[10] Responsibility for fewer children during a proportionately shorter period of the lengthening female life cycle, combined with restricted productive functions, meant an increasingly purposeless existence.

The feminists' solution to female underemployment, lack of financial compensation, and accompanying status loss was obvious; only gainful employment, "if not in the old places then in the new," could remedy the cruel fate that had robbed women of productive labor and self-esteem within their family settings. Many single women had discovered the satisfactions derived from work during the previous decades, and also that they need not retire from the labor force upon marriage. Employment for wives was especially feasible because the residue of functions in the home continued to diminish. Feminists recounted the blessings of the new labor-saving appliances that supposedly reduced housekeeping to a minimum, at the same time deprecating the tasks that did remain, repeatedly describing them as menial and degrading, "the meanest, most irksome, most heartbreaking job in the world."[11]

Advocates of working wives who denigrated homemaking were bolstered by a medical study of neurasthenia among housewives. Various manifestations of emotional disorders—hysterias, depressions, lethargies—

had been prevalent among middle-class women during the late nine-teenth century. Dr. Abraham Myerson insisted that this neurotic be-havior was directly related to the social isolation of the home and the disagreeable routine of domestic chores. In *The Nervous Housewife*, he criticized the home as an inefficient social arangement for women and as a poor atmosphere in which to socialize children. Although his rem-edies emphasized the projection of "mother feeling" into community uplift activities rather than in gainful employment, Myerson furnished marriage and career advocates with valuable evidence of the salutary psychological benefits that would accompany the paid employment of wives and mothers.[12]

Feminists stressed the emotional rewards that would accrue to the wage-earning wife. Economic independence, according to Emilie Hutch-inson in a survey of women's changing roles, was the foundation of responsible adult life; therefore, work after marriage was the key to in-dividual esteem as well as to enhanced economic status. The advice columnist of *Woman's Home Companion*, who earlier in the century decried the working wife, reversed her stand. "Probably no man," she wrote, "who has not experienced it can conceive the ravages of financial dependence on character, the having nothing in the world he could call his own, except as a gift from someone else." Alice Beal Parsons, in one of the full-length studies of the work-marriage issue, prescribed paid work as a miracle cure for the "woman who has been listless and unhap-py." Not only would the working wife derive personal satisfaction from productive functions that were rewarded monetarily but she would also experience a complete metamorphosis of personality. From being a listless housekeeper, the employed wife would become imbued with "vigor, confidence, physical and mental alertness." Educator Ethel Puffer Howes agreed that the lack of utilization of a woman's ability in her trained field could only result in undermining her physical and emotional well-being.[13]

The emphasis on economic independence and the personal rewards derived from employment fell within the bounds of the individualistic, private ethos of the 1920s; but where women were concerned, "the in-creasing emphasis on self-development and the supreme importance of the individual in society" conflicted with conventional feminine virtues of renunciation and self-sacrifice on behalf of their families. Dorothy Bromley could proclaim the emergence of the working wife whose world was no longer completely circumscribed by husband and children, "a full-fledged individual who is capable of molding her own life," but the marriage and career issue was more often conceived in terms of conflict in need of reconciliation. "The deepest problems of modern family life center in the effort to adjust the new freedom of women, and its new demands for individual developments in customary lines of vocational work, to the ancient family claim." Even the self-proclaimed feminists of the National Woman's Party, who took an unequivocal stand on the imperative of economic independence for women and consequently on the necessity of employment for wives, believed that the issue was "linked so closely . . . with the welfare of the home and the family" that advocating expanded economic roles for women had to be reconciled with traditional expectations and institutions.[14]

New-style feminists tried to mitigate the conflict inherent in what was variously described as "woman's dilemma" or "the vocational divide" by balancing the individual advantages that would accrue to women against the social benefits derived from the increasing numbers of stable families. They insisted that society in general and marriage rates in particular suffered unnecessarily when home and work were conceived as mutually exclusive options. An editorial in *Independent Woman,* the publication of the National Federation of Business and Professional Women's Clubs, stated that it was absurd to "hold to the old idea that a woman must either 'stay at home' or definitely give up all idea of having a home of her own when seeking a career."[15] Many first-generation female college and university graduates had faced those alternatives, and they had opted for careers to the dismay of social critics. Neither society nor individual women had gained from that decision which "necessarily involved celibacy or sterility." Voluntary spinsterhood had proven "half a theory," only partial emancipation. Only the woman who married and also participated in the labor force was truly free. And in allowing women access to all spheres of activity, in obviating their need to choose between alternatives, marriage rates would increase.[16]

New definitions of the family as a cluster of interpersonal relationships and of marriage as affectionate in nature gave feminists, who did not wish to belabor the issue of personal gratification alone, a viable framework within which to state their case. While the emerging ideal of the husband-wife relationship during the 1920s stressed loving companionship and stimulating friendship rather than social and economic

partnership between equals, advocates of working wives argued that
only the employment of married women could change the marital arrangement from one of economic support and dependency to one of
truly mutual interests and affection. Satisfying work, with its economic
rewards and stimulating contacts, would create a healthy and intelligent
outlook on life, which was the only true basis for a sharing, stimulating,
and loving relationship. New standards for ideal marriage should be
carried to their logical conclusions with the complete reconstruction of
mutuality that had been undermined by industrialization and the rigid
sexual division of labor. Nostalgia for the past as well as a vision of the
future infused the call for readjustment:

> I believe that there is an impulse for partnership in marriage, for the feeling
> that the man and the woman are working together, both contributing to
> the support of the family (as they both did in pioneer families), which has
> been weakened by the new family economics in which one earns and the
> other spends; one creates and the other enjoys it.[17]

Mary Ross found the actual, rather than the proposed, increase in the
employment of married women unrelated to feminist rhetoric. Still she
explained and defended new and expanded economic activity for wives
as inherent in the desire for partnership in marriage, as part of the
search for "some new alignment of the fundamentals of work, love, and
play which will meet the demands which life puts upon [women]."[18]

But new definitions of the family and new social and economic arrangements within the familial framework involved more than enlarged
roles for women. Some redefinition of husbands' roles and status seemed
necessary as well. Conservative social critics were certain—although
their reasoning was inconsistent—that men would lose "ambition, pride
and the sense of responsibility that all male creatures seem to be born
with" if wives worked for wages.[19] Feminists discounted these frequent
forecasts of doom, but they did anticipate some reallocation of responsibilities between working husbands and wives. They hoped for considerable contributions from husbands toward lightening the burden of
domestic chores which, contrary to claims that homemaking had been
stripped of time-consuming functions and effort, still existed. Nancy
Mavity, working wife and member of the National Woman's Party,
discovered a dilemma resulted from unrealistic expectations: "With
open or secret unwillingness the husband shares the household tasks, or
the wife bears the entire burden to her physical and nervous undoing."[20]

Another writer correctly gauged the seriousness of the problem. Either men must accept a new distribution of functions, she insisted, or "we will never have any proper adjustment of the matter" of wives' successful participation in the labor force.[21] Evidence of male reluctance to assume activities associated with domesticity revealed an undercurrent of frustration in the testimony of some working wives.

Most advocates of combining marriage with careers preferred to ignore or circumvent male recalcitrance and rely on domestic servants to alleviate the burdens of homemaking. They justified this arrangement by proclaiming the virtues of efficiency, professionalism, and rationalization of labor in ways reminiscent of Progressive Era programs and characteristic of the economic rhetoric of the New Era. Not all women, they said, were equally skilled at homemaking. Working wives should use their talents in the business world while trained, competent domestic servants maintained comfortable homes for them and their husbands. There was no acknowledgment of "the servant problem," that perennial cry of upper- and middle-class women that good household help was difficult to find and impossible to retain, or the class bias implicit in the belief that homemaking was mundane and unworthy of their aptitudes but suitable and even enjoyable for those they employed. Nor was there any sense of identification with the supposedly efficient cooks and maids who figured so prominently in descriptions of the household routine of married women workers and who were most likely to be working wives themselves.[22]

Even if husbands were freed from the assumption of household responsibilities, the possibility of negative psychological impact of wives' employment still haunted the women who recognized the prevalence and force of the ideal of the male-supported family. An advocate of employment for married women confessed, "Because jobs and careers were so new to those of us who were married, . . . in our enthusiasm for them we ignored some of the very elementary laws governing the attraction between men and women."[23] Methods of handling income were suggested to maintain the image of husband as sole breadwinner. He would assume responsibility for all financial matters, paying bills and allocating the two incomes in such a way that his earnings covered family expenses, but the wife's income would contribute to the support of dependents or would be deposited in their savings account. Admittedly, these arrangements were compromises on the part of women whose goals were equality in family economic responsibility and contribution, but at least it would allow "masculine dignity to assert itself."[24]

In 1919, the Bureau of Vocational Information was opened in New York to provide occupational guidance materials to college women, other individual applicants, and institutions. As an advocate of the employment of married women, the bureau undertook a study of 100 well-educated, professional women who were also wives and mothers. The sample was carefully selected and undoubtedly skewed. While admitting that some husbands were still subject to public approbation, the experiences of most of the wives and the encouragement they reported they received from their husbands led the interviewer to assume that "a new man is rising to demand a new woman."[25] This conclusion gratified new-style feminists, who recognized that a secure and supportive husband was an essential factor in the attempt to combine economic and domestic roles. But less formal surveys and the testimony of "fifty-fifty" husbands revealed less positive attitudes toward working wives and little revision in the conventional concept of the male role.[26]

Yet, with tact, a domestic servant, or the energy to perform two jobs, feminists believed the employed wife could overcome the obstacles created by a reluctant mate. Children presented a different problem. Explicit Freudian concepts may have been rare in the child-rearing literature of the 1920s, but the belief in the importance of infant and childhood experience in determining the quality of adult personality and behavior was widespread. John B. Watson, the behavioral psychologist, extrapolated the stimulus-response core of his system of explaining, controlling, and inducing human behavior to the subject of child rearing. His *Psychological Care of Infant and Child* emphasized the application of rigid schedules and the limitation of over-affectionate interaction between mother and child. Yet the goal of this restrictive regimen was not an obedient, diligent, respectful individual, the nineteenth-century ideal, but rather a personally contented and socially well-adjusted youngster who would carry these traits through life in an increasingly complex society. The U.S. Children's Bureau accepted and popularized the behaviorist child-rearing advice, along with the focus on individual contentment, in a 1928 pamphlet with the revealing title, "Are You Training Your Child to Be Happy?"[27]

New attention to the importance of the mother's impact on the emotional health of her children placed new stress and responsibilities on the women of the 1920s. Not only did these child-rearing practices reinforce the defenders of women's traditional role as full-time mothers in their attacks on new-style feminists, but they also split the ranks of career proponents themselves. Many advocates of combining work with marriage distinguished between working wives and working mothers. They believed that employment should extend only to the time of child bearing, after which two jobs could be in direct conflict, and the child should have a prior claim on the mother's time and energy. " 'Being there' is the greatest contribution we mothers can make in the lives of our children," according to one firm advocate of vocational training for women and their employment after marriage.[28]

Reconciling this dilemma taxed the ingenuity of home and career proponents. The most common solution involved regulating occupational activity to the woman's family life cycle: continued employment after marriage, retirement upon child bearing and child raising, and the resumption of work when the duties of motherhood were completed. All women were entitled to "two bites at the cherry—a career, a period of child rearing, and a career again," which would satisfy women's right to "demand both work and affection as necessary parts of life during their active years." Only the "postgraduate" mother should resume economic activities outside the home.[29]

Fitting work within the framework of the family life cycle raised serious questions concerning the maintenance and marketability of a woman's occupational skills. What was she to do with her training and ability during the period of forced retirement? Whether they were trying to regain an occupation with possibly rusty skills or were job hunting for the first time after their children were raised, married women were apt to encounter difficulties. For professional workers, in particular, continuity in job holding was imperative, and for most women, age, as well as marital status, was a factor in hiring practices. "The woman of forty who has spent fifteen years keeping house must start over again at the beginning, with a beginner's ignorance of conditions and little more than a beginner's opportunities." Here lay the ultimate choice. The job required full attention and continuity, and to pursue it successfully meant an inevitable clash with the "deepest needs of children —and mothers."[30]

One group of feminists, displaying the same faith they placed in the well-trained housekeeper, reasoned that an efficient and affectionate nurse, followed later by the services of the nursery school, could effectively substitute for the mother's daytime absence. Pressure for the creation of more and better day nurseries was, by necessity, an important part of the program of these women. Child-care centers did grow in number, and a tour of selected facilities by the working women's advisor of *Woman's Home Companion* brought rave reviews. But problems remained. Costs were high, locations were often distant, and Saturday closings of the schools hampered women at a time when the six-day work week was still the norm.[31] Yet this institutional support resolved the dilemma for those home and job proponents who altered the definition of the nature and influence of mother-child relationships on child development. Sons and daughters needed mothers, they argued, but not on a twenty-four-hour-a-day basis. Constant companionship only stifled and smothered children, retarding their emotional growth. After the early stages of childhood, the results could be a debilitating infantilism and other assorted emotional disturbances. By not totally possessing her children, the working mother would avoid raising "impossible egoists" who dominate the home. Watson should have had no difficulty in accepting such reasoning, but he did. "The having of children is almost an insuperable barrier to a career," he wrote. Child rearing, along with homemaking, made demands on women "second to none."[32]

Bored, frustrated women who were dissatisfied with the domestic routine did their children no favor by staying home, according to advocates of working mothers. Just as the wife with outside interests became a better companion to her husband, so she became a finer parent. Children thrived, they insisted, on freedom from overwhelming parental control and enjoyed the stimulating company of a mother with worldly interests. And there were material advantages as well. Feminist arguments were replete with allusions to improved education, music lessons, and attractive physical surroundings, all of which resulted from the raised standard of living of two-income families.[33] Yet doubt surfaced from time to time. "I can't judge the wisdom of my methods until my children grow up and I see the results," admitted one mother who was committed to her career.[34] With a healthy dose of both feminist defiance of traditional roles and personal uncertainty, another working mother admitted:

> In spite of hesitations, doubts, and questionings, I hang on like grim death to my newspaper job. My reasons are simple and selfish. My monthly paycheck is a welcome addition to the family budget, and a degree of financial independence is heartwarming to one who has tried the sentimental

role of partner-homemaker with its uneconomic "allowance" dole. Housework as a life job bores and enrages me. Writing, even such hack work as I do, lights up windows for my soul. . . .

As for the children, time alone can tell the story. . . . Whether or not they will suffer from the repeated injunction, "Now run away and play. Mother must pound the typewriter," remains to be seen.[35]

In spite of numerous misgivings, career and marriage advocates clung tenaciously to their program and searched for methods to solve conflicts between new and traditional roles. One option lay in educating women for marital, maternal, and domestic responsibilities as well as for careers. Historians have viewed the proliferation of home economics programs during the 1920s as a clear indication of the decline of feminism, a reflection of reduced interest in vocations by young, educated women and as a "back to the home" conspiracy by opponents to female employment.[36] The latter judgment is not incorrect. Many critics of working wives assumed that dissatisfaction with domesticity was a major motivating factor in the growing employment of native-born, educated wives, and that upgrading the status and the image of the homemaker was an alternative to the presumed attractions of work. While wages for wives were proposed as one means of satisfying women's desire for economic independence and of rewarding them as producers, arguments focused on the family budget and the need to convince women that new responsibilities, such as careful, intelligent consumption, were replacing old functions. Opponents of working wives suggested co-opting the career image and applying it to the homemaker along with the essential accoutrement of professionalism—formal training. Therefore, supporters of the status quo encouraged home economics courses that focused on consumer budgeting, child rearing, and family living.[37]

The popularity of home economics courses with their new emphasis on economic, sociological, and psychological subject matter[38] and the social conservatism of most champions of curriculum changes masked the vocal support feminists gave to courses in homemaking, child care and family consumption. Preparation for married life would help break down the barriers between work and home, they believed, and improve performance in both areas for women who had two vocations— successively, if not simultaneously. "Education will be sounder where existing conflicts will be resolved and where there will be no antagonisms between careers and home-making."[39] Both the Smith College Institute for the Coordination of Women's Interests, with its emphasis on household arrangements to support the working mother, and Vassar's Euthenics program, which adhered more closely to a narrower home economics approach, were hailed as examples of educational advances that would "make the combination of professional activity and home-making mutually possible."[40] But asking colleges to instruct women in proficient housekeeping and motherhood so that they could both work and marry was self-defeating.

The rationale of economist Chase Going Woodhouse illustrated the shortcomings inherent in feminists' advocacy of training for homemaking. To propose the professionalization of the domestic routine, on the one hand, while firmly believing in the employment of married women, on the other, for the mutual benefit of both, was an intellectually precarious balancing act.

> May it not be possible that with the right help and a bit of direction the present-day college woman with her wide interest, her ambition to continue her professional work, her refusal to be tied to a house, will be the one to reform the home and make it a more desirable and efficient place in which to develop future generations?[41]

Regardless of her insistence that the very necessity for education for domesticity undermined the traditional notion that all women were born homemakers, home economics courses were too closely identified with conventional female roles. Supporting and stressing their importance only reinforced sex stereotypes and confused subsequent analyses of the movement's significance.

Career-and-marriage feminism was hampered by other shortcomings and inconsistencies. Support for training in home economics reflected proponents' preoccupation with gainful employment for married women within the context of the nuclear family and the isolated home. Few advocates heeded the early twentieth-century suggestions of Charlotte Perkins Gilman concerning the need for cooperative household arrangements to counter the inefficiency of the home and to alleviate the domestic responsibilities of working women. Alice Beal Parsons devoted a full-length study to the possibility and need for these institutional changes, and Ethel Puffer Howes experimented with some implementation at Smith College.[42] But in her review of Parsons's book, Virginia MacMakin Collier, who was so pleased with the success of the working mothers in her survey, reflected the framework within which most of the feminists of the 1920s operated. Parsons's ideas were worth considering, Collier wrote, but in the final analysis "it is still an individual dilemma which each woman must, perforce, work out in the way that best fits her individual situation."[43] How women were to combine two jobs successfully remained a question that was to be answered by each woman alone.

Individual solutions precluded organizational attention to and support for the familial role re-orientation and societal support necessary to counteract the conflict between the "two-job wife" and the "fifty-fifty marriage"—contradictory terms the feminists used synonymously. From the time of its founding, the BPW considered the issue. "The New Triangle: Women, Home and Business" was featured on the program of their first annual convention in 1920, and the organization's publication continued to give the question much coverage and working wives encouragement. However, advice for working women focused on new and improved opportunities in business and not on altered patterns of responsibility for homemaking and child care at home. Members of the National Woman's Party (NWP) made the employment of married women a major plank in their platform, and they alone recognized, publicized, and protested discriminatory practices encountered by working wives. But they, too, failed to analyze the implications of economic equality on family functions and relationships. In 1929, the American Association of University Women supported the establishment of the Institute of Women's Professional Relations under the direction of economist Chase Going Woodhouse. The sponsoring organization and the director had expressed interest in work for married women, but from its inception the institute served primarily as a clearinghouse for vocational information for college-educated women and expressed no special concern for working wives.[44]

Without relinquishing domestic responsibilities, individual feminists espoused the values associated with the work ethic as they strove to enlarge and redefine economic roles. Work outside the home represented all the aspirations for personal accomplishment and social equality that confining domesticity vitiated. Retrieving the traditional association between productive labor and moral virtue, feminists pleaded that the ideal Victorian woman of leisure should be relegated to the junk heap. The positive attributes associated with meaningful work must be extended to all adults so that the time would not be "far distant when the married woman who does not employ her leisure productively will feel herself to be an undesirable member of society." Financially rewarding work was the cure for the great sin of idleness, and "regardless of sex, no one has a right not to be busy and to be busy about something that is real and eternal." New-style feminists even extolled work as a guarantee against the vicissitudes of life. "Love may die and children may grow up, but one's work goes on forever," proclaimed Dorothy Bromley. The ramifications of enforced idleness were seemingly limitless. In their demand for employment, proponents of working wives barely concealed their attack on the legacy of nineteenth-century constraints on women in general.[45]

Yet, as advocates of working wives as the "new woman" glorified presumed qualities of gainful employment, workers and intellectuals alike were seriously questioning the intrinsic values of routine work. In their intensive study of the social structure and value systems of Muncie, Indiana, Robert and Helen Lynd found that the "routinized easily learned movements seem to have wiped out many of the satisfactions" formerly associated with the jobs of wage earners, while the gratification experienced by businessmen devolved from the leisure and status which, in turn, derived from earned income. For both classes, the Lynds concluded, the instrumental rather than the intrinsic features of work dominated attitudes toward employment. To Floyd Dell and other intellectuals of his generation, conventional work patterns were inimical to personal freedom, inseparable from the middle-class values against which they mounted their self-conscious revolt. Yet, to the feminists of the 1920s, work was perceived as inherently satisfying as well as the panacea for all personal and social liabilities.[46]

In a society where paid employment remained the moral and social imperative of men, the means of self-identification and status definition, marriage and career advocates adopted the most readily available model at hand. No matter how alienating, confining, or divorced from the positive attributes traditionally associated with work, they vowed to have jobs just as men did. And since men also had families, women should marry as well. "If only men would measure us with the same yardsticks with which they measure themselves," one working wife pleaded, they would understand feminist goals and assist women in attaining them.[47]

Proponents of working wives failed, however, to devise acceptable means by which the gospel of success, which traditionally accompanied the work ethic, could apply to working women as well as men. Dorothy Bromley envisioned female careers lasting forever, but in reality the work commitment of the employed wife often lacked continuity. Lorine Pruette could castigate the leisured wife as an emotional cripple and a social liability, but her solution was part-time employment, which implied that married women still retained domestic and child-rearing responsibilities. And while Pruette admitted that part-time jobs were limited, Katherine Angell, a married member of the editorial staff of the *New Yorker,* noted other serious handicaps. "Except in the most rare cases, no serious professional career can be accomplished by [part-time work]." In the end, women continued to bear the major responsibilities for homemaking, in theory and practice, and careers—part-time, discontinuous—reinforced the employers' assumption of lack of commitment, an impediment to promotion and related earmarks of success.

Besides accepting the cultural values and institutional patterns of their society, feminists suffered from the narrow class appeal of their program. The ideologies of feminism have seldom reached working-class women. Charlotte Perkins Gilman and Olive Schreiner had been unconsciously biased in their unqualified praise for paid work as the solution to women's inferior status and parasitic lives. They failed to examine the harsh, exploitative, and increasingly demeaning nature of much of the labor performed by many of their female—and male— contemporaries. Their perspective was distinctly middle-class, and their successors of the 1920s maintained the same class-biased message, tone, and imagery. The working wives described in academic studies, portrayed in periodical literature, and interviewed in case studies, were well-educated, impeccably dressed professional and business women who left lovely homes in the hands of competent servants as they set out to expand their horizons. They mirrored the social and economic backgrounds of authors and anticipated audience alike. Feminists had little to say to married working women outside the ranks of white-collar occupations. Reference to the impact of a second salary on a family's standard of living was only one feature of their detailed analysis and advocacy of outside employment for wives. By understating economic motives, feminists perpetuated the distinction between working-class

women, who worked because they had to, and business and professional
women, who supposedly worked because they desired an outlet for their
energies and talents, needed the psychological gratification, and deserved
the enhanced status that derived from paid work.

Class distinctions also marked the opposition to working wives.
Critics who addressed the issues of personal discontent and desire for
elevated status and who suggested upgrading the position of the homemaker through education accepted the assumptions and spoke to the
same middle-class audience as new-style feminists. But other defenders
of the traditional family structure and sex roles concentrated on working-
class women and stressed the economic impetus underlying their employment. The Women's Bureau of the Department of Labor, created
in 1920, conducted numerous surveys of the working conditions of
women and published the information in official bulletins. Ostensibly committed to the principles of occupational freedom, equal pay
for equal work, and elevating women's economic status, the bureau concentrated its surveys on low-status jobs in urban areas where high
proportions of foreign-born and black women worked. The focus was
intended to counter the notion that women worked only for luxuries
by demonstrating the economic dislocation that forced them into the
labor market, the extent to which they met family need by combining
occupational with domestic responsibilities, and the necessity for legislation to regulate the poor working conditions they encountered. Where
female workers were married, the bureau was explicit on economic
cause, social effect, and necessary cure. Married women worked because of the inability of male heads of household to earn adequate income for family support. Outside employment by mothers "frequently
means inadequate and casual care of children" while home work tends
"to upset the normal relations, since any diversion of a home to such
purposes impinges upon its efficiency as a place of relaxation and of
nurture of family life." The solution, the bureau believed, was better
wages for men, and mothers' pensions for divorced, separated, or
widowed women with dependent children.[49] William Green, president of
the American Federation of Labor (AFL), advocated strong unions to
raise wages to achieve the former, and advocates of the latter insisted
that they be better financed and administered.[50] Like the proposals
of the Women's Bureau, these remedies assumed the working-class
wife belonged at home.

Opposition aside, common ground did exist upon which working wives of varied social and economic backgrounds and their proponents could have met. Work histories displayed the same discontinuous work patterns; wage analyses demonstrated that married women had the lowest earnings within their varied occupational fields; and interviews revealed similar motivations and satisfactions as well as difficulties. In her study, Collier found that the working mothers with whom she spoke did, indeed, want an outlet for their abilities and ambitions. However, she also found "these women want money in order to give better homes, better education and greater advantages of all sorts to their children."[51] Their attitudes and expectations differed little from the wife of a pipe fitter in Muncie who worked as a cleaning woman:

> We've built our own home, a nice brown and white bungalow. . . . I have felt better since I worked than ever before in my life. . . . We have an electric washing machine, electric iron, and vacuum sweeper. I don't even have to ask my husband any more because I buy these things with my own money. . . . The two boys want to go to college, and I want them to.[52]

An awareness of common problems and benefits that existed across class lines might have led feminists to a more penetrating analysis of the difficulties involved in these new combined roles.

Advocates of marriage and careers for women underestimated the importance of economic factors in the propulsion of wives into the labor force. Mary Ross recognized that economics rather than ideology constituted the foundation for the reconstruction of family life through expanded productive functions for women. She noted that hundreds of thousands of individuals were exploring the means to establish new marriage, work, and leisure patterns for themselves and for their families, while at the basis of this process was "one of the most vexing questions of this generation: *Is economic support of the family a normal and continuing part of the lives of women as well as of men?*"[53] But the conjunction of forces that had occurred to raise these issues in the public consciousness and to boil over into vociferous debate during the 1920s escaped close examination. Changes in the physical setting of income-earning production were well described by new-style feminists as they proposed that married women should secure economically rewarded work outside the home, but possible alterations in consumption patterns and values that could necessitate increased family income and, in turn, motivate women to seek paid employment received much less attention.

Studies conducted throughout the 1920s revealed the disparities between prevalent income levels and estimated cost-of-living needs. The U.S. Bureau of Labor estimated that the minimum income needed for a family of five in Muncie was $1,920 in 1924. A sample of 100 working-class families studied by the Lynds revealed that three-quarters of them earned less than the minimum standard even if the family had more than one wage earner. The Lynds also noted an essential element in this gap between presumed needs and the ability to satisfy them: changes in the concept of acceptable living standards. In the home, in recreational activities, in educational aspirations, "every sector of living is exhibited by such new tools and services commonly used in Middletown today, but either unknown or little used in the nineties." The notion of economic necessity was changing as America became more consumer-oriented, as a staggering variety of new goods and services flooded the marketplace, as an expanding advertising industry informed and persuaded potential purchasers and as material expectations, judging from income levels, often exceeded the ability to satisfy new demands.[54] Home and job proponents overlooked the relationship between the role of married women as consumers in a society increasingly concerned with satisfying material wants and married women as possible producers, contributing their wages to help close the gap between family income and desired expenditures.[55]

Admittedly, even if feminists had examined more closely the relationships between the expanding consumer society and the increasing numbers of working wives, their opponents would not have been swayed. Economic need retained its narrow definition. The "pin money" theory of female employment continued to haunt married women as it had single women earlier in the century. Raising the family's standard of living was too broad a generalization for many of those who censured the working wife. A high standard of living merely masked the simple desire for comfort, hid an unconscionable surrender to consumer-oriented tastes. For conservative social critics, two salaries fed an insatiable desire for material goods, reduced savings, and created a new plutocracy which has "much more than is necessary to keep them in the way they would have lived two years ago, when only the husband would be in work." Those who cherished traditional roles for women would be likely to cling to other conventional values as well, and the working wife undermined the virtues of thrift. The concept of an economy of abundance based on spending for goods and services did not easily replace entrenched attitudes constructed around the notion of scarcity and the necessity of saving.[56]

This conflict in values was more subtle than the more vocal and volatile one over female roles to which it was partially related. Numerous polls revealed that, feminist rhetoric to the contrary, young women would select marriage and homes over careers. The sophomore class of Western Reserve University's College for Women dramatized the issue, anticipating Moss Hart's *Lady in the Dark* by a decade and a half in the process. The heroine of the 1922 skit wants a career, consults a psychoanalyst who advises marriage, dreams she is president, narrowly survives an assassination attempt, awakens, and returns to the arms of her boyfriend, career abandoned.[57] The scenario reinforced the delight with which investigators of women's attitudes concluded that "women are not deserting the role of home-maker in any such numbers as the popular press would lead us to believe." The audible sigh of relief masked the failure to recognize the extent to which the very nature of the questions asked in polls assumed and perpetuated the notion of alternatives or that some respondents chose a combination of roles. The numerous surveys and the reassurance derived from the results did, however, reveal the extent of societal anxiety that accompanied perceived and actual changes in female activities.[58]

Signs of disparities among feminist rhetoric, female-role expectations and actual behavior were surfacing. Young, educated women reported their preference for marriage over jobs, indicating that they did not heed advocates of combining homes with careers and were not convinced that socioeconomic changes and personal needs demanded new vocational expectations. Yet these women were also increasing their participation in the labor force and lengthening their employment span. During the 1920s, working wives increased 40 percent with perceptible growth in the twenty-to-thirty-five-year-old age group. Married women increased from 21 to 28 percent of all female workers. They still lagged behind single women in occupational distribution but continued to enter the ever expanding white-collar categories (which accounted for almost 44 percent of the women in 1930) at a greater pace than single women. Instead of retiring upon marriage, growing numbers of young women continued to work at least until the birth of their first child. For reasons that apparently had little relationship to conscious feminist activity, which women themselves ignored but in fact refuted, work was becoming identified with a new phase of the female life cycle.[59]

In spite of opposition to their program, failure to convince their logical constituency, and shortcomings in their own analyses, career and marriage feminists were closer to actual developments than their critics. Feminists of the 1920s ignored the benefits that were supposed to accrue to women in the aftermath of the suffrage victory and turned instead to proposing change in women's economic roles. They advocated paid employment for married women to improve the social and economic status and the psychological self-esteem of wives. They believed women had abilities beyond those required by familial responsibilities and domesticity and deserved the opportunity to utilize them without relinquishing the emotional gratifications that derived from love, marriage, and motherhood. Above all, they argued that women required financial compensation for productive labor, since economic independence lay at the foundation of freedom and equality.

Given time, feminists might have examined the rigidities of social patterns and attitudes and discovered and analyzed the complex factors behind the actual increase in working wives. They might have waited for numbers of employed married women to reach a level whereby a significantly large audience could relate to feminist goals and understand the conflicts inherent in new roles within traditional work force and familial patterns. Time, however, was not on their side. Before they could assimilate new census statistics and evaluate their own impact on trends, the nation was in the midst of economic chaos. Instead of refining their arguments, feminists were forced to recognize the extent to which hostile sentiment could influence employment policies. They diverted their attention to the defense of wives who had already obtained jobs and were subjected to pressure to relinquish them.

chapter 3

Governments, Working Wives, and Feminists

Opposition encountered by advocates of working wives during the 1920s was not just verbal. Throughout the decade, reports surfaced of attempted and actual dismissals of married women in both the public and private sectors of the economy. With the exception of the National Woman's Party (NWP), whose members discovered and publicized virtually every type and instance of discrimination experienced by women, few other proponents of the employment of married women noted or protested the translation of social sentiment into employment policy. A decade of depression turned that neglect into troubled awareness, then awareness into singular preoccupation. While hostility toward married women workers and economic constraints imposed on them were greatly exacerbated during the 1930s, the rationale that underlay discrimination remained constant. For the anxious leadership of women's organizations, however, growing apprehension over bitter denunciation and burgeoning restraints against working wives—and the deterioration of women's economic status generally—resulted in increasingly defensive, expedient rebuttals which eventually negated the feminist basis of their concern.

When initiated by employers, the refusal to hire or the discharge of married women was explained in terms of conventional social attitudes and values: that by hiring wives employers were somehow contributing to the demoralization of the home, to the reluctance of these women to bear children, and to the neglect of children already born to working mothers.[1] When pressure to circumscribe jobs for wives stemmed from workers, the motivations were ostensibly economic in nature. During the 1920s the Baltimore and Ohio Railroad agreed with the Brotherhood of Railway and Steamship Clerks to prohibit the employment of all wives as clerks. While never explicit about their intentions, male clerks may have feared economic competition in the wake of the 1922 strike of railroad shopmen, which resulted in programs of increased efficiency throughout the industry and possible personnel cutbacks in offices as well as in engine cabins and railroad yards. Printers, whose union vacillated for decades over the position of women in the industry, singled out married women for condemnation during the 1920s. A resolution introduced at the convention of the International Typographical Union in 1925 would have discouraged wives from retaining their jobs in printing shops where their husbands were also employed. The union president was instrumental in defeating the proposal, but only after impassioned debate.[2]

The two-pronged attack against the married woman worker during the 1920s—that she abrogated her social responsibilities on the one hand while competing economically on the other—remained the basis for discriminatory practices as the Depression intensified and levels of popular apprehension kept pace with mounting numbers of unemployed. The area in which the most concerted efforts to send married women workers back to their homes became the public sector, for there conflicting American values pertaining to the role of government converged with conventional ideals of women's place in society.

While dramatic growth in government employment, expenditures, and services is usually attributed to the policies of the New Deal and the exigencies of World War II, government activity had expanded perceptibly at all levels since the turn of the century. Post-1933 growth, especially at the federal level, accelerated developments that were part of long-term trends. Between 1900 and 1930, the number of local and state employees (excluding educators) increased almost 400 percent; workers associated with schools grew two and a half times in number; civilian employees at the federal level tripled. Even before the advent of the New Deal, federal agencies were established, and their sphere of activities increased while national, state, and local governments undertook a variety of regulatory, welfare, construction, and maintenance functions necessitated by a consolidating industrial and expanding urban and motorized society. In a nation where the virtues of self-reliance and minimal government activity were still matters of faith if not fact, these trends were cause for ambivalence if not outright apprehension.[3]

With the onset of the Depression, all levels of government experienced decreased financial resources. Even as new welfare needs begged for a share of diminishing public funds, the call for economy prevailed and resulted in a "wave of budget slashing which has lately become epidemic."[4] When economy measures necessitated reductions in personnel, decisions had to be made concerning the relative expendability of workers by function or social characteristics. Precedents existed for utilizing the latter criterion as a basis for discharge. Although they were confined largely to teaching, social welfare services, and the clerical forces affiliated with expanding bureaucracies, women constituted a significant segment of the expanding public work force, and approximately one-fifth of these were married. During the 1920s, married women teachers had experienced widespread discrimination at the local level,[5] while in 1925, without official sanction, married women were dismissed from the federal Bureau of Printing and Engraving. With growing numbers of jobless men pounding the pavements of the country's cities and towns, wives in public jobs became increasingly popular targets for censure. By early 1931, New York Assemblyman Arthur Swartz, among others, announced that the employment of married women was reprehensible and admonished "our federal, state and local governments [to] cooperate to remove these undeserving 'parasites.' "[6]

Officials at various levels of government reacted. Cities from Syracuse and Racine to Seattle either ordered the dismissal of wives from their jobs if their husbands earned "living wages" or undertook investigations into the feasibility of initiating such practices. When state legislatures convened in January 1931, representatives in Massachusetts and New York introduced bills stipulating that married women be discharged if their husbands also held government jobs. The governor of Kansas proposed a policy to bar married women from state employment if their husbands could support them; the California State Assembly considered three bills concerned with either the dismissal of working wives or the refusal to allow them to take Civil Service examinations. These legislative attempts failed, but, with little debate, the Wisconsin legislature passed a joint resolution declaring "it to be public policy of this state to distribute opportunities for employment in the State service, during periods of depression, as widely as possible." Refusal to hire the husband or wife of a state worker and to discharge either husband or wife if both were employed by the state were the means by which the Wisconsin legislature hoped to accomplish its goal. While the resolution applied to spouses, the individuals who resigned or who were discharged were overwhelmingly female.[7] And the federal government had a formula to follow.

Early suggestions to dismiss wives from federal government jobs made by President Hoover's Organization on Unemployment Relief and attempts by Congress to legislate that policy failed—but not for long.[8] What eventually became Section 213 of the 1932 Economy Act, the "married persons clause," originated in the House Subcommittee on Appropriations to Executive Departments, chaired by Congressman John Cochran of Missouri. Clothed in language that stressed the social necessity of preserving the American home by keeping the wife in it, Cochran initiated and insisted upon legislative implementation of his views. The clause stipulated that whenever personnel reductions took place in the executive branch, married persons were to be the first discharged if their spouse was also a government employee. It received little attention when it reached the floor of the House, seemingly an insignificant part of an omnibus bill that dealt with the reorganization of executive departments, creation of a department of national defense, establishment of a public works administration and provisions for veterans, in addition to sections detailing plans for salary reductions and personnel policies to effect interdepartmental economies. Congressmen concentrated on the suggested 10 percent pay cut for all government workers earning over $1,000 per year, and they debated the advisability of the salary reductions versus nonpaid furloughs for workers. By the end of May, the House had defeated the plan for a defense department, raised the limit on salaries designated for subsequent cuts to $2,500, increased the cut to 11 percent and sent the measure to the Senate where, for the first time, opposition to the married persons clause surfaced.[9]

Edwina Avery, member of the National Woman's Party and president of the Government Workers Council affiliated with the feminist organization, protested Section 213 in a letter which was inserted into the record during the Senate debate. The upper chamber struck out the original clause and substituted its own whereby discrimination against married persons would apply only in future appointments to the Civil Service. In the joint conference report, however, both the original and the Senate versions were recommended for passage along with the Senate's plan for a nonpaid furlough plan instead of specified salary reduction. (The

Senate proposal amounted to an 8.3 percent cut and was still considered the heart of the bill.) In the wake of conference recommendations, NWP members drafted additional letters to senators, paid personal visits to Capitol Hill, and issued press releases. As the Senate debated the conference report, one senator noted that the issue, which had originally aroused little interest, now dominated the debate. The Senate's decision to recommit the bill was frustrated, however, when the Speaker of the House, James Garner, refused to appoint new House conferees to replace those attending the Republican National Convention. Many senators were furious, equating the inaction with a deliberate attempt to force acceptance of the House-approved conference report. But time was at a premium. The Economy Act had been attached to a general appropriations bill, the end of the fiscal year was two days away, and even senators who adamantly opposed the discriminatory clause admitted it was impossible "to get the Government into the trouble that we would bring about by rejecting the Conference Report merely because of that one item in the bill." The Senate joined the House in passing the measure.[10]

President Hoover signed the Economy Act but specifically censured Section 213. "It imposes unnecessary hardships on government employees in minor matters of little consequence economically," he stated as he expressed confidence that the next session of Congress would remedy the inequities. The Government Workers Council praised "his just and clear-sighted stand in the matter," while NWP leader Gail Laughlin deplored the explicit indication that in "this era of depression, the first impulse seems to be to 'wallop the ladies.' "[11] Leaders of the Business and Professional Women's Clubs joined in denouncing the clause and stressed the broad implications of the measure, themes that would be developed during the struggle for repeal: "Such legislation is not only a blow to married women, but through implication to all women workers, and to marriage itself, so that there is a serious social side to such prohibition, as well as the economic one, affecting standards of living and so on."[12] At their annual meeting, Zonta, a service organization of women executives, joined the growing chorus of opposition. The national government was setting an example for both public officials and corporation managers "to make it an open season on married women, and vent their suppressed prejudices against giving them employment."[13]

Some of the predicted social consequences quickly materialized. The day the Economy Act passed, the *Washington Herald* carried a notice placed by a woman concerned over the plight of "lose-a-husband-and-save-a-job widows." "Married women planning to separate temporarily from their husbands owing to recent legislation and desiring comfortable home, communicate with Box A-33 *Washington Herald.*"[14] In September the Civil Service Commission, in order to deter this development, ruled that maintaining separate residences did not signify that a couple was not technically married and that doing so would not prevent the discharge of one of them.[15]

Organized efforts on behalf of repeal waited until the nation underwent a presidential campaign, struggled through the worst winter of the Depression, and inaugurated a new administration. In the meantime, discharges and furloughs had begun. Women threatened with dismissal from the Census Bureau complained bitterly that discharge with less than fifteen years of federal employment deprived them of all retirement benefits, even though their pension contributions were returned with small interest payments. Furlough without pay at least held out the possibility of eventual reemployment and the ability to complete the qualifying term of service. A few departmental officials did make use of the furlough option, but the Economy Act established no uniform rules, so bureau chiefs who personally opposed the employment of married women happily implemented the provisions of Section 213 and made economy cuts by outright discharge. In August 1932, fifty married persons, most of them women, were placed on indefinite leave by the Federal Farm Board. All forty-five married women in the Office of the Adjutant General were dismissed. By spring 1933, the new secretary of labor was receiving distraught letters from fired women, principally post office clerks and substitute rural letter carriers. By the time the clause marked its first anniversary, 1,505 married persons had been discharged, and an additional 186 had resigned in order to protect the positions of their spouses. The vast majority were women employed in the post office, treasury, war, navy, and veterans administration departments.[16]

In May 1933, representatives of nine women's organizations met the new budget director, Lewis Douglas, and appealed for an end to the dismissals. League of Women Voters President Belle Sherwin expressed her objection to this "administrative discrimination against women," and the league's legal counselor, Dorothy Kenyon, offered aid to embattled women workers.[17] A serious setback occurred when President

Roosevelt asked his attorney general for a ruling on the effective duration of the clause. Because the Economy Act was attached to an annual appropriations bill, there was uncertainty whether it should be construed as temporary, for the fiscal year, or permanent legislation. The attorney general ruled that the legislative history of Section 213 indicated it was intended to establish legislative policy and "it was therefore my opinion that this Section is permanent legislation."[18]

A plea to Roosevelt from the National Woman's Party that he use his powers under the Independent Offices Appropriation Act to halt dismissals and, at best, substitute a uniform furlough policy was ignored.[19] The president's role was ambiguous. Hardship letters from discharged women written to the White House were routinely forwarded to Douglas at the Bureau of the Budget and then returned to Presidential Aide Louis Howe or Administrative Secretary Marvin McIntyre, with perfunctory notes requesting that they draft appropriate responses. Howe replied to a woman from Birmingham, Alabama, who had described the financial difficulties resulting from her discharge, assuring her that the president "realizes the hardships which result in many cases on account of such reductions in Federal expenditures, but he feels that it is an essential part of a comprehensive program for the economic recovery of the nation." And Howe concluded by insisting that the president was without the authority to modify Section 213.[20]

At the same time, Roosevelt issued a press statement declaring that civil service personnel dismissed under the stipulations of the clause would have preferential hiring for positions in federal agencies—a policy that was not carried out. When the story of the economic deprivation of a woman dismissed from the Bureau of Foreign and Domestic Commerce reached the president's desk, he ordered McIntyre to investigate the situation because charges of inconsistent application of the measure and accusations of favoritism had surfaced. Political expediency required greater concern, and the president directed the Civil Service Commission to investigate. A detailed memorandum prepared by a commission member was highly critical of the manner in which the clause was implemented, but the administration remained inactive. Predictably, the only expression from the White House of unequivocal opposition to Section 213 and its enforcement came from Eleanor Roosevelt.[21]

While government officials wrangled over interpretation and implementation, women's organizations worked for repeal. At the end of

1933, the League of Women Voters formally declared its opposition and encouraged Congressman Emmanuel Celler of New York to introduce a bill repealing the clause. Celler's measure was sent to Cochran's Committee on Expenditures, where it was doomed. The author of the original section was more interested in the extension of constraints on the employment of wives than in repeal. A subcommittee within the Women's Joint Congressional Committee (WJCC), comprising representatives of women's organizations formed to lobby for reform measures of interest to some or all of its constituent groups, was then established to devise a more efficacious repeal route through Congress. With the aid of the president of the American Federation of Government Employees, Celler and the WJCC members decided to circumvent Cochran's committee by proposing an amendment to civil service legislation that would prohibit discrimination based on marital status. Celler's new bill was then sent to the House Committee on the Civil Service, and hearings were scheduled for April 1935—almost three years after the passage of the Economy Act.[22]

The Celler bill did not pass until July 1937, after another round of national elections was concluded, and a vote to turn the House of Representatives into a Committee of the Whole House finally dislodged the measure from the Rules Committee. Public opposition to working wives made Section 213 a politically advantageous symbol that government officials were reluctant to abandon. During the course of the final debate Cochran proudly acknowledged to advocates of repeal that he was "the villain of this drama," for he attributed his continued reelection to the importance of this issue in his district. Whatever other factors were also responsible for Cochran's electoral successes, if his mail bore any resemblance to letters written to national periodicals and local newspapers, his assessment of public attitudes toward married women workers was correct.[23] By the mid-1930s, with the advent of public opinion polling, it was possible to determine how accurately those letters reflected national sentiment. Regardless of demographic and geographic variables, numerous surveys revealed that Americans were overwhelmingly opposed to the employment of married women. George Gallup concluded that he had never seen respondents "so solidly united in opposition as on any subject imaginable including sin and hay fever."[24]

No polls indicated the level of public familiarity with Section 213 itself, but a reasonable amount of awareness can be assumed from a.

variety of references. Journalist Adela Rogers St. John wrote a series of articles for the Hearst newspapers depicting instances of physical hardship and economic deprivation complete with melodramatic cast of crippled children, sick relatives, and old grandmothers who had lost their means of support because of the federal legislation.[25] Columnist Franklin Pierce Adams versified:

> *Oh for a play by Bernard Shaw*
> *On the Federal Marital Status Law!*[26]

Shaw expressed no interest, but popular novelist Rupert Hughes wrote a six-part serial, "Section 213—A Story Behind the Headlines," which was published by the *New York Herald Tribune*. Readers suffered with a distraught couple caught between their careers and needed salaries and the renunciation of marriage plans. And an official history of the Civil Service, published in the immediate aftermath of the Depression, described the Economy Act and acknowledged that Section 213 was "the best known of [its] provisions."[27]

If Section 213 was politically expedient for government officials, it was socially and economically abhorrent to the women who opposed it. From passage until repeal, before congressional committee hearings, in their publications, and in public pronouncements, the leaders of women's organizations maintained their opposition in the face of a hesitant administration, recalcitrant Congress and hostile public. Repeatedly, the spokespersons of groups ranging from the National Woman's Party and the Business and Professional Women's Clubs to the League of Women Voters, the Women's Trade Union League, and General Federation of Women's Clubs, demonstrated the futility of a handful of dismissals in the face of overwhelming national unemployment. But for these women the clause represented more than just an attack on 1,600 married government clerks. The attempt to proscribe the employment of married women was perceived in broader context, as a government-sanctioned blow to marriage and career feminism in particular and a blatant attempt to undermine female occupational status in general.

Within this framework, the NWP warned that economic stress too often masked the desire "to place a brake on the steady advance in the gainful employment of women which is a necessary accompaniment of our changed social and economic conditions."[28] While comparatively

few women had been affected by Section 213, the Government Workers
Council stressed the wide-ranging ramificatons of such curbs:

> The mania to take jobs away from married women and give them to men,
> if not checked, can easily grow to include all women. Such laws . . . have a
> vital bearing on the whole social status of woman—her education, her
> career. If she is to be deprived of the privilege which all men enjoy of
> equal continuity in employment and promotion, the incentive for prepara-
> tion is gone . . . she finds herself deprived of the privilege of choice as to
> how she shall shape her life.[29]

BPW reported that restraints on working wives and the "strain of long
continued depression [have] raised in the minds of American women
questions acute and arresting as to their place in the occupational
world," and BPW leaders warned women "to protect themselves from
further loss of those opportunities which they have gained at such cost
in the past." The YWCA enrolled in efforts to "hold the gains in freedom of choice in work which women now have and allow no new laws
and policies to be enacted to limit that freedom."[30]

The spokespersons of women's organizations not only demonstrated
their feminist concern for the social and economic status of American
women by combatting the "married persons clause," they were also
sensitive to developments abroad that they considered inimical to wom-
en's progress. By early 1934, Alma Lutz of the National Woman's
Party and writer-psychologist Lorine Pruette were both equating American discriminatory policies with the "back to the home" movements in
Italy and Germany.[31] Witnesses before the House hearing on Section
213 made the analogy, and in 1936 the League of Women Voters introduced its pamphlet devoted to the constraints encountered by married
women workers with the warning that "an attack of this sort directly at
married women very soon becomes an attack on opportunities for employment of all women, an attitude of mind which has come to be
characteristic of that philosophy of government which we know as
Fascism."[32] Constant comparisons with German and Italian attitudes
and practices toward women workers became an important theme in the
rhetoric of those defending working wives. It was an indication of the
extent to which they feared the deterioration of women's occupational
gains at home as well as their early and continuing awareness of the
social implications of fascism abroad.

Concentration on the policies of fascist countries, however, concealed the existence of attacks on the employment status of married women in most Western industrial nations, which were then reeling under the impact of economic dislocation. Worldwide depression led governments, regardless of their political orientation—but usually for political considerations—to adopt similar policies in their attempts to cope with severe economic distress. U.S. and German attempts to foster recovery in industry and agriculture, deal with the problems of unemployed youth, and blunt potential class conflict had much in common. Among the similar approaches to common problems was the attempt to circumscribe employment opportunities for married women, an appealing solution to unemployment to which many countries resorted. By emphasizing the situation in Germany and Italy, the leaders of women's organizations singled out these nations as pariahs and dramatized their own opposition to all curbs on working wives, but they also understated the pervasive international phenomenon of which Section 213 was only one example.[33]

Still, it was the federal clause that heightened the self-perceptions of its female opponents as an embattled class, the only ones who could be counted upon to insist that married women must not be made the "sacrificial lambs to the need for more jobs."[34] Their sustained and eventually successful battle seemed to justify a period of self-congratulation when the Celler amendment finally passed in July 1937. They were mistaken, however, in their assumption that relegating Section 213 to the junk heap removed and discredited the model for state governments to emulate. States' efforts to circumscribe the rights of married women workers, which began in 1931, continued sporadically during the years when attention centered on the federal measure and then burgeoned at the end of the decade.

Some state institutions did not wait for legislation or resolutions to sanction action against working wives. Antinepotism rules that had developed since the early years of the twentieth century gave colleges and universities a useful lever. Originally conceived as a reform measure to free schools from political patronage appointments, they became the instruments for increasing opposition to the employment of faculty wives during the 1930s when retrenchment became prevalent. In some instances, marriage itself and not a relationship to a faculty member became adequate grounds for denial of employment. Two land grant colleges refused to hire married women, and another replaced its married dean of women with the admonition that "marriage itself was for a woman an adequate career."[35]

Another case involved historian Caroline Ware, who had been hired to teach at the University of Wyoming during the summer session of 1935. The institution discovered that she was married to government economist Gardner Means. Administrators explained their policy prohibiting the hiring of married women and apologized profusely for the oversight. Ware refused to accept the situation without formal protest. "My concern is not with the loss of a summer job and salary but with the integrity of American education and the status of American women." For the state that had been the first to grant women suffrage to engage in such policies was especially galling. Her publicized protests and panoply of arguments failed to regain her appointment or to alter the university's policy.[36]

The united efforts of state-based branches of women's organizations together with the passage of social reform legislation and temporarily improved economic conditions stemmed efforts to enact discriminatory legislation in a number of states during their 1935 sessions. But two years later, reduced federal expenditures precipitated an economic downturn and the specter of extensive, perhaps perpetual, unemployment and stagnation grew. By this time, the simplistic, appealing Depression cures of Doctor Townsend, Huey Long, and Father Coughlin had been largely discredited, and in the midst of renewed search for remedies, a government report on unemployment bolstered those who saw a direct relationship between labor force participation by married women and unemployment among men.

John D. Biggers, who administered the voluntary, week-long mail survey of national employment and unemployment, studied the data and reached one definitive conclusion. The number of workers with or without jobs anticipated by projecting 1930 figures forward on the basis of expected population increases and changes in overall age composition was exceeded by 2.75 million. According to Biggers, that figure was equal to the unexpectedly higher number of women who had either entered the labor force or had not withdrawn as anticipated. Increases were marked among white and black women, in farm and nonfarm occupations, and in all age categories. But women between twenty-five and thirty years of age represented the largest single group.[37] Commentators speculated that these new workers were "apt to be recently widowed, separated or divorced persons, or they may be wives forced into the labor market when the family income is inadequate."[38]

At the beginning of the 1939 legislative session, a virtual epidemic of proposed "married persons clauses" broke out in twenty-six states. In some cases, discharge was mandatory if the spouse was also employed by the state; in others, arbitrary income levels for one earner were established above which a spouse would face dismissal—maximum annual earnings permitted ranged from $800 in Utah to $3,000 in one proposed Massachusetts bill; $1,200 to $1,800 was most common. In some cases, any gainfully employed spouse disqualified a married woman from a state job.

Massachusetts became the center for renewed opposition to the employment of married women. In 1937, the lower house of the state legislature passed a measure barring wives from the civil service, and although it progressed no further, efforts to gain discriminatory legislation continued. The following year, heated hearings took place over the issue. The Massachusetts Women's Political Club, a group of socially and politically conservative women, and its president, Florence Birmingham, were especially active in lobbying for the measures. The organization had campaigned against working wives during the entire decade. They had written letters to the White House early in 1935 protesting the preference granted to married women yeomen in government service, had lobbied and picketed in Boston against all married working women the following year, and had written to Representative Cochran supporting Section 213 as well. [39]

The Women's Political Club operated in a hospitable climate. Even without legislation, exclusion of married women in private industry, as well as in public employment, was widespread in Massachusetts. Court decisions removing the protection of tenure from married women teachers resulted in the dismissal of these teachers in seventy-two municipalities in the state. In 1938, the club promoted a referendum in thirty cities and towns in fifty-seven districts on the issue of granting the legislature the right to enact bars against the employment of married women. The voters approved, two to one. With this indication of popular support and additional pressure from Birmingham's organization, five bills were introduced into the Massachusetts legislature when it met at the beginning of 1939.[40]

In the midst of these developments, Birmingham became embroiled in a verbal duel with Eleanor Roosevelt. During a press conference in Boston, in response to a question on the employment of married women, the first lady replied that she hoped "we will not be stampeded into a drive against working wives." Birmingham was incensed, accused Mrs. Roosevelt of meddling in the affairs of the state, and challenged her to debate the issue "at your convenience, publicly or privately." The mayor of Northampton joined the fray and advised Mrs. Roosevelt to "attend to your own knitting" and emulate his neighbor, Grace Coolidge, who had let her husband do the talking (!) on public matters. Roosevelt declined to debate, not because Mrs. Coolidge was her model but rather because "a more important opinion than ours has been rendered in your state." The Massachusetts Supreme Court had ruled that married women could not be excluded from public employment unless the general public and not merely a particular class of citizens—presumably men and unmarried women—would benefit.[41]

Birmingham refused to acquiesce to the court opinion. She vowed to seek an amendment to the state constitution while her fervent supporter, the mayor of Northampton, asserting that "woman's place is in the maternity ward," sought procedural advice from senators Walsh and Lodge in Washington on amending the federal constitution.[42] But on the basis of the court decision and adverse committee reports, the state legislature defeated all five proposed bills, whereupon the Massachusetts Women's Political Club adopted resolutions "condemning the interference of Eleanor Roosevelt in Massachusetts' legislation and her refusal to debate on the issue of working wives although she assumed the initiative in this state and became their mouthpiece." The organization was especially critical of Mrs. Roosevelt because she had affirmed her belief in debate during an appearance before the Workers'Alliance, "a communist-sponsored and dominated organization," and "the Communist party in this state went on record as opposing our proposed legislation to bar married women from employment." At the same time, Mrs. Roosevelt refused to debate the president of "an organization composed wholly of loyal American citizens."[43]

Redbaiting and invective masked an essential factor in the issue of female employment during the Depression: the rivalry between married and single women workers. The Massachusetts Women's Political Club spoke on behalf of unemployed single women as well as jobless men and demonstrated the economic competition among women that often erupted into undisguised bitterness and hostility. Appeals on behalf of the unmarried female indicated the extent to which societal expectations for women during the time between school and marriage had come to include gainful employment. According to the opponents of working wives, married women workers not only deprived male breadwinners but also young women of jobs during a distinct phase of the female life course when their employment was anticipated.

Defenders of working wives were conscious of this important source of criticism and deplored it. During the battle against Section 213, the National Woman's Party warned single women who attacked working wives that they jeopardized their own employment status should they marry. Later in the decade, the New York Federation of Business and Professional Women's Clubs criticized the short-sightedness of young, single girls, and the Women's Trade Union League tried to shame those "whose faces will be red in a few months hence when they find themselves on the other side of the argument, with a wedding ring on the left hand and the right hand unwilling to give up a job secured at long last."[44] In the midst of intense competition for employment, these pleas for unity went unheeded. Birmingham appealed to a significant constituency. Events in Massachusetts were just the most dramatic examples of widespread attempts to curb employed wives which erupted in 1939 and "swept this winter like an epidemic over the entire country."[45] No other state dealt with so many separate proposals or hosted a formal organization devoted to banning married women. But twenty-five additional states tried to pass similar restraining laws, and a Chicago-based group distributed a folder outlining its plans to "Put the Married Women Back in the Home." The Wage Security Plan called for the cooperation of employers and governments at all levels. While unemployed men pounded the pavements, "married women continued to usurp the rightful place intended for man by the Creator."[46]

The veterans of the fight against Section 213 reactivated their forces. The American Association of University Women joined the ranks. Earlene White, president of the BPW, warned allied groups to heed the lessons learned at the national level; proposed legislation should be stopped before enactment because the battle for repeal could be long, time consuming, and distracting. In a few states, organizations were able to marshal their forces quickly and effectively. Pressure from the

Washington BPW prevented that state's proposed bill from getting a second reading, keeping it in committee until the legislature adjourned. Testimony of representatives of YWCA, BPW, League of Women Voters, and Zonta at hearings in Connecticut convinced state senators of the ill-advised nature of their bill. In Oklahoma, leaders from women's organizations testified and succeeded in postponing consideration of that state's attempt to discriminate.[47]

With or without the lobbying efforts of women's groups, almost all of the proposed legislation failed. Only the lower houses of Ohio and Utah passed discriminatory bills. The combined lobbying and testimony of the Ohio BPW, League of Women Voters, and the Dayton branch of the National Woman's Party convinced the Ohio Senate to postpone consideration, and the proposal died. The Utah Senate also defeated a "married persons" bill, but the legislature proceeded to pass a joint resolution declaring that preference in public employment should be given to applicants who did not have other members of their families so employed. Several states discovered that resolutions and governors' executive orders could accomplish discriminatory aims when legislative proposals floundered.[48]

A specific "married persons" bill passed in only one state. Louisiana was the scene of political struggle between the entrenched Long machine and reform factions. The support of discriminatory legislation became part of a power play between opposing forces. When the governor of the state resigned because of ill health, he was succeeded by his lieutenant governor, Earl Long, heir apparent and brother of Huey. In January 1940, the interim governor failed to get the necessary majority of votes in the Democratic party primary, thus necessitating a run-off election. Long immediately called the Louisiana legislature into special session and offered twenty bills, including one to dismiss a person in state employ whose spouse was also employed by the state and earning $100 per month or more.

Long's opponents criticized the obvious bid for public favor when this host of appealing legislation was rammed through the legislature filled with his lame-duck supporters. But the life of the specific measure affecting state-employed spouses was short. Earl Long was defeated in the run-off election. The Louisiana BPW, which admitted that the earlier political situation and time element had made it impossible to marshal its opposition forces, now lobbied quietly and effectively for repeal. The new governor concurred, and after just six months on the record books the measure passed from the scene.[49]

Women's organizations and concerned individuals stood virtually alone in the face of the flood of state proposals. In the battle against Section 213, they had active support from the American Federation of Government Employees, but the principal union that had organized state workers during the last half of the 1930s remained aloof from the problems confronting some of the female members of their constituency. The American Federation of State, County and Municipal Employees gained a charter from the parent federal union in 1936 and made great organizational strides afterward. Although their strategy focused on expansion and enforcement of civil service requirements and coverage, union records indicate that it had no concern with marital status as a possible bar to public employment. A Congress for Industrial Organizations (CIO) rival, the State, County and Municipal Workers of America, was much more sensitive to the "married persons" issue, but that union and its concern were both short-lived.[50]

As BPW officials warned that the plethora of state bills represented "the most serious problem confronted since the organization formed in 1919,"[51] additional voices were raised in behalf of working wives. Eleanor Roosevelt used her newspaper column to inform her readers that "it seems to me so obvious that married women should not be discriminated against that I cannot imagine anyone who would really consider such a proposition."[52] Since the public and their elected officials did consider just such propositions, Virginia Gildersleeve, dean of Barnard College, novelist Margaret Culkin Banning, historian Mary Beard, and entertainer Kate Smith all expressed their opposition to discrimination and its intensification.[53] Even women's magazines, the bastions of domesticity and proponents of traditional female roles, published articles and editorials defending married women and their jobs. An editorial in *Woman's Home Companion* questioned limiting women to homemaking if they have time, talent, and energy for additional undertakings. The epidemic of efforts to curb working wives "has been becoming cruel and often vicious," according to a writer in *Good Housekeeping*, and the editors of *Ladies' Home Journal* agreed.[54]

The apprehensions aroused by the intensified assault on married working women created a unity among women's organizations and institutions unmatched since the passage of the Nineteenth Amendment.

Like the suffrage movement twenty years earlier, however, opposition to this distinct form of economic discrimination proved a narrow issue around which women of disparate views could unite, and the extent of their concern was shallow. Leaders of women's organizations confessed that their outrage was not always shared by the rank and file. The chair of the LWV Committee on the Legal Status of Women, who led the group's defense of working wives, reported that "you will find that many of our own members are not thoroughly convinced that the League's point of view is the right one." Her counterpart in Zonta noted that some members opposed that organization's resolution calling for the repeal of Section 213.[55]

As the attack on working wives grew, arguments on their behalf became increasingly narrow and defensive as well. Emphasis, earlier in the decade, on women's right to work, the desirability of productive employment as a means of self-fulfillment, and the necessity to sustain economic opportunity became less prevalent. Instead, the spokespersons of women's groups stressed the predominant role economic need of families played as the motivating factor in the gainful employment of married women. Just as Women's Bureau bulletins of the 1920s had concentrated on the important income contribution of working wives to family welfare, the bureau continued to conduct similar surveys during the Depression in order to underscore the deleterious impact on families of efforts to proscribe the employment of married women. BPW publications quoted widely from Women's Bureau reports insisting that "even before the Depression studies tended to show that as high as ninety percent of working women were doing so because of family necessity."[56] Early in 1937, however, the BPW could still reconcile the economic responsibilities of working wives with the feminist goal of autonomy and self-definition through gainful employment. "Revealed for the most part as a worker outside the home from family necessity," the married woman worker still symbolized "that freedom to seek self-realization that men and women should guard jealously," according to *Independent Woman*.[57]

In response to intensified attacks accusing working wives of abdicating their traditional roles and responsibilities in the home, defenders increasingly depicted married working women as praiseworthy individuals who were meeting economic obligations to their families when, in fact, they would rather be at home. An intensive BPW study at the end of the decade concluded that constraints on the employment of married women were unconscionable, for these women worked "only because their families needed the money they earned. They preferred not to work outside the home." A syndicated columnist defended the right of wives to work because it was common knowledge that "90 percent of these women would rather be at home sewing on buttons, arranging flowers, and baking beans for their families." Furthermore, the willingness of young women to assume the burdens of work made marriage possible, given the economic uncertainties and inadequate wage scales of the period. Alma Lutz of the NWP attacked discriminatory practices because they penalized marriage, and those who believed "in high moral standards and the sanctity of the home may well be alarmed." Since few couples could marry on the salary of one, according to a Woman's Party colleague of Lutz, the issue was not "Can married women work?" but rather "Can working women marry?" The right of a wife to work must be protected, for even though her "place is in the home . . . she must have a home in which to stay, which her employment makes possible."[58] The traditional behavioral trait of self-sacrifice combined with the conventional social expectation of marriage to form the rationale protecting married women workers.

As the rhetoric of the leaders of women's organizations increasingly emphasized the self-denial and family-oriented values of working wives, defenders also insisted that these virtues precluded the personal desire to work and the satisfaction that one derived from employment. A BPW survey, published and circulated in order to blunt opposition to working wives, minimized the commitment of women to occupational continuity and success. "The number of married women who work simply for a career is negligible, despite the vast sums spent on specialized education for women. . . . These women are exceptions to the rule as to why married women work."[59] The *Ladies' Home Journal*, basing an editorial on behalf of working wives on the BPW study, popularized the argument that "no selfish desire for a career prompts [them] to work, simply the pressure of financial need."[60]

While interest in economic advancement was deprecated, the occupational structure itself was used to counter critics who stressed the threat working women posed to "legitimate" breadwinners in a contracted labor market. Defenders emphasized the noncompetitive nature of female employment and the futility of attempting to solve male unemployment by dismissing women. According to Mary Anderson of the Women's Bureau, "the important fact is that women compete very little with men for jobs since all available data show that their occupations usually differ markedly from those of men." Low-status, sex-stereotyped jobs simply were not "the kind men could or would take for their own employment."[61] Like the economic motivation underlying the work roles of most wives and the anticipation of marriage by most young women, the description of female occupational distribution was well grounded in fact. But this argument made a virtue of occupational segregation by sex as well as serving as an implicit attack on those women in, or anticipating entrance into, nontraditional fields of employment. Together with the denigration of careerism, it represented a self-defeating plea for the occupational status quo.

As the content of the feminist response changed, the very concept of feminism withered. In the 1920s, Dorothy Bromley had described "feminist—new style" in terms of individual women combining marriage and careers. The combined efforts of women's organizations opposing Section 213 provided the context within which the president of the National League of Women Voters defined "a 1935 new-style feminism." It had become "a movement which demands women making good in positions of responsibility, other women backing them up, and all preparing themselves for similar service."[62] At the same time, writer Genevieve Parkhurst believed erroneously that feminism was dead because women's organizations were not active on behalf of embattled working women.[63] The focus had shifted from personal achievement in expanded roles to group solidarity in defense of those roles, but it was still conceived of as feminism.

Early in 1935, the Institute for Women's Professional Relations sponsored a conference on women's work and women's stake in public affairs. In her formal remarks, Chase Going Woodhouse, director of the institute, urged women to become more involved with public issues and help to discover solutions to cyclical unemployment. Economic dislocation led to attacks on married working women and presented a threat to the political and social fabric. Recovery was essential. "Today feminism and democracy will be saved together or go down together," she declared.[64] But by the end of the decade this union was severed. The married woman worker issue was publicly articulated in terms of freedom and liberty within a democratic society, not as a feminist concern.

Why, asked Alma Lutz of the NWP, do those "guarding women's hard earned freedom . . . watching business and government policies to see that they do not discriminate against women . . . shy away from the designation 'Feminist'?" Allies in the defense of working wives indicated it was a matter of expediency. Members of Zonta warned that defenders of married workers should be careful "not to become feministic and create psychological barriers between men and women that will result in lingering discrimination once the Depression ends." Officers of the BPW advised their members that "it was easier to get the vote than it may be to retain our jobs." The fight over the means to a livelihood was, she said, unlikely to make men gallant or just. While women must be firm in preventing the passage of state bills, they must also be sympathetic toward the bitterness of men and single women without jobs. The public must be educated to the futility of the discharge of working wives as a solution to the unemployment crisis, but the campaign should be undertaken with diplomacy and understanding so that women will not appear "too aggressive or pugnacious." A special BPW committee concurred. "All plans must be adopted and modified to the atmospheric pressure of public opinion."[65]

One practical way to capture popular support was to downgrade the feminist aspects of the battle on behalf of married working women and place the issue within the framework of political and diplomatic developments. A few years earlier, Section 213 was conceived as the precursor of an attack on all working women with the fate of female progress and social and economic status hanging in the balance. Later in the decade, the ultimate stakes had changed. According to Earline White of the BPW, proposed state restraints "are but the entering wedge of an attack upon all women who work, and hence upon democracy." Being "vigilant to guard the economic freedom of women" was an important ingredient in the struggle to preserve liberty and democracy, a spokeswoman for Zonta wrote.[66]

In an address before the National Conference of Social Workers entitled, "The Danger to Democracy of Legislation Against Minority Groups," Mary Winslow of the Women's Bureau stressed the political significance extended beyond the married woman worker to "those who would preserve the fundamental demands of democracy—the right of any citizen to work, to earn and to share in the constructive tasks of democracy. . . . This is not a feminist issue."[67] The YWCA reprinted her speech. Significantly, their publication titled it, "This Is Not a Feminist Issue."[68]

It is difficult to determine the extent to which defenders of working wives internalized predominant social values and growing political fears and expressed them in their rhetoric or merely bowed to external exigency. To their own membership, women's leaders continued to insist that "a married woman should have the opportunity to develop by using all her talents and skills as she chooses." It was essential "to combat the traditional point of view that 'woman's place is in the home,' " and to educate a "society grimly determined to 'put the married woman in her place.' "[69] The defense that concentrated on portraying the married working woman as a gainfully employed female carrying on traditional functions may have been cleverly expedient.

On the other hand, the American public was becoming increasingly apprehensive over events abroad. Not only was German aggression viewed as a military threat to world peace, but the belief that the nation and its political principles and institutions were menaced by a dangerous new ideological force was growing as well. After war erupted in Europe, and especially after Great Britain remained the only apparent bulwark against encroaching fascism, public concern for the survival of American values and institutions erupted. Even the intellectual community perceived democracy as an endangered political species and reexamined the conceptual and methodological underpinning of its various disciplines, while it groped for philosophical theories and moral props for the democratic system.[70] Identifying the right of married women to their jobs with the essence of a free democratic society was probably more than an efficacious maneuver. This reasoning undoubtedly reflected the anxieties of the defenders themselves, as the American community added new apprehensions about events abroad to old concerns about lingering economic ills at home.

Through a decade of Depression and then impending war, one issue captured the interest of articulate women and their organizations: the question of the gainful employment of married women. In retrospect, it was of short-term significance. With economic recovery and wartime labor shortages, overt hostility, if not quiet misgivings, over married women workers disappeared. Of more lasting impact was the erosion of feminist rhetoric and thought. Defenders explained and supported the employment of married women on the economic basis of why they worked and not on feminist assumptions of why they should work. Married women's right to employment was based, it was said, on their overriding concerns for their families and not on earlier hopes of enhancing women's status. By the time the employment of married women burgeoned during and after World War II, a positive ideology encouraging personal and occupational progress and equality had vanished—a casualty of the Depression decade.

chapter 4

Even Spinsters Need Not Apply: Teachers in the Depression

Fourteen percent of the female labor force was classified as professional workers when the Depression struck. Two-thirds of the women engaged in these professional pursuits were teachers. Proportionately they dominated the teaching profession. Changes were occurring in the economic status of teachers and in the institutional structure of schools that had already influenced and would continue to affect the sex composition of the nation's teaching staffs. But with women constituting four-fifths of all teachers in 1930, to describe the impact of the economic crisis on this group of workers is to describe, in large measure, a female experience.[1]

During the 1920s, several developments enhanced the status of the teaching field. The lengthening of the years of compulsory education, an expanding curriculum, and consequently growing numbers of secondary schools resulted in increased demand for teachers. Greater employment opportunities were accompanied by improved training facilities, more exacting qualifications for admission to normal schools and university departments of education, longer and more uniform courses of study, and more rigorous certification policies. These constant goals of critics, who insisted on raising the standards and consequently the status of the profession, made the teaching degree more difficult, time consuming, and costly to obtain. But enrollment in teacher preparatory institutions continued to grow.[2]

Prospective teachers were encouraged, in part, by the overdue rise in salaries relative to other employment fields and especially in relation to wartime and postwar soaring living costs. Financial compensation

remained lower than incomes in government, industry, and other professions. Only clerical workers, another predominantly female field, received
lower annual incomes than personnel associated with public schools;
but after 1922 teachers' salaries did rise perceptively. By mid-1931, just
as wage retrenchments began, the buying power of teachers' incomes
approached that of other wage earners. Improved financial status
was an additional factor in attracting young people into the profession,
especially men. The feminization of teaching, which marked the history of the field, was reversed during the 1920s.[3]

For the first time since the movement for the establishment of public
schools, the supply of teachers approached demand by the middle
of the 1920s. This situation was not universal; urban areas were most
likely to experience oversupply where higher pay and better facilities
drew the growing number of graduates from preparatory institutions.
Competition for positions grew. Pressure was exerted in two directions:
on women generally by increasing numbers of men entering the profession, and on married women teachers already employed by young,
single women. These conflicts over contracted occupational opportunities
were greatly exacerbated when the full impact of the economic collapse
of the 1930s hit the nation's school systems.

Few Americans or their institutions survived the Depression intact,
but the public schools and their teachers were particularly vulnerable.
Economic contraction accentuated the ambivalent attitude toward public
education that had been a constant feature in the debate over the role
of the school in a society where the expressed desire for extensive,
quality education countered public reluctance to assume the costs.
(Low-paid teachers had been one solution to that dilemma.) By the
early 1930s, the failure of high school graduates to find employment,
thus casting doubt on the time-honored relationship between education
and economic opportunity, caused some devaluation of education and
raised innumerable questions about the quality, function, and cost of
schools.[4]

Virtually all systems encountered financial difficulties because they
were so dependent on local property taxes for support. Widespread delinquency among taxpayers and lowered assessments to grant relief to
hard-pressed mortgage holders who did pay their tax bills depleted
local treasuries. In addition, some school districts saw funds evaporate
in failed banks while others had monies frozen for extended periods

of time. Communities often turned to their states for aid, and by the end of the 1930s the proportion of school budgets assumed by local and state governments had shifted perceptively. But as the economy deteriorated during the early 1930s, states were more concerned with relief for the unemployed, and school systems resorted to a variety of financial retrenchments. These policies encountered little public opposition, but for teaching personnel they were disastrous.[5]

Before the end of the school year in June 1931, reports surfaced of numerous cases of inability to meet teacher payrolls.[6] This development was a mere warning of the storm that was to hit the schools during the 1931-32 terms. Schools either closed or shortened sessions. Closings were especially prevalent in rural areas. Seven hundred and fifty schools, affecting 36,000 students, closed in Arkansas alone during the year; almost 5,000 rural schools shut their doors throughout the country. In cities, costs were cut by curtailing programs initiated over decades and suddenly viewed as unnecessary frills. Kindergartens and classes for adults closed, health services ceased, and expenditures on art and music instruction, for vocational training, and physical education either ended or were severely cut. For teachers in these areas, the result was unemployment. Staff reduction was also achieved by refusing to fill vacancies as they occurred by transferring assistant supervisors into teaching positions, and especially by increasing the teaching load through larger classes or increases in the number of class periods assigned. In New York City, the average high school class jumped from twenty to thirty-one. In Manchester, New Hampshire, where depressed shoe and textile manufacturers demanded and received reduced property evaluations, rural schools closed, and their students were transported to the city. Nineteen high school teachers were dismissed, and those remaining taught six sessions instead of the previous five, and department heads' work loads increased from three classroom periods to four and five. Outright dismissals and school reorganizations across the nation resulted in approximately 80,000 unemployed teachers by the time classes resumed in fall 1933, about 8 percent of the 1930 teaching force. By January 1936, when schools began recovery, the Work Progress Administration (WPA) still certified 40,000 teachers as eligible for relief. Since the vast majority of unemployed teachers were women, and since certification of women for federal relief programs was more stringent than that of men, this figure does not represent the full impact of joblessness among teachers.[7]

Additional factors compounded the numbers and problems of the unemployed teachers. In New York, teachers declared eligible to teach had to engage in their profession within four years or lose their certification. An Unemployed Teachers Association formed and demanded that the time limit of the 1928 roster be extended so that expirations would not occur through no fault of the currently unemployable but certified teachers. And in New York, as in hundreds of communities across the country, the numbers of unemployed and deferred employables were augmented by applications from new graduates which simply were not processed.[8]

For the teachers who retained their jobs, fortunate as they were, the Depression meant combinations of decreased salaries, deferred salaries, difficult working conditions in the classroom, and constant anxiety over where the next retrenchments would fall and whom they would affect. By the time the 1932 school term began, salary reductions were a nation-wide occurrence. Minneapolis reduced salaries 10 percent and opened school two weeks later than usual, thus effecting an additional half-month deduction from salaries. A plan suggested by the New York school board to save $750,000 by requiring absent teachers to share in the cost of paying substitutes failed, but savings were achieved by filling vacancies with substitute teachers who retained their rank rather than being promoted to a full-time position with an annual salary. In the fall of 1933, salaries across the country were 5 to 40 percent below 1929-30 levels, one-fourth of all city schools were on shortened terms, and in rural areas, where closings were becoming endemic, 700 schools expected to run three months or less.[9]

The size of salary reductions varied as widely as teachers' pay. In 1930, the average teacher received $1,400, but great disparities existed according to the size and the location of the school. The median salary for a teacher in a one-room, rural schoolhouse was $788; the average pay for urban personnel was $1,771. But even within these divisions, there was wide state-to-state divergence. Arkansas paid the typical country schoolmarm $477 per year; California, $1,360. The same states paid city teachers an average of $967 and $2,249, respectively. During the Depression, those receiving the lowest pay at the beginning of the economic debacle experienced the greatest reductions. By 1935, the salaries of rural teachers were cut by an average of 33 percent while those of urban teachers fell by approximately 10 percent.[10]

For workers during the Depression, wage cuts and part-time employment (a shortened school term for teachers) were hardly unusual. For short periods of time, public and private employers even reverted to payment in scrip to survive temporary monetary crises. But few workers experienced the long, payless periods of employment that became commonplace among teachers. In a few localities, contracts actually specified that payment of salaries was not guaranteed. Boards of education simply stated that they would pay what and when they could. Minneapolis teachers sued over wage cuts and the lack of promise to pay. They lost. The judge merely castigated the school board for requiring teachers to accept contracts that failed to assure compensation. The teachers' complaints and insecurity were well founded. In the summer of 1933, the National Education Association reported that teachers were owed $37 million in back pay.[11]

In eighteen states, some teachers were paid in warrants which were usually cashed at discounts, thus compounding the salary reduction. In Arizona, pay cuts rose as high as 40 percent, and when salaries were then issued in warrants, teachers experienced an additional 10 percent loss.[12] Few school systems equaled Chicago's in its inability to meet teacher payrolls. The city's financial problems predated the Depression. In 1928, city property owners revolted against increased assessments, and the city was forced to raise funds by selling tax warrants; cash salaries to teachers ceased. By the fall of 1931, they were paid with 6 percent interest-bearing warrants. How well they managed depended upon the storekeepers with whom they dealt. One teacher recalled that some stores accepted the warrants at full value, and "old timers like us still go there." Another teacher received full value for her warrants by using them to pay her rent. Her landlord used them, in turn, to pay his real estate taxes. The city, at least, was obligated to accept its warrants at par. More often, teachers had their warrants discounted 50, 60, and even 75 percent. And then, during 1932-33, Chicago teachers received no compensation at all.[13]

The reactions of Chicago's beleaguered teachers ran the gamut of human behavior. Some women discovered a new activism traditionally unassociated with their profession. "We marched down LaSalle Street, we marched down Dearborn, we marched down Michigan Avenue. We marched everywhere. People were appalled. Teachers are supposed to be meek and mild. We were supposed to be the bulwark of the status quo and here we were, joining the revolution."[14] Others depleted their savings, carefully recorded their mounting debts, and wondered how long before they, too, would join the public protests. And for a few there were reports of nervous collapse and suicide to testify to years of economic deprivation and emotional strain.[15]

Like the national economy, the financial plight of the schools reached its nadir in 1934-35. By late summer, 1935, three-fourths of the cities reported at least partial restoration of salaries with the largest urban areas displaying the best recovery. Indianapolis restored half of its original 11 percent cut; Muncie introduced a new salary schedule, planning a phased four-year return to pre-1929 levels; New York salaries were already 2 percent higher than pre-Depression levels by the end of 1934. A survey conducted by the National Education Association (NEA) revealed that nationally the average teacher salary by the 1938-39 terms was $1,360, only slightly below the 1930 average of $1,400.[16]

Recovered salaries retained their geographic and sex differentials along with the disparities that existed among elementary and secondary scholteachers. When Cleveland boosted pay at mid-decade, high school teachers received $100 per year raises; junior high school teachers, $90; elementary school teachers, $80. This trend was inimical to women who monopolized positions in elementary schools and whose numbers thinned at higher grade levels. In Muncie, the superintendent purposefully planned to secure higher salaries for men, and, according to the Lynds, when the men asked how he planned to accomplish this feat, he replied, "Well, by golly! I'll say that you do better work than the women." However differentials were accomplished or maintained, they were part of a national pattern. By the end of the decade, junior high school teachers in cities received 13 percent more than their colleagues in elementary schools; senior high school teachers' salaries were 22 percent higher.[17]

Salaries, paid and unpaid, falling and recovering, do not tell the entire story of teachers and their Depression-decade experiences. Even at the end of the period, after the restoration of most pay schedules, 40 percent of elementary school teachers and almost half of high school teachers complained of heavy or extreme professional loads. No comparable study was made prior to 1930, and teacher dissatisfaction may have predated curtailments, but retrenchment policies undoubtedly affected the classroom as well as teachers' perceptions of their functions and performance at the same time that economic hardship and demographic trends had dramatic effects on the student population.

By 1933, additional class loads meant an estimated increase of eighty students per day over 1928 levels, and the discharge of clerical help increased teachers' duties. In Muncie, the average class size was thirty in 1923, but it rose to thirty-five by 1935. The Lynds found elementary schoolrooms with fifty and fifty-five children. Teachers in many communities found themselves instructing thirty-five to forty students with aging or even nonexistent textbooks and other instructional materials in deteriorating rooms designed for twenty-five.[18]

Accompanying larger classroom load, a significant shift took place in school population which was part of a long-term trend and was partly the result of Depression developments. During the first three decades of the twentieth century, the number of secondary school students increased 750 percent. By 1930, 4.75 million youngsters, one-half of the eligible age group, were enrolled in junior and senior high schools. At the same time, the disparity between boys and girls attending secondary schools narrowed. By the onset of the Depression, boys constituted 48 percent of high school students, an increase from a little over 40 percent in 1900.[19]

During the 1930s these trends continued. The elementary school population, as a result of lower birth rates and restricted immigration, diminished. While economic pressure might force sixteen-to-eighteen-year-olds to seek employment in order to aid their embattled families, diminished job opportunities resulted in even greater numbers of them remaining in school. As the school term began in 1932, New York announced an increase in enrollment, "wholly in the junior and senior high schools, where many boys and girls are remaining in school, owing to the difficulty of obtaining work." By the beginning of 1934, the enforcement of National Recovery Administration (NRA) codes prohibiting child labor also added to the size of school enrollment. Later in the decade, National Youth Administration funds and jobs kept older students in the classroom. From New York to Muncie to Minneapolis came reports of larger high school enrollments. The trend was not confined to larger cities, nor was it greeted joyously by all educators. Showing undisguised elitism, an English teacher in Aberdeen, South Dakota, complained of the difficulties of coping with the "physical, mental and social misfits" flooding the high schools, youngsters "who in better times would have left school to go to work as truck drivers, maids, section hands, or waitresses."[20] In addition, secondary school teachers encountered an entirely new addition to the school population

—the returning postgraduate. Idled young women served as unpaid aides to teachers while young men became janitors' helpers.[21]

The changes that teachers encountered in their students were qualitative as well as quantitative. If teachers were ill prepared for older students, who may have been as dissatisfied attending school as some teachers were in having them there, teacher preparatory training had failed to introduce them to theories and methods designed for the instruction of children so hungry that their attention spans were negligible, so ill clothed that the warm school building was in reality a temporary refuge from unheated homes. A New York survey in the fall of 1932 revealed that one-fifth of the city's schoolchildren were suffering from malnutrition. Teachers often dipped into their own depleted resources to help students. In New York, with some resentment at the element of coercion involved, teachers were requested to donate 5 percent of their salaries to meet the needs of children and their families for free lunches, shoes, and clothing. In many locations, the response was more spontaneous and voluntary. "When we discovered that some were dropping out of school because they did not have shoes or stockings," wrote a Chicago teacher who was watching her own debts climb, "we teachers began to bring for distribution what garments we could round up among our friends." Occasionally, teachers were on the receiving end of assistance. Chicago mothers organized a bake sale to raise funds for the transportation expenses of teachers for whom the twenty cents per day streetcar fare had become a major expenditure.[22]

Economic survival and professional performance monopolized the concerns of teachers, but they had additional problems peculiar to their chosen occupation. Teachers had always played an anomalous role in American society. "At no time in our history," wrote one historian of the profession, "have lawyers, doctors, and other professional workers been expected to maintain a comparable level of righteousness with that required of schoolteachers."[23] Their moral conduct was carefully scrutinized by the communities in which they worked. Like ministers, they were expected to adhere to prescribed, rigid moral standards that were often evaded by the public they served. Some restraints diminished after World War I, especially in large, urban areas in the North, but in other sections of the country and in smaller communities, smoking, drinking, and dancing were activities in which teachers engaged at the risk of their jobs. In the early 1930s, contracts in Protales, New

Mexico, and Twin Falls, Idaho, explicitly forbade women from attending public dances. A young woman who was hired to teach English and dramatics in a small town near Pittsburgh in 1930 remembered the "little lecture" at the first teachers' meeting, where she was informed that weekends should be spent in town and church attendance was "suggested." She recalled that smoking cigarettes would have resulted in instant dismissal so she only smoked in her bathroom after dinner with the skylight open. The Board of Education of Red Lodge, Montana, adopted a resolution in 1932 giving hiring preference to teachers who did not smoke. Originally intended to apply only to women, the ruling was extended to men as well.[24]

As the economic dislocations of the 1930s intensified, concern over teachers' personal habits was replaced by a growing anxiety over their political views and affiliations. Teachers' commitment to patriotism, as defined by self-appointed guardians of such virtues, and their allegiance to the American social and economic systems, as esteemed by those business interests with the largest stake in their survival, became major issues. Highly vocal and visible members of communities, who often determined the level of tax support for schools as well, brought great pressure on teachers and school administrators during the 1930s as matters of morality were superseded by questions of loyalty.

The movement to require teachers to sign loyalty oaths had begun during the 1920s, but it spread rapidly because of fears engendered by the Depression. By 1937, twenty-two states required oaths swearing obedience to the Constitution or pledges to promote, teach, or refrain from teaching certain subject matter. Few teachers were actually dismissed for introducing "questionable" subject matter into their classrooms, but a majority polled by the NEA reported that they were extremely cautious about discussing political, economic, and religious topics for fear of punishment. Subtle penalties were sometimes imposed. A teacher in one large city who defended the recognition of the Soviet Union in her civics class was removed from the class and reassigned a course in medieval history. A history teacher considered "too radical" found herself the typing instructor. Advocating membership in the World Court elicited an editorial in a Muncie newspaper reminding teachers that schools were supported by public taxation. Academic freedom was seriously compromised and, with good reason, was a source of major concern to teachers and their organizations throughout the 1930s.[25]

To further complicate the status of teachers, a variety of discriminatory employment practices mirrored the religious and racial prejudices of individual communities. Catholic and Jewish teachers could seldom secure employment outside Northern, urban areas, and Protestants often complained of what would now be termed reverse discrimination. Blacks taught in the most poorly funded, backward, segregated facilities in the South and in schools with predominantly black student bodies in the North.[26]

Within this matrix of economic adversity, conflicting educational values, and social prejudices, extensive hostility against married women teachers took place. By 1920 almost 10 percent of the female teachers were married, and a decade later the proportion had almost doubled. Bars to their employment became common during the 1920s, but when the Depression compounded the social pressure against working wives generally, the economic competition for jobs, and the financial hardships of school systems, the status of married women teachers deteriorated further. Nowhere was proposed and actual discrimination against working wives more pronounced.

Legal ambiguities exacerbated the precarious position of married teachers. At the turn of the century, neither state legislation nor certification regulations referred to women's marital status. Since laws failed to dictate to the contrary, the right of local school boards to hire and fire at will could only be challenged in the courts or through formal complaint to state boards of education. By 1920, the principle was established in a few states in which it had been tested that the dismissal of women teachers, solely because of marriage, was untenable and that school boards must adhere closely to their stipulated guidelines for discharge. However, most states did not specify guidelines, and, in those that did, their elasticity in application went unchallenged in the courts. Tenure laws could protect the teaching wife, but only five states had enacted such legislation by 1920. As the decade began, the legal status of 62,000 married women teachers was precarious and subject to the whims of authorities in most local jurisdictions.[27]

By the mid-1920s, when competition for teaching positions first began, reports of refusals to hire married women and to dismiss those already married became more frequent. The situation rapidly became "a question of intense interest" as numerous cities announced the initiation of policies inimical to teaching wives, including those who married while employed. In St. Paul, Minnesota, teachers were informed that "such marriage shall immediately terminate your appointment." Kansas City teachers were not only dismissed upon marriage but also had to give two weeks' notice of their forthcoming change in marital status or forfeit two weeks' salary. Any female teacher in the Cleveland school system was forced to resign immediately upon marriage and retire for one complete semester. She could then return as a substitute for an additional semester. After that period of time, if her ability rating placed her in the upper quarter in teacher evaluations, she would be fully reinstated at her original salary level.[28]

An analysis of 427 teacher contracts published in 1927 revealed that contracts in eighteen states specified that marriage would void the agreement. An amazing 30 percent of large communities with populations of 100,000 or more issued no contracts at all—an indication of the precarious status of teachers generally.[29] A more detailed survey by the National Education Association revealed the widespread nature of discrimination by the late 1920s. Sixty percent of cities and towns refused to hire married women, and half of the communities forced a teacher who married to retire—either immediately or at the completion of the school term.[30] Census figures, however, failed to reflect the impact of discriminatory practices. More than 150,000 married women were working as teachers by 1930, over two and one-half times the number enumerated ten years earlier. Their proportion of all female teachers almost doubled during the decade, from 9.7 percent to 17.9 percent. Their increase was more spectacular than two simultaneous trends, the continued growth in the number of all teachers from three-quarters to slightly over 1 million and the reversal of the feminization of the profession. During the 1920s, the proportion of men who taught increased slightly.[31]

The renewed interest of men in teaching careers portended a new source of economic competition in the event of increased job scarcity. The Depression created that situation. But in no way can opposition to the employment of married women teachers be attributed solely to the ensuing economic chaos. The Depression exacerbated a preexisting condition and accelerated a prominent trend. By the 1930-31 school year, even before schools felt the full impact of economic crisis, only 23.4 percent of all cities hired married women, compared with 39 percent three years earlier. Increased reluctance to retain a female teacher who married was also evident. Whereas almost half of all cities surveyed earlier had allowed a woman to continue teaching after she married, in the later study only 37 percent reported that they kept the newly married women on their staffs.[32]

Few studies examined discriminatory policies in rural districts. One survey of Ohio taken during the first year of the Depression revealed that 74 percent of the cities and towns of the state did not hire married women and two-thirds required termination of employment upon marriage. In rural areas, however, married women were both hired and retained in two-thirds of the cases. The U.S. Office of Education confirmed that higher proportions of married women taught in rural schools, but it also pointed out state-to-state variations. Almost half of all rural teachers in California were married, whereas 92 percent of those in predominantly rural Nebraska were single. Teacher supply seems the most plausible variable. Low salaries, inadequate facilities, and social isolation made teaching outside urban areas less desirable. Proximal cities and towns in populous states could deplete the supply of teachers available in rural districts and limit the ability or desire to discriminate. In vast agricultural areas, however, young single women could not improve the location of their employment without migrating some distance, an undertaking less likely during the Depression. The numbers who remained close to home in rural states, augmented by recent graduates unable to secure employment in cities, and the numbers of rural schools closed or curtailed inflated the supply and permitted policies that were increasingly prejudicial to married women teachers.[33]

The financial crises of school systems sometimes played a role in attempts to discharge teaching wives already under contract. In Cleveland, salary schedules were based on years of experience. Many married teachers had lengthy employment records and high salaries. An estimate of the savings that would result from their replacement by new teachers paid minimum salaries was almost $500,000, a financial boon difficult for a hard-pressed system to resist. In 1932, the city's acting superintendent suggested that in twenty cases where both husband and wife were employed in the schools the wife should be replaced so as to reduce the payroll by almost $28,000.[34] The plan was defeated, but when

Cincinnati schools faced a $450,000 deficit, a printed circular appeared, attacking teaching wives and advocating salary differentials based on sex. "Did You Know," the caption read:

> That Cincinnati pays it *[sic]* men and women teachers the same salaries? . . .
> That approximately 90 percent of the men and 20 percent of the women teachers of Cincinnati are married?
> That a large majority of the homes of women teachers have more than one wage earner?
> That a differential in salary between men and women teachers will easily absorb the reduction of $450,000 in the school budget?[35]

The Hoboken, New Jersey, school district found a more devious method to force married women teachers to bear the burden of budgetary problems. Lower student enrollments and reduced operating income forced the closing of two schools. The board transferred twenty-six married teachers to these two schools before closing them. New Jersey had a tenure law, but the court ruled that the board's actions were justified as long as nontenured teachers were not holding positions that tenured ones were qualified to fill. In an unrelated case, a New Jersey court ruled that the Lyndhurst school board could refuse to include married women in the same salary bracket with single teachers when pay increases were granted.[36]

The economic disarray within the teaching profession, and not just the financial straits of school systems, intensified the attack on married women teachers. Their dismissal seemed a logical method for easing unemployment among young single women. According to one vocal school board president, graduates of teacher-training institutions were not finding jobs because of "mercenary wives who persist in pursuing a pedagogical career." One young graduate complained that she was deprived of work "because of the greed and selfishness of the married teachers who insist on holding their positions." Critics related competition for the contracted numbers of jobs to concern for the future of the profession. Fears were expressed that chronic unemployment would discourage bright young women from embarking upon teaching careers, and that openings in normal schools and university departments of education would go begging. Furthermore, married women teachers were undermining the profession from within. They were accused of inefficiency, irresponsibility, and failure to keep abreast of new developments because their dual responsibilities at home and at work were so time consuming. Studies were cited to substantiate claims that teaching wives were more subject to illness and had poor attendance records.[37]

While some critics stressed the detrimental effect of double duties on teaching performance, other opponents emphasized the deplorable repercussions of outside employment on family life. The assumption that a teaching career would necessarily result in the neglect of domestic responsibilities was compounded by the accusation that these wives were failing to fulfill their biological duties. Promoting their employment leads "to the restriction of children in homes that really should produce more children." Either place constraints on married teachers, their critics implored, or "you tacitly endorse and encourage such practices which are the most reprehensible sins of the upper and middle classes." Educator and eugenicist David Snedden echoed these sentiments. Teachers, by virtue of their social backgrounds and educational attainments, were precisely the women whose low birth rates had alarmed many social observers since the turn of the century. Enlightened public policy, wrote Snedden, should encourage child bearing by "the kinds of women (usually considerably above the average both in heredity and in cultural rearing) who commonly become teachers."[38]

These explicit class-based anxieties help to explain why the debate that swirled around married women teachers was so intensive and actual discriminatory practices so extensive. By 1940, communities that hired wives as teachers fell to 13 percent, and those that retained a teacher who married fell to 30 percent. Superintendents from districts that had initiated or strengthened their discriminatory practices during the Depression admitted that popular sentiment and the desire to palliate overt agitation were major factors for adopting discriminatory policies.[39] What helps to account for the public opposition was the high visibility of this group of women workers in their communities, the fact that they were paid by public funds, and especially, their social-class backgrounds and the presumed duty such women owed to their families, their government, and their society. Studies confirmed that the typical schoolteacher was native born, from a small town (traditionally the repositories of conventional social values and attitudes), and "recruited from a social background characteristic of a middle economic level of American life."[40] Teaching wives were perceived as and actually were middle-class women who were challenging middle-class social values. They were not just economic competitors for jobs at a time of economic distress but also social threats to treasured institutions and behavioral patterns. Married charwomen who cleaned the schools were not subject to the furor that raged over the status of married women teachers.[41]

Teaching wives did have defenders. They were included under the umbrella of concern held aloft by women's organizations that were distressed over the plight of women workers in general. The Cincinnati teachers who were threatened with dismissals and wage discrimination successfully defeated the proposals with the aid of the Dayton branch of the National Woman's Party. Alma Lutz, party spokesperson, protested the dismissal of teaching wives in Everett, Massachusetts, and the feminist organization fought compulsory retirement of married teachers in Norwalk, Connecticut. At its 1935 convention, the National Association of Women Lawyers decried the moral implications of the report of migration to Nevada for "convenient divorces" by female teachers who continue to live with their husbands.[42]

Throughout the decade, the National Education Association, whose ranks swelled to 200,000, passed resolutions opposing discrimination of any kind but admitted that the policy was violated on every point. Superintendents, who comprised their own department within the association, were not overwhelmingly opposed to the employment of married women, but one NEA survey indicated that in 80 percent of the cases investigated, employment practices were determined by school boards and not principal administrators. Even the superintendent held his job at the pleasure of the school board, and one group of superintendents admitted to an investigator that their advocacy of hiring and retaining married women would have placed their own jobs in jeopardy.[43] The NEA conducted excellent, detailed studies on all aspects of the status of the profession throughout the Depression, but action on behalf of beleaguered members was minimal.

The American Federation of Teachers (AFT) was also outspoken in its opposition to all discriminatory practices. Throughout the 1930s it maintained its position that "teaching efficiency shall be the basis of teacher tenure and that there shall be no discrimination against any teacher on account of sex, race, religion or social status." But the union had little leverage, and its membership was limited until the mid-1930s when New Deal policies and the new-found militance of some teachers gave its organizational drives greater impetus. At the moment of greatest growth in the later 1930s, however, the union was both wracked by internecine disputes and attacked from without because of the activities of some Communist-dominated locals.[44] Disagreements over teaching wives surfaced, too. Clara Roe of the Flint, Michigan, AFT local deplored the fact that wives were made scapegoats for the inability to solve unemployment problems, but another local official informed the national board that his group at a vocational high school supported the dismissal of married women teachers.[45]

Besides lack of unanimity, efforts of women's groups, professional organizations, and unions on behalf of teaching wives failed because of the institutional structure of the nation's schools. Thousands of individual, autonomous school boards determined policy. Defenders of married women teachers did not have the forces to combat the pervasive public hostility to which school board members responded and to exert counter-pressure in so many independent jurisdictions. In addition, discrimination against the married women was just one of many impediments encountered by teaching personnel. A more useful approach to protect teachers from the vagaries of employment practices was tenure legislation, and both the NEA and the AFT pressed for enactment. But by 1940, nineteen states still had neither tenure laws nor provisions for long-term contracts. Of those states that had passed tenure legislation, only five were statewide in their applicability. One of those states, Massachusetts, consistently refused to extend the shield of protection to married women. A 1936 court decision equated marriage with "other good cause" for which a teacher could be discharged.[46] In their 1937 law, Kansas legislators appeared oblivious to the value judgment implicit in their juxtaposition of offenses exempted from tenure coverage: "Causes for the discharge or demotion . . . shall be immoral character, conduct unbecoming an instructor, insubordination, failure to obey reasonable rules promulgated by the board of education, marriage of women instructors, inefficiency, incompetency, physical unfitness.[47] By the middle of 1938, the moral behavior, political opinions, and social characteristics of almost two-fifths of the nation's teachers were still unprotected by any type of tenure guarantees, and the status of the married women teachers was the most precarious of all.[48]

While defenders of teaching wives won few battles, they did polish their verbal arguments and countered the attacks of their opponents point by point. No defenders denied the existence of seemingly chronic unemployment, but they stressed the professional rather than the economic functions of educational institutions. School boards were established to administer education and not to solve economic problems. Merit and efficiency should be the only criteria of employment of teachers, married or single. Not only would schools gain educationally, but the profession would benefit in the long run. The fact that there were fewer students in teacher training facilities would not endanger the occupational field to the extent that large-scale turnover of experienced, efficient personnel undermined the profession. Why, proponents of teaching wives asked, would girls train as teachers if the ability to put that training to use were circumscribed? Discriminatory policies were tantamount to usurpation of the monetary funds invested in gaining professional training. Only teaching efficiency mattered. Independent studies that found few, if any, differences in performance between carefully matched groups of single and married teachers were widely cited.[49]

Many individuals and groups who came to the defense of married women teachers, however, carried their arguments one step further. They stressed a variable absent from the more formal investigations of comparable abilities and effectiveness in the classroom. Teaching wives, they said, were not simply equal to single women of equivalent age, education, and experience but were actually superior just because they were married and had families of their own. These teachers would be better able to deal with children in the school where they could use their "mother understanding and mother love and mother experience." Rather than dividing the interests and attention of women, marriage resulted in more settled and less distractible attitudes so that the married woman "brings more sympathy, understanding and experience to her teaching service than can the single women." Married women were best suited for teaching courses that incorporated the study of child development and family relations.[50]

The ban on married women, their defenders continued, resulted in faculties dominated by older, single women who created the image of schools as population centers for bitter old maids. Yet, perhaps they were unmarried because they feared for their jobs, a choice that necessarily undermined "the domesticity and natural impulses of normal women." To the extent sexual gratification had become valued as an essential element in the life of well-adjusted women, celibate spinster-hood could have unfortunate effects. In a much less insightful book than her earlier studies of waitresses and salespersons, Frances Donovan attributed the moodiness and tyrannical behavior of the "queer teacher" to the sexual frustrations of her unmarried status. Even Lorine Pruette, advocate of married women's employment and perceptive analyst of the cultural and institutional impediments that lay in their paths, concluded that "the important task of educating the young should be entrusted to women who lead a normal life of the affections and who have ex-periences with children outside the classroom."[51]

According to the advocates of teaching wives, the answer lay in the realization that "the attractive woman who finds it easy to marry and establish a home is the kind of woman that the schools need and cannot secure or retain under regulations against marriage." Society must decide if schools were created for educating the young or for providing havens for spinsters, if the ultimate qualification was celibacy or merit. Defenders of married women teachers could equal the jeremiads of their opponents as they warned of the social costs of marriages forsaken. They were, in effect, adopting the same set of prescriptive norms, assuming that marriage was the normal, desirable, and necessary goal of women and that no roadblocks should, therefore, be placed on the road to the altar.[52]

Unlike their critics, however, married teachers and their proponents insisted that the qualities and benefits derived from marriage and child rearing should be projected into the public sphere through professional employment. The result was a rationale of "professional motherhood" analogous to the concepts and activities of prominent women earlier in the century. But while reformers like Jane Addams had engaged in vicarious maternal functions and social housekeeping and educator M. Carey Thomas had "raised" a generation of college women, they remained respectably single and celibate. Praising the attributes of the married teacher and attacking the "old maid" implied that the unmarried woman was deviant. This negative value judgment did not go unnoticed. Virginia Gildersleeve, dean of Barnard College, who iden-tified with the older cohort of female educators, decried "the tendency of today to regard celibate teachers as 'frustrated.' " While she blamed psychoanalysts primarily for propounding theories that amounted to "cruel and unwholesome discrimination against unmarried women," the rhetoric of well-intentioned supporters of teaching wives accomplished the same end.[53]

Linking merit and efficiency in the classroom to traditional female roles and behavior not only served to perpetuate those ideals but also had limited value as expeditious defense of teaching wives. The presumed nurturing qualities of women were effective factors in promoting their employment in an earlier period when public schools usually had eight grades and diminishing enrollments at the secondary levels. The student population was young, and the maternal qualities women supposedly brought to children seemed appropriate. But with the expansion of secondary education, these attributes were no longer so highly prized. By the late 1920s and 1930s, the wisdom of employing female teachers, especially in junior and senior high schools, was seriously questioned as anxiety grew that the schools were actually contributing to the feminization of Americans. Critics expressed concern that women could not handle disciplinary problems encountered with older male students, that boys did not perform as well as girls because of the lack of appropriate role models, and that the general result of years of exposure to female instructors would be "weak" citizens. A *Fortune* magazine poll asked, "Do you think it would have a better influence on schoolboys over thirteen years old if they had men teachers instead of women?" and almost half of the respondents replied affirmatively. "The public is coming to demand more of the masculine influence for its growing young people," announced the bulletin of a teachers' college.[54]

Besides these vaguely defined public fears over poorly influenced students, many educators (generally male) believed that the feminization of the profession was a major reason for its relatively low status and that men should be encouraged to reenter the field to enhance its prestige. In his compendium of infringements on the freedom of teachers, historian Howard Beale suggested that one reason for removing all proscriptions was that "only then will many young men again enter the profession."[55] Young men were apprised of the opportunities for male teachers in secondary schools and for principals in elementary schools, the Depression notwithstanding. And while the Depression necessitated economy measures, men were assured that "only the strongest teachers, those who can handle large classes" will be retained.[56] One displaced woman did not recall the presentation of such elaborate rationale, only her own summary replacement: "I had just finished my first year teaching when the Depression hit hard in Pittsburgh. Women were laid off so that men could be put in their place. There I was . . . after a very short career. I was out, and I had spent my life preparing to teach."[57] Men did make considerable inroads into the teaching profession during the 1930s. Male teachers increased from 19 to 24.3 percent of the total during the decade, and the proportion of men enrolled in teacher training institutions, with portents for the future, grew from 31 percent in 1931-32, to 40 percent ten years later.[58]

While vocal hostility and pervasive discrimination were directed against married women teachers, they not only maintained their precarious hold but even increased their proportionate representation slightly. In 1940, 22 percent of female teachers were married. While this was only a slight gain and much reduced from the great increase of the 1920s, any growth was remarkable. The figure does disguise regional variations. Married women's gains were greatest in southeastern and southwestern states where employment policies were more liberal. Teaching wives experienced regression in employment status where discrimination was more blatant and extensive. Gains by male teachers, however, were national in scope.

In several respects, the debate that swirled around married women teachers, while reflecting genuine economic despair over massive unemployment and social anxiety over the challenge to sex roles and family structure, was a smoke screen. Married women teachers maintained their foothold in the profession, but young single women, on whose behalf so much of the intense antagonism against their married sisters centered, lost ground. Economic competition, structural changes, and public sentiment all worked to the advantage of men at the expense of female teachers generally. The professional progress of women during the previous decades, even within this feminized field, came to a halt—a Depression decade legacy for women that continued beyond the 1930s.

chapter 5

"He Wants My Job!":
Working Women, Women's Work,
and the Depression

The negative impact of the Depression on women teachers was duplicated in other female-dominated occupational categories. While trends in the social composition of the female labor force continued, competition for fewer jobs between men and women as well as among women themselves reverberated along the entire occupational ladder. Women unwilling or unable to postpone entry into or to drop out of the work force often responded by accepting any available employment, waiting for the crisis to pass. But for the female worker, economic dislocation was not temporary; the losses were not regained with wartime recovery and postwar prosperity. Economic hardship and psychological disillusionment left imprints on the vocational aspirations of many women, a development intricately entwined with the deterioration of women's economic status generally.

Nowhere was occupational decline more dramatic than in the professional category. Predominant in the feminized fields of teaching, nursing, librarianship, and social work, women failed to maintain their position even in these areas, which had represented the acme of their economic accomplishments. The proportion of women in all professional pursuits declined from 14.2 percent to 12.3 percent during the Depression decade so that the overall distribution of women in this classification was barely higher in 1940 than it had been twenty years earlier. Unlike teaching, increases occurred in the absolute numbers of nurses, librarians, and, especially, social workers by the end of the 1930s, but not in proportion to men in these areas or to the rest of the female labor force.[1]

Women in the feminized professions experienced and articulated concern over the increasing deterioration of professional standards and economic compensation from already low pre-Depression levels. Depprecation of self and occupation occasionally surfaced as positions diminished in number, salaries were cut to the bone, and working conditions worsened. Some professional women vied with one another in denouncing their chosen vocations.

Librarians often complained about salary levels, work loads, and their own complicity in their misfortunes. Like teachers, they were employed primarily by public institutions and had, by 1935, experienced income reductions ranging from 3 to 60 percent from the comparatively low 1929 levels. The 20 to 30 percent salary cuts in Detroit and Chicago were typical. One unhappily employed librarian insisted that the "worst paid profession is still the worst paid profession. Librarians have sustained their reputations of being nobly genteel, ineffectually patient, and grossly underpaid." Many women agreed that library work remained basically clerical in nature, although seldom "was the wage scale equal to that of the intelligent office girl." In addition, librarians denounced their own form of "speed up." Library circulation increased 40 percent during the 1930s as Americans substituted no-cost reading for other forms of leisure-time activities that lay beyond individual and family budgets. Smaller staffs with reduced salaries served millions of new readers.[2]

Dissatisfaction among social workers echoed many of these complaints. Unlike most other occupational categories, this field boomed during the Depression as most Americans, more or less reluctantly, accepted welfare measures as an essential response to economic despair. But while one social worker noted the contrast between business at its nadir and "social work at a peak," personal discontent over previous low and presently declining salaries surfaced constantly early in the decade. "Social workers have never shared in the benefits of the rising wage scale during times of prosperity," protested the Association of Federation Social Workers as early threats of salary cuts were heard. Objections to the contrary, by the end of 1931, the budget committee of the Cleveland Community Fund made 10 percent cuts on all salaries over $1,200 per year. Pittsburgh held the line but "encouraged" workers to make special contributions to their agencies or to general community welfare funds. When Detroit's charitable drive fell hundreds of thousands of dollars short, welfare activities and many social workers were eliminated. As local governments assumed increasing relief responsibilities from private organizations and were supplanted, in turn, by federal programs, social workers encountered an entirely novel problem. Salaries stabilized and job opportunities proliferated, but the average American taxpayer, ambivalent toward this new concept of large-scale public relief, made the social worker along with the welfare recipient an object of criticism and even contempt. As local and state politicians passively watched huge sums of federal relief money passing them by, they echoed the barely disguised criticism of Governor Davey of Ohio, who called for the transfer of funds from "young college students clad in furs" to the "hands of the respected civic leaders and township trustees who know their people."[3]

Besides public scorn, young women who entered social work encountered huge caseloads which required great outlays of physical energy and played havoc on their emotions as well. It was difficult to remain immune to human suffering when one sat "hour after hour, facing stark realities in the lives of men, women and children asking for help." One caseworker in California remembered her caseload increasing until it included 800 families who "were starving or they wouldn't have been able to qualify." Her principal function was to check their homes "to see if people had one crust of bread too many, to see if they could get along for another day or two without another relief check."[4] Another social worker described the constant pressures and dilemmas: "You see, the investigators are terribly overworked, and always afraid of being fired and having to go back to a relief allowance themselves. We're under pressure to give as little help as possible, to refuse relief on the slightest excuse, to miss some families with the checks occasionally."[5] Women played major, if sometimes unwilling or unwitting, roles in creating the insensitivity and inefficiency that became associated with bureaucratized social services.

For many caseworkers, however, the conflict among personal response to the needs of clients, inability to meet those needs, and occasional displeasure from superiors and the public proved overwhelming. The social worker in California maintained her caseload, became especially concerned over the plight of old, sick women, and finally "got so I couldn't stand it anymore. It made me sick all the time, and I quit and went home to Woodland." Another woman with a temporary emergency relief group in Pittsburgh worked with many families living in unheated hovels. She was powerless when children picking up bits of coal around train tracks were discovered and arrested. "I worked for nine months in those conditions, and then I needed a vacation. I was very young and dedicated. I stopped sleeping, and I wouldn't allow myself a day of sickness." Such was the toll on the sensitive worker.[6]

These two women also dramatized issues surrounding the professionalization of social work. Both women were college graduates but not specifically trained in social services. One had lost her job as a teacher and was hired by a former professor from whom she had taken a few courses. The other graduated from college with a major in botany and bacteriology, tried a number of make-shift jobs, and was finally offered work in a settlement house. She recalled several of her former college classmates suddenly appearing, like herself, as caseworkers by 1932 and 1933.[7] These women brought compassion and hard work to their jobs but no apparent training, and thus could do little to upgrade and standardize qualifications, the constant aims of professionals. On the other hand, as they bowed to caseload and emotional pressure and abdicated the burgeoning field to the trained professional, they removed one impediment to the development of an impersonal, inflexible bureaucracy.

While public and private welfare and relief agencies were absorbing workers of varied educational backgrounds, the nursing field was an economic disaster area. Like many industrial workers whose employment patterns had always been irregular, nurses experienced intensified but not new economic insecurity.[8] Young women had graduated at incredible rates from hospital-administered schools of nursing since the turn of the century, and because hospitals continued to utilize (exploit, according to some critics) their own students for ward duty, the trained nurse had been and continued to be forced to turn to private duty or public health nursing in order to earn her living. Unstable employment was endemic prior to 1929. A graduate nurse could depend on an average of eight months' work netting an income of about $1,300 per year. (Since nurses often waited days or weeks between private duty assignments, longer interim periods during the 1930s were accepted as a matter of course, and nurses were seldom counted among the unemployed.) During the first four years of the Depression, nursing schools, which remained deplorably inadequate in terms of formal instruction, graduated 100,000 additional nurses. Hospitals not only ignored a government suggestion that graduate nurses be employed at salaries that at least matched those paid aides and practical nurses (who were surviving hard times better than their more highly trained sisters), but hospitals also made the financial exigencies of the 1930s an excuse for perpetuating "the system of apprentice training" at the expense of upgraded, truly professional education.[9]

Critics of the continuing subservient status of nursing placed much of the blame on the passive, obsequious behavior of the women themselves. Elizabeth C. Burgess of the National League of Nursing Education condemned nurses for "their apathy, their lack of understanding, and because of their long domination by hospital interests."[10] The charges yielded no results. The only notable gain for nurses during the Depression involved a shorter workday for the private duty nurse. By mid-decade, the eight-hour day became commonplace. Spreading the work made employment more stable and compensated for reduced fees. The shorter shift was a boon to the nurse who had come to accept twelve- and twenty to twenty-four-hour shifts based on arguments of efficient administrative necessity that resembled the rationale that had perpetuated the twelve-hour shift in the steel mills. The public quickly accepted the reduced workday. By 1937, the American Nursing Association announced that the eight-hour day was common in a growing number of hospitals and that calls to nursing registries revealed that requests for nurses to serve on shorter shifts increased dramatically.[11]

For the public health nurse, daily experience paralleled that of the social worker more than that of her hospital-based colleague. "Depleted funds, salary cuts, uncertainty as to how long her decreased income can continue" were accompanied by heavier work burdens that became more social than medical in nature. Lillian Wald, founder of the Henry Street Settlement House and a pioneer in public nursing, believed that the social worker and the public health nurse had much in common, especially in terms of their emotional responses to their clientele. "The worker who goes into the home to give financial relief or to watch over the health of the family," she wrote, "must daily gird herself as though for battle."[12]

Although the number of female librarians, social workers, and nurses increased during the 1930s, like teachers, women in these feminized professions could not maintain their proportionate dominance. While the most feminized of fields, nursing, experienced no dramatic change, the comparatively insignificant entrance of men into the profession was just large enough for the U.S. Office of Education to note male enrollment in nursing schools for the first time. Men made considerable inroads into other bastions of female employment, despite continuing complaints of overabundant numbers, low status, and poor pay. Just as the proportion of male teachers grew during the decade, so did that of male librarians—from 8.7 to 15.1 percent during the ten-year period. The situation among social workers was especially revealing. As relief and welfare services expanded, the number of workers in these fields more than doubled, from a little over 30,000 in 1930 to almost 70,000 at the end of the decade. And the proportion of those welfare workers who were male increased from one-fifth to over one-third.[13]

Women's status also deteriorated at higher rungs of the hierarchical ladder within these professional categories. Just as male teachers expanded into secondary schools and administrative positions, men dominated administrative posts in libraries to a greater degree than ever before, continued their control over nurses as doctors and hospital administrators, and followed suit in the burgeoning field of social work. Grace Abbott, social worker, teacher, and reformer, commented on the problems encountered by women at higher administrative levels in relief and welfare work. "Fewer women than men have an opportunity to demonstrate capacity, and failure by one woman still leads to general conclusions as to the competency of the whole sex." Private agencies were most likely to discriminate, she found, and even though women were chief administrators of relief in Philadelphia and New York and in Georgia and Arizona, within New Deal programs "women usually have had a 'Ladies' Aid Society' status."[14]

If women could not maintain their position in fields with which they were traditionally associated, it was little wonder that they lost their limited and precarious foothold in nonconventional professions and high managerial positions. The small number of women in medicine and dentistry decreased, continuing a trend that had begun in the 1920s. The Lynds discovered that Muncie had eight female physicians and one woman dentist in 1920. Only two women doctors remained in 1935. In addition, the Lynds found that women made no inroads into areas that had grown in spite of the Depression.

> The lone woman lawyer continued, while male lawyers increased from sixty to seventy-three. The three women in the classification Designers, Draftsmen, and Inventors dropped to two, while men rose from forty-two

to eighty-five. Middletown had in neither period any women Chemists or Technical Engineers, while men in the former rose from three to thirty and in the latter from forty-three to ninety-eight.[15]

Women in responsible managerial positions found themselves especially vulnerable to economic retrenchment and male pressure. Female buyers in department stores sometimes lost their jobs when two positions were combined and the new post was then given to a man. A concerned placement bureau official in New York asked, "Are Women Losing Ground?" Without hesitation she answered affirmatively on behalf of highly trained, well-educated female executives "who rode the opportunity train of the 1920s." They were now forced to accept any available job, which invariably downgraded their abilities. Some of these women could find no substitute employment because they were considered overqualified. Supervisors, department heads, and publicity experts found themselves replaced by men more often than they experienced outright job elimination.[16]

The position of women in higher education clearly indicated the refusal to hire them and the tendency to substitute men for them. Total employment in colleges and universities increased more than 17 percent during the 1930s, but the number of women remained unchanged. As a result, female administrative officers and faculty fell from 32.5 to 26.5 percent. Occasionally, a well-publicized instance of female replacement drew protest. In 1937, the Mt. Holyoke board of trustees appointed a man to the position held by retiring President Mary E. Wooley. Board member Frances Perkins was furious, and the National Woman's Party publicly protested the move. The organization was astounded that the college with its long record of training women to leadership would relinquish "its own leadership to a man as long as outstanding women educators are available for the high post."[17]

Female faculty, especially in women's colleges where they had predominated, lost ground throughout the decade. Between 1930 and 1940, the increase in the numbers of male faculty at Wellesley College was dramatic. At Vassar, 83 percent of the faculty were women during the 1924-25 academic year. Ten years later, the proportion was 70 percent. As in public education, the trend continued for decades. Smith and Bryn Mawr joined other women's colleges in precipitous decline in female faculty, a decline accompanied by lower proportions of women who received graduate degrees generally. The relationship between these developments did not go unnoticed. As a dissenting member of the Mt. Holyoke board that appointed a male president, Frances Perkins recognized the importance of positive role models for educated women and wrote to a female colleague: "In this Mid Century where women need very much to learn to respond to leadership of other women, a college headed by a vigorous and inspiring woman is one of the ways in which they can learn."[18]

In the face of the assault upon women in professional and managerial fields of employment, the replacement of women by men in colleges and universities produced a multiplier effect. The absence of models of achievement in visible academic pursuits reinforced a sense of futility where female aspirations and goals were concerned. Fewer women, therefore, obtained the training necessary for attaining high professional status in the future. The presumed passing of the serious career woman from the national scene has been largely attributed to the generational shift that marked the period after 1920. The assumption that the serious female college student passed from the scene has seldom been questioned. Not only did academic achievements decline but, according to one historian, "those who earned advanced degrees put them to less and less use."[19] This presumption of voluntary withdrawal on the part of educated women may be unfounded. One recent investigation of women scientists indicates that academically oriented women may have shared a common fate with female executives who did not retire from the labor force willingly but, rather, gained "alternative" employment in less visible and prestigious areas. Women continued to gain doctorates in the natural and social sciences through the late 1930s, but as academic posts closed many found jobs in government or as research associates. Elaborate surveys conducted during the decade by Lewis Terman on marital and sexual behavior and by C. Wright Bakke on the impact of unemployment among working-class men were based on data gathered and tabulated by staffs of female research personnel. High unemployment rates (9.5 percent compared to 1.3 of men in the study's control sample) and participation in less visible and rewarding endeavors indicated that female scientists did not retire willingly but struggled to salvage professional employment in the face of great difficulties.[20]

The tentative conclusions of the study of women scientists can be extended to female workers in general. Demotion, not withdrawal from economic activity, appeared to be the most typical experience of women during the Depression. Added to the disappearance of positive role models were reduced possibilities of attaining occupations commensurate with their education. Uninspired and discouraged, women may have gradually lowered their career goals, dropped academic pursuits accordingly, and sought security in marriage, with work playing an ancillary role. The process by which levels of aspiration and accomplishment were reduced was more complex than the explanation that implicitly blames women for the inability to maintain and improve their economic status. College women were subjected to countless polls during this period on the question of their goals. The overwhelming numbers who replied said that they preferred marriage and a family to a career, thus supposedly revealing the dissipation of the career impulse among younger women. Most young women probably always have preferred marriage, and increasing numbers of them attended institutions of higher education between the wars. But other factors influencing choice can be the nature of the economic scene, the degree of economic opportunities, and the potential for realizing one's aspirations.

Guidance literature did not ignore "the recent sentiment against the employment of women, combined with their greater need to earn under difficult economic conditions." Authors complained that women appeared less enthusiastic about careers than they had been in the recent past. But diminished ambition was attributed to "dissatisfaction with the limited success which women have won in business." Advisers blamed occupational immobility, in turn, on the discriminatory "brambles which society has placed in their paths," and they admitted that labor force withdrawal because of marriage and child rearing reinforced employers' beliefs that female employment was sporadic and temporary. These were realistic appraisals of working women's inability to gain "promotions and posts of responsibility" as well as of the complex factors affecting vocational aspirations. Still, once having defined these problems, counselors were not inclined to examine the underlying structural bases of discrimination and interrupted career patterns.[21]

While they noted the obstacles on the path to occupational advancement, vocational advisors generally ignored the prevalance and possible impact of economic demotion on career commitments. If the devaluation of the graduate training of female scientists were not discouraging enough, the examples of a small group of educated working wives in Ames, Iowa, hardly proved inspiring. Three women, who had worked as teachers prior to their marriages, were employed as a factory operative, a domestic, and a house-to-house canvasser after their weddings. One former postmaster was currently working as a janitor, and a stenographer found employment as a store clerk after she married.[22] Altrusia Clubs had no doubt about the source of this pressure that crossed the female educational and occupational spectrum. "There is on foot a far more formidable campaign aimed to introduce men in large numbers into teaching, librarian work, secretarial work, and into better paid or more authoritative white-collar positions in both private and public service." At a time when the predominant public attitude toward working women—especially working wives—was that they had usurped the jobs that rightfully belonged to men, Grace Nies Fletcher titled an article in *Independent Woman* that described economic pressure on women "He Wants My Job!"[23]

The ability of men to replace women at high levels of economic achievement and to enter traditional feminized areas increased competition among women all along the occupational scale. For many women the result was a dramatic downward plunge. An unemployed teacher described her attempt to secure a position in a retail store where, she discovered, only the most experienced saleswomen were retained, and they were working on commission, not for salaries. She eventually found two days' work as a domestic servant for one dollar a day and meals. The YWCA reported that in Washington, D.C., scores of young women who once had worked as stenographers and typists were taking jobs as domestics, if they could find them. Intense competition between high school and college-educated women further depressed wages and other working standards along with occupational attainment, while employers raised the educational qualifications of job-hunting women. Universities recognized this development. A promotional pamphlet of Flora Stone Mather College in Cleveland, published in 1937, encouraged women to seek higher education because offices and department stores would not hire clerks without a college degree.[24]

Concerned women suddenly realized that much heralded gains in business and the professions had been overestimated. And the higher the position reached, the more precarious the female hold. They now discovered and deplored increased competition among women for employment in "subordinate" fields.[25] In a survey of American Woman's Association members of New York City, Lorine Pruette described individuals "who belonged to a generation of women which stressed and exalted in the importance of jobs for women, and [who] had known the crest of the wave that began during the World War." While the unemployment rate among the organization's business and professional women's membership was lower than national estimates and many did find new employment, it was often on a lower economic scale. As many as two-thirds of the women, unemployed at some time, found new jobs but in less desirable positions. "Some of those who have found reemployment,"Pruette reported, "have secured this at the sacrifice of the occupational career on which they embarked."[26]

Pruette was also concerned with the long-term impact of the Depression on women's aspirations. A "generation of women has grown to maturity in the belief that nothing was impossible for which they were willing to work and struggle." Now, Pruette worried that the newly acquired sense of insecurity would result in lower goals, as women acquiesced to the realities of the contracted demand for their labor. Psychologically, she believed that women could survive these developments. She had been concerned with the reasons women did not succeed in the business world to a greater extent prior to the Depression. She suggested that the socialization process instilled few expectations for success. The presence of options, whereby women could retire or reduce their commitment to work, was an additional reason "Why Women Fail." Therefore, "as society is set up, the woman who fails has less to lose in personal and social status, and this definite handicap during prosperity periods becomes an equally definite advantage in times of depression." As women discovered that their declining economic status was not accompanied by a concomitant loss of prestige, they could endure the "psychological adjustment of going from the top of arts and business to menial clerical work."[27]

Emotionally armed for the assault on their economic status, women with some degree of education and training were bombarded with advice on job opportunities in the midst of hard times. The information dispensed by vocational guidance counselors, employment placement personnel, and authors of advice literature displayed two principal features. Writers stressed specific, noncompetitive, feminized occupations and encouraged the display of sex-typed behavior on the job.

Chase Going Woodhouse, director of the Institute of Women's Professional Relations, illustrated the first response. "Rather than competing with men, [women] are finding jobs in developing lines of work which are primarily women employing," she reported. While she sometimes regretted that "too much distinction is made between men's work and women's work," she contributed directly to the continuing tradition of occupational segregation. Woodhouse noted growing numbers of wives in the labor force and believed that numerous business trends she observed worked to the advantage of working women, married and single. Growing concentration on the consumer, greater emphasis on fashion and beauty, more service industries in the private sector, and social welfare responsibilities by government all were developments which she believed were conducive to female employment. New opportunities in consumer service areas, which had "not had time to become labeled men's jobs," and in food and institutional management were especially welcome. Here were opportunities "to translate a feminine viewpoint into industrial services, design and distribution." For the married woman especially, she insisted, home economics-related work in the private sector was preferable because there her special perspective would be welcome.[28]

Pruette reiterated the special attributes that wives brought to certain occupational endeavors. "Women who maintain their own homes have obvious advantages in the work of the decorator, the professional shopper, the renting agent, etc." The increased emphasis on the passive role of consumer could be turned into productive efforts with jobs as saleswomen. Articles in a vocational guidance journal encouraged young women to seek training in semiprofessional, health-related areas as well. A positive attribute of the new field of dental hygiene was the absence of men. Occupational therapy was desirable because it was "almost exclusively a woman's field."[29]

Female executives encouraged young women to enter retail establishments where they believed the outlook was particularly favorable. But the emphasis was placed on feminine behavior and on jobs at less than the highest levels. Hortense Odlum, president of Bonwit Teller, informed female aspirants that "the greatest asset of the business woman is feminine charm and feminine clothes." Opportunities for advancement were undefined. "Don't wear the pants," she suggested. "Men are the leaders, but women belong in the business world and have a great field there." One vocational guide acknowledged the "sex war which has recently been introduced into business and has been fostered by the Depression." The author's advice on achieving cordial relations with men then concentrated on flattery, sex appeal, deference, dress, and manners.[30]

Few efforts to identify a subordinate female occupation with sex-linked characteristics and behavior exceeded the 1935 *Fortune* magazine series on working women. Advocates of the gainful employment of women had often referred to any woman in an office, beginning with the file clerk, as a business woman, and they had held out the promise of unlimited promotion. During the 1920s, *Independent Woman* extolled the ladder of success on which the stenographer climbed to office manager and business executive. The author of the *Fortune* articles identified "Women in Business" with the private secretary. She was nothing less than the office mate of the harried male executive, and she dutifully fulfilled the emotional and business needs of her boss. In direct imitation of marriage, in which the wife derives her social status from her husband, the private secretary achieved her exalted position through the man to whom her services were indispensable.[31]

The author of the series did not overlook women who had achieved financial success and fame in executive capacities but stressed the non-competitive, female-oriented markets of their products. The success of Helena Rubinstein could not be ignored, but she represented no economic threat to Henry Ford. To salve any fears of *Fortune* subscribers that women in offices harbored secret desires for upward mobility, the author insisted that the sample of women executives consisted of "sixteen exceptions to prove the rule that woman's place is not the executive chair." Business acumen and aspirations did not characterize private secretaries who "are where they are, not because they have mastered business, but because they have mastered the art of being invaluable to the men for whom they work. . . . It is a triumph for their womanhood and not for their ambition."[32]

While this writer lauded the victory of femininity over ability and ambition, vocational guidance counselors and students of occupational trends through most of the 1930s cautioned that openings for private secretaries were diminishing. The "help wanted" advertisements in newspapers for stenographers, typists and secretaries moved en masse to "situation wanted" columns during most of the decade. Numbers competing for limited openings were swelled by young women who stayed in school longer because of the employment situation, college graduates unable to work at professional levels, and second-generation immigrant daughters and working-class women seeking white-collar status. Those fortunate to find and retain office jobs usually earned less than twenty dollars per week—as little as six to eight dollars a week in small office firms—from which they still had to purchase "silk stockings, permanent waves and smart clothes." These strains on the budget, however, made office work outwardly acceptable to women skidding down the occupational slide and especially appealing to those with aspirations of upward mobility.[33]

While intense competition for clerical jobs was a phenomenon of the 1930s, the decade was also marked by reorganization in office structures and procedures. These developments had more permanent effects on the nature of office work and workers. Specialization of clerical functions and decreased promotional opportunities had been noted before 1930, but new technological advances and Depression-induced economies forced businesses to centralize their clerical operations even further. "Squads of stenographers" using newly installed dictating machines were rapidly supplanting private secretaries. Teachers of commercial courses in public schools and in private business schools were encouraged to direct their female students into developing careers as transcribing, billing, and bookkeeping machine operators.[34]

The private secretary as "office wife" left much to be desired as both image and occupation, but the position still retained a degree of individuality now superseded by faceless pools of female workers. *Office Economist,* published by a firm that manufactured office furniture and equipment, lauded the great economies that followed in the wake of new office machines. A stenographic department of interchangeable stencil cutters, transcribers, and typists would rationalize office procedures, reduce the overdependence of executives on their secretaries, and save money. With no attention to the impact of monotonous routine on work performance, one office manager wrote to extol the virtues of combining and centralizing the secretarial pool with new dictating equipment. Time would be saved and work would be standardized and so "promote a feeling of good will and build up the morale of the employees."[35]

Perceptive observers were less sanguine about these developments.

The Women's Bureau noted that in some offices "workers tending machines in the performance of their duties are not unlike the factory worker tending a machine in the factory." Besides having processes "as monotonous and meaningless as the machine tending of most industrial workers," business organizations were growing in size. Historian Caroline Ware noted that "the day when the typical white-collar job was that of a clerk, bookkeeper or secretary in a small office, working closely with the boss and having a hand in the running of the office, is rapidly passing." One result was less contact with management, and increasing depersonalization.

Yet, in some offices employers economized by fusing instead of specializing functions. One bookkeeper gradually absorbed the duties of two fired saleswomen, a stenographer, and a general clerical worker. She worked eleven-hour days and most of Saturday for half of her former wages and refused to complain for fear of losing her job. During the mid-1930s, the YWCA organized summer institutes at Oberlin College for activist stenographers, typists, and clerks analogous to the summer classes held at Bryn Mawr and the University of Wisconsin for women in industry who displayed leadership potential. The office workers who attended the sessions addressed problems concerned directly with the Depression as well as those that involved changes in office procedures. "What meaning do their 'white collars' have in view of wage cuts, insecurity and unemployment?" asked some of the activists (one-third of those who attended the 1935 institute belonged to clerical workers' unions). "What will become of office jobs with growing mechanization of business?" asked others.[36]

In the short run, white collars for clerical workers were clearly no protection against the economic vagaries of the decade. But, by the end of the 1930s, statistics revealed that specialization of office functions had not reduced the number of jobs. Clerical occupations actually increased 25 percent, but the work required less skilled and less experienced women than ever before. By the middle of the decade, a student of occupational trends noted that employers placed greater emphasis on the "type" of woman—her personality and appearance—rather than on her abilities. Women who sought reemployment after losing managerial positions were encouraged to display passive, compliant, "feminine" qualities. One employment bureau official discovered that she not only had to deprecate the abilities of a female applicant, but she also emphasized the woman's "ability to take orders and to conform, to stress her willingness to adapt herself and be contented with a small wage." A vocational counselor reported that the job market looked brighter for women, especially those endowed with a "pleasing appearance, attractive personality and youth." Writer Meridel LeSueur noted that younger, prettier girls could get jobs in stores or restaurants. Age was assuming great significance as women over thirty were refused jobs as waitresses, stenographers, or salesgirls.[37]

While the thrust of the advice to working women—married or single— was toward female-stereotyped occupations and behavior, vocational guidance manuals continued to list their job categories topically, usually describing less traditional areas of employment as well. By the end of the decade, however, one popular guide formally segregated vocational information along sex lines. Nursing, home economics, teaching, office work, dental hygiene, library, and social service all fell within the division labeled "Ladies First." "Free for All" included some sex neutral options like factory work, advertising, selling, and writing. High status business and professional pursuits were labeled "For Men Only—Unless." Readers were advised not to allow the last section to inhibit their vocational choice, but the authors admitted that their object was to be practical.[38]

Even advice to women in traditional male professions increasingly dwelled upon areas of specialization that were supposedly more suitable for women because of their emotional qualities. Aspiring female dentists were apprised of opportunities in textbook writing, dental research, and on hospital staffs—everywhere but in private practice. Trust departments in banks seemed especially appropriate for women "where sympathetic understanding, patience and tact are essential in relations with customers, frequently widows or minors." Noting the difficulty experienced by female physicians in obtaining internships and residencies, the Institute of Women's Professional Relations suggested that more women should enter the field of clinical research and solve the hospital problem "quietly and tactfully." And, if it were still possible for women to achieve executive positions in business, it was because of the close relationship between office and home management. "Both require tact with people, a genius for detail, and a knack at buying." Whatever else women lost in terms of economic achievement during the Depression, they apparently cornered the market in tact.[39]

Occupational segregation did not stem solely from encouraging women
to enter areas of employment "considered feminine in type and background" nor from yielding to barriers erected in nontraditional fields.[40]
Sex differentiation in the labor force predates and extends beyond
the 1930s. Recent examinations of the phenomenon describe the sexual
division of labor in the work force as "a major reflection of the generalized
segregation that characterized all aspects of Western social life." It is
one highly visible manifestation "of a massive institutional subculture."[41]
Numerous complex factors (demands of the labor market, demographic
characteristics of the female labor supply, explicit laws, and the socialization process which conditions motivation and expectations) have created
and continue to perpetuate the bifurcated occupational structure. But
the active, purposeful role of women who have encouraged segregated
patterns has received little attention. Embattled advocates of working
women during the Depression placed a higher value on vocational
segregation than earlier in the century. Noncompetitive occupations
appeared to offer the safest route to employment and security. But,
because feminized jobs have inevitably ranked low in status and compensation, the protectors of women's economic roles inadvertently
contributed to the perpetuation of women's inferior occupational
status.[42]

While women generally struggled to maintain employment, wives
experienced the added liability of discrimination based on marital
status. Unemployment among female scientists was 9.5 percent, but
over 22 percent of the married women scientists were without gainful
employment. After a period of time in which many of these wives held
tenuous, marginal positions, they often lost their hold on any semblance
of work within the scientific community. Educated wives in feminized
professions did not encounter constraints to the extent experienced
by teachers, but difficulties were common. A survey of members of the
AAUW revealed that of all forms of sex-linked discriminatory practices
described, almost one-fifth involved marital status. Of the married
women who were employed, about half stated that they had encountered
refusal of employment in hiring or retention at some time during their
careers. The figure undoubtedly reflects the large proportion of female
college graduates who entered education-related occupations. The
fact that these women were still working also indicates the determination to maintain and the ability somehow to obtain alternative employ-

ment. The survey revealed additional forms of discrimination related to marital status: smaller starting salaries if married, salary reductions or job demotions upon marriage. Since the wives who responded were less often employed in teaching, nursing, and librarianship than in sales, publishing, and social work, the compiler concluded somewhat timidly, "One may question whether exclusion of married women from schools and colleges or from libraries has taken place."[43]

The extent of discrimination encountered by married librarians is more difficult to determine than the experience of married women teachers. The American Library Association reported little incidence. Members of the Denver Public Library staff surveyed fifty-seven institutions and found the majority employed wives. Yet, twelve of the libraries required resignation upon marriage, nine reported that wives were retained with temporary status, ten stated they would not place a married woman in a position that entailed responsibility. One guide to administrative procedure in personnel management suggested a ban on hiring wives. "Since the library will have many members of its staff marrying and retaining their positions, it may be wiser not to complicate matters by making original appointments of married women." Like married teachers, only one-fifth of librarians in 1940 were married, compared to 35.5 percent of the total female labor force.[44]

The official publications and proceedings of the American Nursing Association reveal little evidence of or concern over married nurses, although Genevieve Parkhurst, surveying the deteriorating status of working wives, reported "they have been removed from the staffs of hospitals." Public health nurses were sometimes affected by employment practices within their particular jurisdictions, and school nurses, like ten in Jersey City, often fell within the boundaries of policies established by school boards. Even allowing for the large number of supposedly single student nurses in the census category, in 1940 married nurses constituted the smallest proportion of working wives in any group of professional women. However, small numbers could have stemmed from the nature of the profession as well as from discrimination. Nurses associated with hospitals were sometimes expected to live on the premises, and private duty nurses often worked longer than average hours even as the eight-hour shift became more prevalent. Both conditions made work combined with marriage difficult.[45]

Wives employed in clerical fields were also vulnerable to discriminatory policies. A survey on the effect of Section 213 on dismissals conducted by the Women's Bureau revealed that the vast majority of women who lost their jobs were typists and stenographers. Few married charwomen or elevator operators were discharged. The Women's Bureau also studied the employment of women in offices early in the 1930s and discovered that the proportion of wives in clerical pursuits was considerably lower than that reported in 1930 census figures. Author Ethel Erickson drew two conclusions. Compared to findings on employment practices in industry, Erickson stated, "There has been more prejudice against women's employment in office work after marriage than any other general lines of work." Furthermore, she explained the discrepancy between census figures and employers' data by assuming that wives were reluctant to inform employers of their marital status. "Considerable prejudice leads to subterfuge on the part of women office workers as to their conjugal condition." The survey found variations in the extent of barriers among cities and among types of business concerns, but regardless of location, "definite and drastic policies barring married women" were especially prevalent in large offices, with banks and insurance companies most likely to discriminate. Studies conducted later in the decade confirmed these patterns. Purdue University found that twice the number of offices it sampled (more than 25 percent of 250), compared to factories, refused to hire married women, and the fewest numbers of wives were working in banks, insurance companies, and public utility firms. Retention policies were generally more liberal, but, once again, factory operatives were much less likely to lose their jobs upon marriage than office clerks—even in the same business concern. Proportions differed somewhat in a National Industrial Conference Board study, but the overall patterns were the same.[46]

For most of the Depression decade, department stores remained safe ports for working wives. They both hired and retained married women as sales clerks more frequently than other employers of white-collar workers. The part-time nature of much sales work appealed to both worker and employer. In some cities, 40 to 46 percent of department store clerks were married women.[47] These large retail establishments could also be a haven for a married woman suddenly faced with the realities of the Depression. The wife of a dentist recalled, "One day in '32 he just went fishing . . . and he fished for the rest of the bad times. . . . So at twenty-eight, with two little girls, I just had to go to work. I took a job as a salesclerk in the J.C. Penney, and worked throughout the Depression."[48] By the end of the 1930s, store employers admitted hostility from customers and labor organizations made it increasingly difficult to "lie low." Still, a survey conducted by the BPW found discriminatory practices in only 13 percent of large retail businesses compared to 43 percent of public utilities. And, when possible, the women's organization countered attempts to initiate practices inimical to working wives in retail stores and mailing houses. Sears, Roebuck executives admitted they were considering formulating a policy under which they would dismiss all married women whose husbands earned over $20 a week, but they discarded the attempt when BPW leaders protested.[49]

Discriminatory practices coincided with occupational status. Wives were most likely to encounter constraints in professional and other white-collar jobs that appealed to single women and some men, although women who worked in factories were not entirely immune. Two married packing inspectors in separate Cleveland plants lost their jobs— one when a fellow worker informed the foreman that the inspector had kept her marital status secret. But the NICB and Purdue surveys discovered that hiring policies barring married women in industrial firms were considerably lower than the incidence in white-collar categories. In some cases, the same company that fired an office worker who married retained a married woman in their factory. In the clothing and textile industries, where a large proportion of the work force was female and married and where working conditions were traditionally exploitative, concern over the marital status of women workers was virtually unknown. And, at the bottom of the economic ladder, among domestic servants, no expressions of outrage over economic competition or abdication of prescriptive social roles were heard.[50]

Related to the higher prestige of the occupations in which wives were most likely to encounter employment restraints was the greater visibility of those jobs. The public was much more likely to come into direct contact with married women in public schools, offices, and stores than with those in factories and private homes. As in the case of teachers specifically, white-collar working wives were most likely to have the social class and educational backgrounds that most seriously challenged the conventional understanding of the proper role for a young matron. The intensity of the hostility leveled against these women was as much a measure of social anxiety as a remedy for economic ills, for the public approbation leveled against working wives and its actual policy implementation in white-collar occupations was entirely out of proportion to their actual participation in the work force. By 1940 only 15 percent of all married women were gainfully employed, and only one-third of them worked in professional, clerical, and mercantile pursuits. Public perception of their numbers and importance was greatly magnified, but it focused on the area where two dominant twentieth-century female labor force trends converged—a growing number of married working women in an increased proportion of white-collar occupations.

The trends were acknowledged in other forms. For the first time, self-help manuals recognized the problems encountered by married women in offices. But the advice was often misleading and contradictory. One author cautioned against keeping marriage a secret because such action conveyed an image of the employee as untrustworthy and "double dealing." If losing a job was a certainty, then the woman was counseled to turn to her conscience to arrive at a decision. Unrealistically, the writer insisted this problem would seldom arise since "there are not many business organizations left that maintain so illiberal a policy toward married women employees."[51] At the end of the decade, the same author admitted that wives "might experience some difficulty in landing a job in the first place," but the single girl who married would not have to resort to subterfuge or endure a scolding for depriving a married man of work.[52] A guide that stressed business etiquette, talent, and hard work as certain ingredients for success also advised aspiring job seekers against concealing their marital status. "It is in much better taste at least to offer to resign, giving the firm an opportunity to ask her to remain, if it wishes to." But the manual proceeded to undermine the efficacy of the suggestion by deploring existing discriminatory practices, especially those policies of banks, insurance companies, and the federal government.[53]

The numerous references to deception were well grounded in fact. The ability of wives to gain and retain employment often meant lying about their marital status. Numerous individual examples exist including the letter signed "A Victim," in the *New York Times*, in which the writer protested her firing after inadvertently revealing she was married. She was immediately discharged for having made a fraudulent employment application. Reaction to registration under the Social

Security Act in 1936 indicated that the practice was widespread. Anna Rosenberg, regional director of the Social Security Board in New York City, reported that she received more than one thousand telephone calls from women who had used fictitious ages and concealed their marital status from their employers. She assured them that they could return registration forms directly to local post offices rather than to employers. If they preferred, workers could fill out forms at their place of employment and then forward the corrected information to the board. Rosenberg guaranteed that cards on file in Baltimore could not be examined by employers.[54]

In addition to outright deception, some moderate increases in the size of most job categories by the end of the 1930s helped account for the ability of the economy to absorb increased numbers of married women. In spite of all rhetorical and enforced opposition to their employment, the proportion of working women who were married increased from 29 percent to 35.5 percent during the ten-year period; the number grew by almost one-half. Although wives increased work force participation rates in all major classifications, they still predominated among servants and factory operatives. Approximately two-thirds of all married women workers were engaged in these major classifications. Arguments on behalf of working wives that stressed economic need were based on this data, although these women were actually least likely to encounter employment discrimination based on marital status.[55]

While married women increased their participation in the labor force, other long-term demographic trends also continued. Single, native-born women sought and obtained employment in greater numbers and proportions relative to foreign-born and black women. Immigration restriction reduced the pool from which the former were drawn, while dislocation accompanying the slowed but continuing rural-urban migration, and inordinately high unemployment rates may have affected work patterns of black women. By 1940, almost four-fifths of working women, twenty to twenty-four years old, were white and native born. Married women did not constitute more than 20 percent of the total employed women in any age group, but their highest rate occurred in the twenty-five-to-twenty-nine-year-old age category. Thereafter, percentages declined, indicating that young women were increasingly less likely to retire upon marriage—consequently, the spate of retention constraints—but waited until the birth of their first child.[56]

While the changing social characteristics of the female labor force were not unduly affected by the Depression, the events of the decade clamped a lid on the occupational shifts that had taken place since the beginning of the century. During the first three decades, while domestic and personal service categories remained almost unchanged, manufacturing and white-collar jobs reversed positions as the principal fields of female employment. Between 1930 and 1940, however, this pattern remained static, with clerical and sales occupations gaining at the expense of the professional pursuits within the white-collar category. Here was the crux of the deteriorating economic status of women during the 1930s. Married women continued to enter white-collar jobs at a greater rate than single women—though at a reduced pace from the 1920s; but the jobs they entered were considerably less demanding and prestigious than even the feminized professions. The contours of the post-World War II labor market had clearly emerged: a work force the majority of which would be white, married women in menial clerical and semiprofessional work.

A decade of public attack and personal suffering had left its mark on women's economic aspirations. Pre-Depresion optimism, which had motivated women to seek training and high vocational goals, dissipated as occupational mobility ceased and the options they encountered "have not satisfied them creatively." The editors of *Independent Woman* reviewed the AAUW survey on discrimination and asked, "Do Degrees Pay Dividends?" Severe limitations based on sex, marital status, and adverse economic conditions were so pervasive that the BPW leaders were forced to answer, "No!"[57] Reduced rates of matriculation, especially at graduate levels, indicated that young women already agreed. Lorine Pruette sympathized with the older women "who thought nothing was impossible" but who had reaped the bitter fruit of Depression-induced insecurity and lowered their expectations accordingly. But she also pondered the fate of the younger generation of women who never knew the earlier excitement of feminist agitation over economic accomplishments. Young women deprived of occupational opportunity and economic security renounced commitment to careers and sought satisfaction in "the good bread of a daily job." Emotionally and materially deprived and discouraged, the female experience of white-collar workers, in particular, could undermine occupational aspirations for years to come. As for the contention that women should not only have rewarding work but fulfilled marriages as well, younger women either ignored or were unaware of "the earlier feminist choice of career versus home of their own for many of them had a chance at neither," wrote Pruette.[58]

She correctly guessed that women's economic gains had peaked during the 1910–29 period and would "stand for a long time as a high-water mark."[59] Women could hardly be blamed for grasping at any occupational straw during a decade of exacerbated hostility and discriminatory practices as well as diminished employment options and mobility. Those who found a straw considered themselves fortunate, for many of them, like men, experienced wretchedly deteriorating working conditions or found no jobs at all. In desperation, they looked to the federal government to protect work standards, provide relief, and promote general economic recovery.

chapter 6

"The Forgotten Woman": Working Women, The New Deal, and Feminism

The official papers of Secretary of Labor Frances Perkins contain a printed resolution of unknown origin. Its authors summarized and condemned what they considered the plight of women workers under the New Deal. "They have been thrown out of jobs as married women, refused relief as single women, discriminated against by the N.R.A. and ignored by the C.W.A."[1] These concerns were echoed at greater length by Genevieve Parkhurst, writer and former editor of *Pictorial Review*, in a 1935 article entitled "Is Feminism Dead?" Women, she contended, have suffered in undue proportion to men because of discrimination in work and pay and because they were denied access to the same recovery programs. Furthermore, she held women's organizations largely responsible for this state of affairs. They lacked ideological consensus and inspiring leadership and were indifferent toward and inactive on behalf of working women. This judgment has persisted. Forty years later, historian William Chafe wrote that by the 1930s the woman's movement was so entangled over the Equal Rights Amendment that "instead of moving ahead together to attack the practical problems of discrimination, women's groups polarized over doctrinaire questions of ideology."[2]

Neither Parkhurst during the Depression nor historians since have underestimated the bitter rift among women's organizations nor the personal animosities aroused by the potential threat to protective legislation for working women that was posed by the ERA. But at a time when the dominant images of the human cost of economic disaster were male images—men at employment and relief offices, men at soup kitchens and in bread lines, men struggling to organize unions—the leaders of women's groups and highly visible women in the Roosevelt administration overcame their internecine disputes long enough to remind those who would listen that the "forgotten man" had female relatives who shared much of the same distress. Like the issue of working wives, the anxieties and activities on behalf of female workers were often narrow in scope, a measure of the limits of feminism as well as an indication of the social and intellectual climate of the period. The watchdogs of working women lacked the foresight that would have enabled them to concentrate on policies with long-term ramifications, such as unionization and the social security system, rather than on the short-run impact of the National Recovery Administration and federally sponsored relief programs. Yet, not even with the benefit of historical perspective is it a simple exercise to untangle the web of beneficial and victimizing effects of New Deal legislation.

The first massive recovery program to gain congressional approval was the National Industrial Recovery Act (NIRA). By the summer of 1933, it was already apparent that several industrial codes written under the provisions of Title I of the legislation contained wage provisions inimical to female workers. Women's organizations quickly discovered, publicized, and protested this development. The National Woman's Party pointed out that twelve of the early temporary codes listed wage differentials based on sex. Officers of the National Federation of Business and Professional Women's Clubs (BPW) immediately sent telegrams to Roosevelt and NRA administrator Hugh Johnson, demanding that codes "assure equal pay for equal work and equal opportunity for equal ability regardless of sex." The League of Women Voters (LWV) joined the protest and complained directly to Johnson who issued a policy statement: "Where women do men's work, they should get equal pay." Women found this guideline unsatisfactory and insisted that industrial operations be clearly described and defined with wage levels based upon the defined job and not on the sex of the employee.[3]

In spite of assurances by Eleanor Roosevelt and Frances Perkins that the wage differentials were temporary and would not survive the public hearing and final approval process, the discriminatory pay features remained. By October 1933, eight such codes had been signed by the president, including one in the coat and suit industry that had earlier submitted its temporary code in which wage scales were based on the nature of work. A ten-cent differential between male and female operatives suddenly appeared in the permanent approved code. Women's organizations expressed opposition and concern. As the first code to gain permanent status, it could establish a dangerous precedent. Disparity between the temporary and final agreement indicated that the public hearing process and the watchdog Labor Advisory Board were mere formalities, easily circumvented. Finally, the code covered an industry with a large female work force.[4]

Dissatisfaction was compounded by the "July 1929 clause," a ruling by the National Recovery Administration that stipulated persons paid below minimum NRA levels on that date could continue to be so paid. Thirty codes incorporated this feature. Six industries established wage minimums except for "employees engaged in light and repetitive work," which served as a euphemism for "female."[5] The Women's Trade Union League (WTUL) protested to Johnson; the National Consumers' League, the General Federation of Women's Clubs, and the YWCA also complained. The National Association of Women Lawyers suggested a selective boycott to force revisions, arguing that half the codes containing discriminatory features were written by industries dependent upon women as consumers. In the fall of 1934, armed with a comprehensive policy statement prepared by the WTUL and a study of the extent of discriminatory codes compiled by the Women's Bureau, organizations affiliated with the Women's Joint Congressional Committee subcommittee appeared before the reorganized NRA Board.[6]

The assistant counsel of the NRA did not dispute the fact that almost one-fourth of 465 codes established lower rates for women, ranging from 14 to 30 percent, and a colleague admitted that there were no logical grounds for the policies other than custom. As many as 25 percent of female workers in manufacturing pursuits were affected by the differentials, and, in many cases, lower rates were compounded by differentials based on region and size of city. Paper box manufacturers were covered by a code that distinguished among minimums to be paid in northern, central, and southern sections of the country. The boot and shoe industry code reduced minimums as the population of a city dropped from 250,000 to 20,000 to under 20,000. One investigator concluded,

"The fact that each region, each city of a certain size, each sex and each industry was considered separately, has resulted in various gradations with women always drawing the lowest wage."[7]

Facts, figures, and protests were futile. Customary industrial wage practices, an ineffectual Labor Advisory Board, and the Roosevelt administration's determination to certify codes with a minimum of delay undermined attempts to delete the wage differentials based on sex. In addition, there were real and perceived benefits for women in industry even in light of discriminatory wage guidelines. Working conditions for men and women in manufacturing had deteriorated rapidly and dramatically since 1929, and industrial codes were welcomed as a means to stabilize, if not improve, the situation. In twelve months, between 1929 and 1930, the average woman in South Bend, Indiana, had lost six hours and $4.45 wages per week. By the summer of 1931, 25 percent pay cuts were common among women in New England factories. Even experienced operatives earned only five to six dollars per week. The New York Department of Labor reported that female factory workers earned eight dollars per week or less. Averages reflected part-time schedules and lower piecework rates as well as standard wage reductions. The shrinking cost of living helped compensate but not in the face of wages that had often been inadequate before the downturn.[8]

Two months before Roosevelt's inauguration, the YWCA described the plight of an experienced, skilled machine operator in a garment manufacturing plant who had sustained constant cuts until she earned $1.95 per 100 pairs of trousers, netting $0.58 for nine hours' work. Still, she continued, "because I know that there are fifty girls waiting to take my job, and where would I find another now?" Finding industrial work was not only difficult because of intense competition but also because managers seldom used private or public employment bureaus through which women could be placed. Women sometimes heard of openings, where they existed, from friends or from unions. Hiring was done "at the gate," and so girls and women rose before dawn in desperate attempts "to be the first in line at factory gates."[9] Hiring often resulted in bedlam. Vera Bush Weisbard, a Communist and labor organizer, recalled seeking work as an operator working on blouses in 1933 during a slack period in a seasonal industry when, Depression or not, only a skeletal force of "relatives or bosses' favorites" would be kept on. During this particular period in 1933,

So many women applied for that miserable twenty-dollar-a-week job, crowding the stairs and pushing into the office, that the boss wild-eyed, shouted, "Get out!" and shoved us all out of the room locking the doors. Whether he hired anyone or not I don't know, but surely at least two hundred applicants were there.[10]

The resurgence of homework added to the difficulties of maintaining some semblance of industrial standards. Women, often with their children, worked on knit goods, earning five cents an hour for seventy hours of work a week. Desperate young girls took artificial flowers home to work on after their regular hours in the plant. Some woolen mills, refusing to pay minimum wages for mending (weaving loose ends), sent the work to retired employees to do in their homes at lower rates. Neither NRA codes, the unions, nor the protests of women's organizations were able to control the increase in sweatshop labor conditions. Given the state of industrial conditions generally, workers could hardly be faulted for grasping the promise of stability held out by the labor provisions that were mandatory in all codes.[11]

Workers excluded from coverage often viewed codes as a possible salvation. A cook in New York wrote to Roosevelt, pleading for protection and expressing the disappointment of servants who found "that the large and unprotected class of Domestics were not thought of. I keenly felt for my kind who you spoke of the robbery of the Bankers but never mentioned the robbery of the Housewives."[12] The YWCA was sensitive to the plight of domestic servants. The organization forwarded a suggested code to Washington, specifying a ten-hour day, six-day week, nine-dollar minimum for live-in servants, and hourly and overtime rates for day help.[13]

Codes were limited to industries engaged in interstate commerce, so by definition domestics were exempted. Household workers remained the stepsisters of the female labor force and invisible to New Deal policy makers. At the onset of the Depression, the shortcomings of domestic employment echoed complaints of the previous hundred years. Hours were always long and time off was often illusionary. Like servants in surveys fifty years earlier, household help in 1930 compared themselves unfavorably to women in industry. At least in the factory "when they get through their work, their time is their own." Although long hours were universal, wages, quality of room and board, and the degree of courtesy received from employers varied greatly. Placing a monetary value on room and board was difficult, but, as the Depression deepened, employers did so by arbitrarily reducing wages "by having the worker live out." While social observers believed increased employment of the servant as day worker was good for the employing family's privacy as well as for the worker's social life, the economic cost was great.[14]

Descriptions of working conditions among household servants during the 1930s read like litanies of squalor and misery. Domestics in California were found sleeping on sofas or on cots set up at night, on back porches where wash tubs and garbage cans were kept, lying sometimes in the same bed with children. Occasionally, women were refused use of the bathtub. In Texas, a weekly wage of one dollar was not uncommon and at least more prevalent than domestics who worked solely for room and board. By the end of the decade, $2.00 to $2.50 per week was typical in the Carolinas; $5.00 in the North. Still, for one black migrant cotton picker from Mississippi, $3.00 per week, room, food, and clothes was a major step up the economic ladder. She even received a dollar raise, although extra duties were then added to the daily cleaning, laundry, preparing and serving of six different breakfasts in bed at six different times.[15]

For many black women, the dreadful conditions of household employment were compounded by racial discrimination. Black women had traditionally found work on the bottom rung of the occupational ladder —as maids, laundresses, and sometimes as waitresses and elevator operators. A few had made their way into the factories by 1930, but "where other women are doing machine processes, she does only the porter work or may help in the cafeteria." To one observer, "the canaille of the American labor market" was an occupational description, not a racial slur. Yet, even willingness to accept the dirtiest and least desirable work at wages below those of white women did not ensure black women employment. With women generally tumbling headlong down the economic ladder, black women could not withstand the dual pressures of competition and racial prejudice. "White only" had appeared in help wanted advertisements for domestics during the 1920s, but a constricted labor market made the employer's preference a reality.

The Urban League reported white women were replacing black do-estics at lower wages from Springfield, Illinois, and Cleveland, to Nashville and New Orleans.[16]

For black women, the ultimate degradation occurred on street corners in the Bronx where open-air "slave markets" were resurrected. Observers discovered hundreds of "forlorn and half-starved" girls who "gathered every morning to offer themselves to the highest bidder for a day's work at from nine to fifteen cents per hour." And those hired often found only a few hours' work.[17] That young women were reduced to such conditions was a cogent indictment of racism and sexism in an economy regardless of its state of health. That individuals came to purchase this labor provided grist for the Marxist mills that proliferated during the period.

Even if it had been possible to devise codes for women in private households, their impact would probably have been more apparent than real, especially for blacks. The benefits derived from codes were mixed. Wage differentials combined with regional ones in the laundry code sanctioned earnings for southern black laundresses below precode levels. Omission of particularly onerous jobs, such as cleaners in the cotton industry code, exempted those workers from coverage altogether. Where codes raised wage levels and employers willingly complied, they replaced black women with white.[18] Other complaints and in-equities were less racially specific. Higher wages, shorter hours, and improved working conditions were sometimes circumvented or nullified by "speed ups," tampered records, once-higher wage rates reduced to minimum levels, and stable rates combined with decreased hours resulting in reduced total earnings. One woman who had run electric riveting machinery in a radio factory, earning eight to ten dollars every two weeks, lost her job when the company hired inexperienced replace-ments because the NRA code specified trainees could be paid 80 per-cent of the minimum wage. While one garment worker complained that she earned less during her shortened week but had a higher quota, another shirtmaker was thrilled to receive the $13.32 per week code minimum even if she did not make her quota and more if she did.[19]

While almost as many women in clerical pursuits—well over 1 million —as in industry were covered by code regulations, the effect was neg-ligible. Those in insurance company offices, where salaries were tradi-tionally low, were exempted. Employers often discovered methods to circumvent guidelines. Typists sometimes received imposing new titles and salary raises sufficient to exempt them from hours regulations. In the newspaper industry code, reporters and editorial workers who earned $35 or more per week had no limitation on hours. One stenographer had her once-reduced $35 salary restored, her title changed to editorial worker, and a host of new duties added to her already heavy stenographic load.[20]

Section 7a, which made it possible for workers to organize and bargain collectively with employers independently of management interference and code standards, produced more tangible economic results. For women in extremely seasonal industries, such as garment manufacturing and food processing, increased union activity enhanced their job security and working conditions. Organization attempts had actually begun in earnest during the late 1920s as unions tried to recoup the membership losses suffered during that decade. Unionization campaigns and strikes among southern textile workers were especially crucial for women workers and demonstrated their capacity to bear the rigors of employer and public hostility, survive eviction from company homes, and endure long-term unemployment while maintaining loyalty to unions. In 1929, before the stockmarket crash, the introduction of the "stretch out," the necessity to tend twice the number of looms at the same eleven dollars per week, twelve hours per day, ignited worker opposition, public dismay, and union activity. For three years, the United Textile Workers of the AFL, the National Textile Workers Union of the Communists' Trade Union Unity League, the Women's Trade Union League, the YWCA, and church organizations worked together and at cross-purposes in attempts to organize the southern textile industry. But, in the end, it was the workers, large numbers of married women among them, who bore the hardships of protracted strikes in violence-prone communities and who were eventually defeated. Ella Mae Wiggins of Gastonia sang ballads on behalf of the union and was shot to death for her efforts; Ida Loving wrote from Danville, pleading for aid and promising, "we will some day repay you when we have our union recognized and have helped make the South 100 percent union." The promise is not yet fulfilled, but the southern women presaged a decade of organizing action by women in industry throughout the nation.[21]

The International Ladies' Garment Workers Union (ILGWU) and

the Amalgamated Clothing Workers Union began their campaigns in 1930 and intensified them after the inclusion of Section 7a in garment industry codes. These unions in large female-employing industries made significant gains, but in spite of specific bans on employer interference with workers' choice of bargaining agent, fear of job loss prevailed in many cases, and company unions were chosen as representative agents. Knitters in a Midwest hosiery mill, where workers had signed yellow-dog contracts, invited union organizers after 1933. They held secret meetings at drugstores, lunch rooms, and at the local YWCA, but still the company union won the election. Only after a violent strike and a ruling from Washington was an outside bargaining agent certified. White-goods workers in a nearby area won a favorable decision, but again only after violent confrontations in which "the police were very brutal to our girls, striking them in the face with batons, tripping them up, and using filthy language." The result was often an increased sense of community and supportiveness. The striking young women "would discuss their grievances on returning to the hall, and the sympathy gained from each other would encourage them to more determined efforts the next day."[22]

Union sympathy was not unanimous, nor was sisterhood all encompassing. Once six arrested women discovered that one of their companions in the paddy wagon was a strikebreaker. "They set about tearing her hair and dragging off her clothes. Finally the police stopped the wagon and deposited her, with some of her clothes in her arms, on the sidewalk." During a thirteen-week strike in Cincinnati, women stationed at strategic downtown street corners pelted scabs "dressed in their fresh summer dresses" with eggs. Women strikers finally established a local of the Amalgamated Clothing Workers Union after picketing all summer in 100-degree heat, which alternated with pouring rain. Victories achieved under the aegis of the NIRA were often fragile. Women forced to sign yellow-dog contracts in one southern plant received a favorable review from the Atlanta Regional Labor Board, but then "the Supreme Court ruled our perfect decision out of court with the sick chickens."[23]

First afraid that Congress would not renew the terms of the NIRA, the watchdogs of the female labor force suddenly had to contend with the Supreme Court ruling that declared the legislation unconstitutional. In an evaluation of the NRA on women workers, probably written in late 1934, Rose Schneiderman undoubtedly spoke for most working women and their advocates. As a long-time organizer for the ILGWU, president of the New York WTUL, friend of Eleanor Roosevelt, and unflinching adherent to New Deal policies, she had resigned her former positions to serve as the only female member of the Labor Advisory Board. Without ignoring sex-based differentials, difficulties in policing homework, and lowered earnings, particularly in the cotton textile industry because of curtailed hours, she still concluded that in terms of wages and hours, women in most industries and in small retail establishments, such as five-and-dime stores, benefited from codes. Most important to Schneiderman, Section 7a sanctioned trade unions, and she remained "fully convinced that the most lasting gains for women workers will come through organization of working women." Women made significant progress in those industries where effective unions existed, and for this alone she judged the legislation a major step in the right direction. In spite of discriminatory features and elusive implementation, most working women probably shared her positive evaluation.[24]

The effect on women of the second title of the NIRA, which created work relief, was less ambiguous: women were ignored. The extent of female unemployment, like joblessness in general, was conjectural. Limited surveys at the beginning of the decade indicated that women fared reasonably well. Heavy industry bore the initial brunt of the economic downturn, and women in consumer goods industries and in clerical work did not feel the impact of contraction until somewhat later. By 1932, however, the incidence of unemployment among women workers increased in all occupational categories. The New York Emergency Relief Committee reported that stenographers were hardest hit, with seamstresses and general clerical workers close behind. In industries employing large numbers of women, only shoe and candy manufacturing escaped serious cutbacks. In 1930, the American Women's Association discovered a small proportion of its New York City business and professionally employed members were out of work, but three years later the number had increased significantly. At that time the estimate of unemployed women was over 2 million nationally. Until mid-1933, classified advertisements and openings at the Pennsylvania State Employment Office revealed continued demand for domestic servants and semi-skilled and unskilled factory operatives. After June

1933, openings decreased (especially in Philadelphia) and the downturn continued. At one point, one-quarter of all job applicants were clerical workers, but only 5 to 6 percent of all available employment was clerical in nature. According to the 1937 voluntary census conducted by the government, two-thirds of the unemployed women, including those on relief projects, were in clerical, semi-skilled industrial, and domestic service occupations. One-fifth were new entrants into the work force, 60 percent of whom were under twenty-four years of age. At a time when less than one-quarter of all workers were women, they comprised about one-third of the unemployed.[25]

Women's organizations recognized the growing problem of female unemployment. The YWCA initiated its own programs after an emergency meeting called in November 1930. Plans were proposed for provision of food, shelter, clothing, medical care, and, most important, means to maintain morale. Club rooms were opened in additional quarters because the organization found decentralization a necessary response to lack of transportation and car fare. Board members in Detroit contributed to a relief fund, while a club of working clerical women in Tacoma raised money to cover the expense of suppers for unemployed women in industry. The YWCA in Kansas City, Missouri, found activities that did not segregate unemployed women were important because "contact with girls who have jobs helps the morale of the girls who have not, much more than the constant association with but those out of work." Typing classes were organized so skills would not grow rusty; sewing classes, to remake their own clothing in order to look presentable when seeking work; English classes, so foreign-born women would make a more positive impression.[26]

As the YWCA discovered it was becoming a private relief agency and an employment bureau, the organization's leadership bemoaned the fact that the needs of unemployed and underemployed women received much less attention and publicity than those of men. To a great extent, "women and girls do not apply for relief unless they are in desperate straits." While women may have been protected from the societal pressure to succeed through work and from the shame that devolved upon a man without a job, women who had familial responsibilities or who were self-supporting still had to meet concrete physical needs. "Where Is Cleveland's Lost Battalion of Jobless Girls?" headlined a feature article in the *Cleveland Plain Dealer*. Writer Meridel LeSueur found "one of the great mysteries of the city [is] where women go when they are out of work and hungry. There are not many women in the bread line. There are no flop houses for women as there are for men." A college graduate who, in threee years, never found a job, tried to sleep in the waiting room of Grand Central Station and discovered that homeless women often slept in railroad stations, pretending to be waiting for a train. She also found women lying behind the heating and ventilating shafts in subway toilets. Only when her own mended dress was tattered and her shoes had more holes than leather did she apply for relief.[27]

Women were not immune from the emotional burdens of joblessness either. An unemployed social worker felt that"a dead weight hung in my chest. It took away the taste for food. Sleeping became difficult. My weight reached a new low. A failure, done for, finished!" Women in industry suffered the same effects on morale as "confidence gave way to bewilderment and discouragement and finally to a feeling of almost complete helplessness." Regardless of class origin or former occupational status, anxiety turned leisure into a lodestone. Women reacted to unemployment with the same sense of humiliation and apathetic behavior that was described throughout the studies of the effect of unemployment on men.[28] And across that most tangible line that divided the worker from the unemployed, hopelessness and desperation stemming from diametrically opposite sources found common outlet in explosions of frustrated anger. LeSueur described the hysterics of a young unemployed girl when the women in charge of a YWCA placement bureau could offer her nothing. The official, who "could hardly bear the suffering she saw . . . couldn't eat sometimes and had nightmares" of her own, returned the outburst in kind:

> So they stood there the two women in a rage, the girl weeping and the woman shouting at her. In the eight months of unemployment she had gotten ragged, and the woman was shouting that she would not send her out like that. . . .
> "We can't recommend you like that," the harassed Y.W.C.A. woman said, knowing she was starving, unable to do anything.[29]

LeSueur found that a clever woman "can get herself a good living from the charities, if she's naturally a lick spittle, naturally a little docile and cunning." But more often, middle-aged women, with families and husbands who were either unemployed or who had deserted them, sat around local unemployment bureaus, their numbers augmented by recent arrivals from the countryside. They hesitated to seek relief. Of 500 early applicants to the New York City Registration Bureau, only ten were women. Besides, public aid for women was limited. At the same time the Los Angeles Business and Professional Women's Club demanded that public relief and employment agencies should allocate the same proportion of their funds to women as the proportion of women in the labor force, San Francisco announced that funds for work projects had dried up. Prominent women in New York raised a $350,000 work relief fund to aid the unemployed "army of women clerical workers" because the city's $8 million program concentrated on male heads of families.[30]

Projects under the NIRA Public Works Program resulted in carefully planned schools, hospitals, city halls, and bridges—boons to unemployed architects and construction workers. Women could not and did not qualify for jobs thus created, and they did not fare much better under other relief programs. The Federal Emergency Relief Administration (FERA), which used grants-in-aid to states but administered relief from Washington, also depended heavily on construction projects. Eleanor Roosevelt's efforts to duplicate the popular Civilian Conservation Corps (CCC) for women eventually created eighty-six camps for 6,400 women. The number was insignificant in relation to the level of female unemployment (estimated to be 3.5 million in 1937) or in proportion to the number of young men in CCC camps; and the financial compensation for the women was fifty cents per week compared to one dollar per day received by men.[31]

The situation improved with the initiation of the Civilian Works Administration (CWA), a short-term program created to meet the unemployment crisis anticipated during the winter of 1933-34. Women benefited after Eleanor Roosevelt convened a White House Conference on the Emergency Needs of Women because of her own genuine concern and the complaints of leaders of women's organizations. By the end of 1933, 100,000 women had received work relief, but at no time did more than 7 percent of CWA jobs go to female unemployed. In addition, the wage structure discriminated. Administrator Harry Hopkins established a one dollar per hour minimum for skilled labor, forty cents minimum for unskilled construction work, and a thirty cent rate for persons on relief and educational projects—largely women.[32]

Ellen Woodward, director of women's projects under various federal programs, insisted no conscious intentions to discriminate existed and that female heads of families and needy single women would receive increased consideration. Her assurances did not quell complaints. Helena Hill Weed of the NWP attacked the low proportion of women (8 percent) who received FERA aid, the wage differentials in CWA projects, and the practice of placing men in more highly paid supervisory positions on projects designed for women. Through the fall of 1934, groups ranging from the Women's Trade Union League to the National Association of Women Lawyers protested, "urgently request[ing] the Federal Government to develop work relief projects for unemployed women."[33]

Significant change began under massive WPA programs. Proportions of women on work relief varied from 12 to 19 percent; in December 1938, over 400,000 women (13.5 percent of total recipients) obtained relief. But WPA applicants had to meet specific eligibility requirements, which often hampered women, especially when programs were administered at the local level where prevailing custom and prejudice also affected certification. No more than one member of a family could receive work relief, and that individual had to demonstrate principal breadwinner status. Louisiana reinforced the concept of breadwinner as male by ruling "a woman with an employable husband is not eligible for referral, as her husband is the logical head of the family." WPA applicants also had to demonstrate they were in the labor market. Michigan defined this requirement narrowly for female heads of family. They were eligible only if they had been working or were seeking work outside the home and were registered at a public employment office. In Louisiana, women had to have previous work histories and prove they were actually seeking employment. In other states, lack of work experience often disqualified a woman forced into the labor market for the first time because of the exigencies of the Depression. Occasionally, women were certified as breadwinners if programs for husbands did not exist, but when new projects were initiated, the women were removed and replaced by husbands as quickly as possible.[34]

In the Southwest, citizenship laws were sometimes used by local officials to refuse certification to female applicants married to Mexicans.

In the Southeast, white administrators and social welfare workers favored white women over black. A written appeal to Roosevelt revealed the plight of those who were black, female, and in need of work relief in the South. "Answer by help your a Negro woman [*sic*] here in Mt. Pleasant, Texas. I am afraid to put my name on this letter."[35]

Women who overcame these obstacles were still not guaranteed work relief. Approved projects had to be available, and availability depended on the size of annual congressional appropriations, the amount allocated to various states, and the degree to which local officials desired to match skills (or lack of skills) with available projects. While skills of male recipients were often downgraded in work relief, they were seldom dismissed outright as often happened to women. Studies revealed that higher proportions of certified men than women actually received work assignments. And for the women who obtained relief over the lifetime of WPA, over half were engaged in the most traditional of female work— sewing. According to two observers, the sewing room became "a female ditch-digging project, a dumping ground for women for whom no other work can be found."[36]

Women's organizations were not oblivious to the difficulties involved in meeting eligibility requirements and in devising projects at the local level. The National Woman's Party warned members that honorable intentions of federal officials in Washington were not adequate protection for women. The leadership encouraged all those concerned with the inability of needy women to receive an adequate share of work assignments to write to Ellen Woodward apprising her of inequities. And when WPA went into effect the League of Women Voters warned, "It will be necessary in the future as in the past for those concerned with unemployed women to exercise great ingenuity in devising projects and securing materials and facilities for them."[37]

Because of eligibility requirements, the characteristics of women on relief reflected family structure more than female unemployment rates among occupational categories. Domestic and service workers on relief outnumbered women in other job classifications, because so many were heads of households. But the availability of projects was also an important factor, and it remained easier to establish a sewing room or homemaking classes than to create projects for former white-collar workers. As a result, three-fourths of all women on the WPA rolls were former service or factory workers; the remainder had been in clerical, sales, professional, and technical work. This situation prevailed, although the actual proportion of white-collar female unemployed was higher, and work histories revealed that many had been out of work longer than the average unemployed woman. Married women—those most likely to qualify as principal breadwinners—had always been less prevalent in clerical and professional pursuits, but their needs were great. Their average length of unemployment exceeded that of single women. The Women's Bureau discovered, early in the decade, that of the married clerical workers unemployed, 30 percent were out of work for more than a year. The WPA was less likely to meet the relief needs of these women than those formerly engaged in lower status jobs.[38]

Unemployed women from white-collar categories did obtain some WPA aid. At one time 16 percent of female workers on WPA rolls included 22,000 teachers, principally in adult education projects, 15,000 librarians and clerks repairing and cataloguing books, 14,000 women on recreational projects, including nursery schools that served as day-care centers for the children of other women on work relief, and 8,000 in the Federal One Program.[39] The latter was comprised of the Federal Theatre, Writers, Music and Arts projects, an innovative departure for the government that was enthusiastically welcomed by those whose sources of private patronage had disappeared. While many women qualified legitimately, others, like their male counterparts, begged and lied their way onto the federal payroll. Writer AnziaYezierska, destitute by the mid-1930s, engaged in "a joyous shouting celebration" with her friends when they learned of government support for artists. Then her friends taught her how to convince officials she was on the relief rolls and therefore qualified. "Remember," they coached her, "Two years residence in the city. No relatives. No friends. No insurance. No money. No nothing—you've got to be starving to death."[40] Applying for relief was not meant to enhance anyone's sense of self-esteem although, eventually, engaging in creative endeavors and keeping from starving could compensate for the initial insults.

While men usually supervised projects designed specifically for women, Federal One projects gave administrative responsibilities to a number of highly qualified women (and some incompetent political appointees as well). Hallie Flanagan directed the Federal Theatre Program, walking a tortuous course among efforts to establish creative theatre, administer social welfare in a bureaucratic maze, and disengage from political controversy and congressional redbaiting. She was adept, but eventually she and the program fell. At the start of the Federal

Writers Project, fourteen women served as state directors, including
Dr. Mabel Ulrich in Minnesota, and Eudora Ramsay Richardson in
Virginia. Both performed admirably, while they were also articulate
defenders of married women workers in other contexts. Audrey Mc-
Mahon abided by her husband's wishes and refused to direct the Federal
Arts Project, but she did administer the program in New York City,
which dominated the artistic scene. The city was a hotbed of conflict
and heartbreak, where radicals on the various projects warred among
themselves over Stalinist or Trotskyite predelictions and fought with
project directors over congressional cuts and personnel layoffs. As
members of craft unions or the radical Workers Alliance or as individuals,
Federal One employees protested pink slips that followed in the wake
of congressional cuts in funds. In June 1937, relief workers staged a
sitdown strike at the projects' New York office. A $19-per-week clerk
on the Writers Project became hysterical over her firing and tried to
jump out a window. Three hundred dismissed theatre workers, sobbing
women among them, attacked the Theatre Project offices, while seventeen dancers (including twelve women) stopped rehearsals with a sitdown
and hunger strike at the Federal Music Theatre.[41]

Such protests only added to growing popular and official resentment
toward WPA relief. The seemingly superfluous nature of the finished
products and particularly the political radicalism of the relief recipients
in the arts programs were only two sources of opposition to the massive
program. Another was the cry of "too many women" on WPA rolls in
general. Ellen Woodward, head of women's and professional projects,
asked her regional directors to increase their news releases on the
positive features of women's programs, and she constantly reassured
critics that in all cases the women on WPA rolls were certified heads of
families. In 1939, only 20 percent of the women on relief projects were
single and without other persons in their families. Earlier surveys revealed that 90 percent of female WPA workers were married, although
only 15 percent of those were living with their husbands. In rural
Missouri, 40 percent were married and living with husbands who were
either handicapped, ill, disabled, or too old to work. To Woodward,
these figures indicated that women in general, and married wom-
en in particular, needed work on a permanent basis and relief when jobs
were not available. Neither the characteristics and demonstrated need of
the relief worker nor the innocuous nature of the ubiquitous sewing
projects quelled the complaints. Critics claimed that materials for

sewing rooms were too costly, although the non-labor expenses on all WPA projects amounted to 26 percent of total expenditures, while the cost of fabric, thread, and related materials was 27 percent.[42]

Woodward was more successful in calming the anxieties of those who feared the relief needs of women went unattended. As WPA expanded and her articles on female projects appeared in the journals of women's organizations, concern subsided.[43] When the NIRA was declared unconstitutional, furor over code inequities ceased. Female leadership concerned with the plight of working women then focused on the issue of constraints against married women workers. By concentrating on short-term manifestations of discrimination in NRA and relief policies and employment practices toward working wives, women's organizations overlooked more subtle, permanent New Deal social welfare policies that also embodied features detrimental to working women.

As originally passed in 1935, the Social Security Act created old age insurance plans covering all workers under the age of sixty-five engaged in commerce and industry. Workers were fully insured if they had $2,000 of cumulative wage credits and had been employed at some time during each year for five years, although important groups of workers were exempted. Otherwise, old age insurance applied to all workers in concerns that employed at least ten persons for at least twenty weeks per year. The act also provided for unemployment insurance, but states were to receive grants-in-aid and determine coverage and benefits. Federal legislation did establish the guideline that firms employing at least eight workers must participate.[44]

The legislation marked an important turn in government assumption of responsibility for social welfare. The United States lagged behind other industrial nations in these types of programs. In spite of numerous shortcomings, which critics were quick to point out, especially in the tax structure of the insurance plans, most reformers who had long hoped for social and economic security legislation were reasonably pleased. The LWV and the YWCA recognized the need to extend protection to neglected workers, "yet many of us who have faith in social insurance believe that the principle is sound."[45] Only the National Woman's Party remarked on a little noticed feature of the measure. The passage of the act coincided with the death of Charlotte Perkins Gilman. The feminist journal eulogized Gilman and acknowledged her ideological legacy to all women by stressing the importance of work and economic independence. According to *Equal Rights*, the Social Security Act reinforced that message. Under the terms of the legislation, adults who did not work for pay received no security. Women who chose marriage over employment or renounced careers upon marriage gave up government protection as well.[46]

The NWP analysis was correct, but it did not go far enough. There was a sizable number of people who worked for pay and still did not qualify under the insurance plans. Women constituted almost all of the domestic workers exempted, as well as large proportions of farm laborers and educational, charitable, and hospital personnel. One critic suggested that business women demand to know why occupations of varying status, "so largely female employing," were excluded. In the case of domestic workers, a high proportion was married. In effect, that one area of exemption alone placed one-third of all married women workers outside the protection of the social welfare program. Industries that engaged large numbers of married women participated in social security, with one important exception: the stipulation exempting firms that employed ten or less workers, for twenty or less weeks per year, was purposefully enacted to free canneries from covering their employees. Canneries had been in the past, and continued to be through the 1930s, large-scale, seasonal, and exploitative employers of married women.[47]

The 1939 revisions in social security legislation altered the focus of coverage from the individual worker to the worker's family. Widows' benefits were added and wives of insured workers were entitled to old age payments equal to one-half of their husbands' when both reached retirement age. The method of computing benefits and eligibility requirements was also changed. In the amended law, a working wife whose primary income benefit was less than 50 percent of her husband's still would receive the higher amount, the same amount she would have received if she had not worked at all. However, she paid taxes on those earnings. The legislation also established a family benefit limit; so if her average earnings entitled her to a benefit that when combined with her husband's exceeded the limit, her benefit was reduced accordingly. Husbands and wives paid taxes at the same rates on their individual earnings, but they received benefits as a family. A working wife also purchased less insurance for the same tax paid. The act introduced survivor and dependents' benefits but only for widows and the children of widows, not for surviving husbands and their children.

A working mother purchased protection for her children only if they were not living with their father or the father was not paying some support. Inherent in the legislation were the assumptions that children were dependent upon the earnings of their fathers and that married women workers were secondary breadwinners. However true in terms of actual family structure and the economic status of family members, it was inequitable to tax wives at the same rate as husbands when they purchased no insurance protection for their husbands or children in case of their own death. In response to the discriminatory aspects and the concept of female dependency institutionalized in sweeping federal legislation and practice, women's organizations were silent.[48]

The unemployment insurance feature of the Social Security Act did not discriminate quite so blatantly. However, as in the case of old age coverage, a large proportion of women workers gained no protection because of the exemption of domestic and agricultural workers. In the cases of all employees who were covered, the federal legislation established minimum requirements, and the states then delineated eligility and benefits. By the end of the decade, twenty-eight states adhered to the government standard of participation by all employers of eight or more workers. Only ten states included all employers in unemployment compensation programs. Working women who were covered but who lost their jobs upon marriage because of discriminatory retention policies suffered additional hardship. Nebraska, Nevada, North Dakota, and Minnesota enacted legislation disqualifying wives from unemployment insurance benefits if they were forced to retire because they married.[49]

Some local WPA officials tried to take advantage of Aid to Dependent Children (ADC) provisions of social security and switch women from relief to ADC rolls as quickly as possible. Hopkins ordered them reinstated until Aid to Dependent Children programs were functional and mothers had time to apply for benefits. In a few cases, women protested with sitdown strikes at welfare offices, because they preferred work to cash relief. This situation represented both economic and work preference aspects of relief problems. Prevailing wage rates in local communities determined work relief payments and were invariably higher than mothers' pensions (later, ADC payments). Two observers believed an additional dimension was present. The conflict between the conventional view that mothers belonged at home with their children and the growing desire of women for gainful employment had moved into the relief office. Eventually, local officials and social workers prevailed. WPA administrators discharged mothers from their work relief projects as a means of pressuring stalling state legislatures to enact the enabling ADC measures.[50]

Like social security legislation, the National Labor Relations Act passed the same year had great long-term impact on social and economic structures. More the work of Congress than of the executive branch, the Wagner Act placed the power of the federal government firmly on the side of unionization after the positive commitments embodied in Section 7a were invalidated with the rest of the NIRA. With specific antiunion practices by employers outlawed and a government board mandated to conduct and certify employee bargaining agents, union organizing—albeit with continued conflict and violence—burgeoned. For women in industry, this development carried new benefits in terms of work standards.

The American Federation of Labor, composed of independent craft unions, had made few commitments to the unionization of female factory workers. From the formation of the Women's Trade Union League in 1903, the federation had given verbal encouragement but little organizational and financial aid to the women's groups. Furthermore, the operations performed by most women in industry were unskilled or semiskilled, and thus organization was necessary along industrial rather than craft lines to bring them within the framework of unions. Before the organizing drives of the Congress for Industrial Organizations (CIO) in the mid- and late- 1930s, only the United Mine Workers, in an industry without female labor, and several unions in the clothing industry, which did include sizable numbers of women, were industrial in structure. According to AFL figures, few more than 200,000 women were union members in 1924, and over half of these were in garment manufacturing. Under the auspices of the CIO, gains were made. By 1938, an estimated 800,000 women had become affiliated with unions. Along with continued gains in the garment industry, organization took place in paper and paper products, cigar and confectionary manufacturing, and in restaurants and laundries—areas with substantial numbers of women workers.[51]

The major thrust of CIO activity was on heavy industry, where comparatively few women were employed. One exception was in textiles where, in the aftermath of an abortive national strike in 1934, CIO President John L. Lewis virtually disbanded the moribund United Textile Workers and created the Textile Workers Organizing Committee. With funding and leadership of proven ability from established unions, sincere efforts to organize the industry were made. But complex structural features, overwhelming employer intransigence (especially in the South), and the effects of the 1937 recession undermined the massive drive. Still, the automobile and rubber industries employed women, and they made gains as the result of difficult, violent, but eventually successful CIO organizing campaigns. About one-fifth of the rubber workers were female, and after suffering severe wage reductions and extended hours earlier in the decade their wage rates doubled, and the eight-hour day became prevalent when the United Rubber Workers gained recognition and bargaining rights. But the contract also designated "men's jobs and women's jobs," with wages in the latter category averaging 20 percent less.[52]

Women employed in industries organized during the late 1930s and early war period gained improved work standards and job security along with their male coworkers. But discriminatory features crept into some contracts, such as wage differentials that had been included in discredited NRA codes and were carried over into negotiated agreements. Job categories remained sex-defined. Seniority lists were separate In addition, one western union forced an employer to discharge married women, and the Idaho State Federation of Labor passed a resolution expressing opposition to working wives.[53]

During this period of acute industrial unrest, women enlarged the scope of their organizing and strike activities which had begun earlier with the encouragement of Section 7a. Women strikers were highly visible in the pecan fields of Texas, the garment plants of Michigan, and retail stores throughout Ohio. They organized an Emergency Brigade in Michigan and engaged in the diversionary tactics that allowed male strikers to occupy Chevrolet Plant 4 at Flint, thus ensuring the success of the most publicized sitdown strike of the period. The sitdown strike staged by a handful of clerks at a small variety store in Akron, Ohio, received less attention, but it was symptomatic of wide-ranging activism on the part of working women.[54]

For a handful of women, already seasoned union organizers, this was a time to be relished. Pauline Newman of the International Ladies' Garment Workers Union, who began organizing strikers during the "uprising" of New York shirtwaist makers in 1909, remembers the 1930s as a time of fulfillment for the trade union movement. Fellow ILGWU organizer Rose Pesotta was a ubiquitous figure during the Depression—among garment workers across the nation, with home-workers in Puerto Rico and French Canadian women in Montreal assisting rubber workers in Akron and auto workers in Detroit and Flint.[55] New activism brought new women to the forefront, some of whom combined radical ideology with union organizing. Socialists and Communists played major roles in CIO unionization campaigns, combin-ing their particular vision of social justice and workers' utopia with trade union organization. One present-day Communist recalls falling in love with her husband and the party on a picket line in New York. Stella Nowicki began organizing workers in Chicago's meat packing industry on Communist party initiative, struggling to overcome hostile employers, hesitant employees, and union suspicion of women workers. To Nowicki, the union was the answer to degrading working conditions and job insecurity as well as the means to bring about a socialist society. Another activist joined an office workers' union in order to attract the attention of the party. She succeeded, and for ten years following 1938 she worked as a union organizer for the Communists. Her description makes it difficult to distinguish between the activities of union and party.[56]

The commitment of women organizers to their unions did not result in commensurate rewards at the leadership level. Only fourteen of 477 delegates to the 1938 AFL convention were women; the same proportion participated at the CIO gathering. The Women's Bureau noted that 5 women and 120 men attended the 1938 convention of the United Rubber Workers and attributed the discrepancy to women's passivity at meetings and the "triple responsibilities of factory worker, homemaker, and active union member." Nowicki concurred. Women often acquiesced to male leadership because of their responsibilities to home and children after a full day's work in the factory. Married women, in particular, did not envision positions of authority as their proper purview, nor did they particularly care for the atmosphere of meeting halls and taverns where male officials often gathered. Unions simply did not make efforts to attract women to meetings or to address women's issues. Nowicki engaged in menial chores which did not entitle her to time loss with pay. Yet she could recall, "It was a privilege and a wonderful experience to participate in the excitement of those times." For another woman, ten years as an organizer were the best of her life. "I'll never have years like that again, that's for sure." These women brought one common feature to their glorious adventures— neither had household and family responsibilities at the time.[57]

With the exception of the amended Social Security Act in 1939, the Fair Labor Standards Act of 1938 marked the last piece of major legislation of the New Deal. The administration hoped to maintain reasonable wage and hour regulations for those workers who had lost protection from defunct NRA codes but did not gain new protection because they worked in unorganized sectors of the economy. The bill that eventually passed contained numerous exemptions, many of which affected female workers, especially working wives. While workers in southern textiles and northern shoe factories—including many low-paid women— benefited, seasonal employees like those in canneries and clerks in retail stores uninvolved in interstate commerce were not covered by the provisions of the legislation. As in so many other New Deal measures, the ineligible included domestic servants.[58] The YWCA sponsored a summer conference for domestic workers in 1938 during which they sang about their treatment under the New Deal:

> *Social Security we need!*
> *Social Security indeed!*
> *March we forth two million strong,*
> *Workers all, but stand alone*
> *While all legislative measures pass us by!*[59]

While recognizing that significant numbers of women workers were not covered by the Fair Labor Standards Act (FLSA), the National Woman's Party believed that by reestablishing the principle of wage and hour regulation for men as well as women—which the NIRA had first accomplished—special protective legislation for women was unnecessary. The main objection to an equal rights amendment by most women's organizations was no longer valid. The NWP had opposed protective laws for women because members believed they impeded economic opportunity and reinforced the concept of female dependency and inferiority. The NWP feminists had always advocated regulation of working conditions based on occupation, not sex. They hailed the FLSA as vindication of their position, calling for all women's groups to eliminate protective legislation by extending standards to all workers not covered in the federal act with comparable state legislation. The Women's Bureau replied on behalf of special laws. The need for wage and hour guidelines for women not covered by the FLSA as well as other protective and prohibitive measures was unchanged; the assumptions that women were physically and emotionally different from men, rightfully filled different family roles, could not compete equally with men in the economic sphere, and therefore continued to require special legislation based on sex, were unchanged.[60] Agreement over definitions of sexual and economic equality and, consequently, compromise among women's organizations remained as elusive as ever.

Yet, on a number of issues, the ideological conflicts and the social class and occupational differences so often blamed for the feminist split had been largely overcome. The NWP and business and professional women's groups vigorously opposed the NRA wage differentials that affected women in industry. Countering the judgment of one historian who believed business and professional women identified with management and viewed industrial women as workers rather than as women,[61] the president of the National Association of Women Lawyers described the discriminatory aspects of the industrial codes as integral parts of widespread retrogression in women's economic rights generally.[62] And the League of Women Voters, the Women's Trade Union League, and the Women's Bureau, whose principal focus remained on women in industry, played major roles in combating Section 213 and related discriminatory action against married women workers, the negative impact of which fell most heavily on professional and clerical workers.

This ability of women's rights advocates to cross class lines was accomplished, in large measure, because of the narrow nature of the issues upon which they agreed. Unity resulted from shared awareness of discrimination against working women in New Deal policies and in attacks on employed wives. They engaged in similar educational, protest, and pressure campaigns, and in defense of married women workers they united to project traditional notions of female attitudes toward work and familial roles. Together they ignored those features of social security legislation that institutionalized those roles and female economic dependency.

Other feminist issues and concerns fell by the wayside. In 1934, two writers noted that as the shadow of the Depression lengthened, "women, with their unlimited capacity for adaptability, abandoned the fight . . . and all other battle cries of the feminist movement." Alma Lutz of the NWP decried the return of feminine fashions and increased deprecation of career women. In two articles in *Independent Woman,* Juanita Tanner flippantly attacked the onslaught of "testimonials to the effect that Feminine Dependence will cure depression, headaches, wrinkles, graying hair, insomnia and that dull feeling." In a more serious vein, she condemned the growing emphasis of advertisers on women as mindless consumers, the constant portrayal of women as sex objects, and the anti-female orientation of Freudian psychology.[63] These protests were rare cries in the wind. The BPW, which had just endorsed the Equal Rights Amendment, published the Tanner articles with the disclaimer stating the author's opinions were solely her own. The NWP remained the vanguard of American feminism and continued throughout the period to ask some of the right questions, but it never developed a coherent, consistent body of answers. Just as the ERA began to receive more favorable reception in Congress, the NWP suffered internal schism over structure and tactics that weakened these committed feminists.[64]

Highly visible and influential women in the Roosevelt administration shared many of the same concerns of the women's organizations. Eleanor Roosevelt was steadfast in her insistence on women's right to work and to obtain relief without discrimination. To observers, friendly and otherwise, Mary W. Dewson's initials stood alternately for "minimum wage" and "more women," as she moved from the Consumers' League and efforts to promote protective legislation to the Women's Division of the Democratic party and attempts to bestow the blessings of political patronage on women. The intersection of social work and social reform with feminist issues was less obvious as Frances Perkins moved up the administrative ladder. However, she never completely forgot the sense of mission so common among late nineteenth-century college graduates to put their education to constructive use and to prove their competence as women in the process.[65] These women belonged to that group of female reformers who represented the continuity between the Progressive Era and the New Deal.[66] But whereas some feminists of the earlier period also engaged in radical feminist analysis, this strand did not carry over.

It is difficult to conceive of the Depression apart from the New Deal and the general intellectual agitation generated by economic collapse. But unlike other periods of major ferment and reform (for example, prior to the Civil War, around the turn of the century, during the 1960s), visible, vocal, and wide-ranging feminism was not a prominent feature of the New Deal era. Feminists in other periods have been explained in terms of perceptions of status loss, or absence of role options or models.[67] No individuals were more aware of women's deteriorating status than the spokespersons who defended working women during the Depression, yet their anxieties were translated into defensive rhetoric and not into agitation to improve female status. Furthermore, a YWCA study indicated that the most ardent defenders of women's economic freedom were those women whose own positions were most secure.[68] Status loss and anxiety were endemic in the daily experiences of the insecurely employed, marginally employed, or unemployed women who, more often than not, supported New Deal measures regardless of discriminatory features. Women protected by a discriminatory wage standard, who had never had a floor under their wages before, cared little for sexist implication. For desperate women on relief, the sewing room represented survival rather than a sex-segregated handout. The concepts of status loss and anxiety remain too ambiguous and do not explain the constricted nature of feminist activity during the 1930s in contrast to women's rights activities at other times.

The nature of the social climate provides a better clue to the defensive quality of activities on behalf of women during the Depression. Feminists in other major reform periods shared surroundings in which extensive questioning of private values and public institutions, as well as experimentation with alternative life styles, existed. Many women were influenced by and contributed directly to the pervasive ferment in which little was sacred or escaped the discovery and analysis of reformers. Some of the more astute women carried their awareness of specific social problems into more intensive analysis of the entire society, women's roles and status within it, and possible means by which their position could be ameliorated.

But the social and intellectual climate differed during the 1930s. Whereas in other reform eras individuals with a variety of interests and perspectives roamed over the entire social landscape, the Depression decade was marked by intellectuals, reformers, politicians, and faddists who shared a single concern. The massive economic dislocation, its causes and possible solutions, riveted the attention of Americans along the entire ideological spectrum. The public arena absorbed all interest. Few individuals were interested in examining or tampering with male-female roles and relationships within the privatized family at a time when the family would, it was hoped, fulfill its emotional function as a "safe port in the storm" when safe ports were in short supply, would perform its social function as the bedrock of social order when order seemed to be dissipating with economic disarray. Issues seemingly unrelated to economic reconstruction were neglected. The diffused social and intellectual ferment that had nurtured (and in turn, had been nurtured by) feminist activities and thought in other reform periods was absent. It is one measure of the Depression's impact that efforts to understand what had happened and to overcome it completely captured and monopolized Americans' energy and imagination.[69]

If would-be feminists in the 1930s lacked an intellectually invigorating climate, they also lacked a group model upon which to focus for comparative analytic purposes. The experiences of women in abolition societies before the Civil War, in civil rights activities in the 1960s, and in the settlement houses or Socialist party in the early twentieth century provided a point of departure for identification with a specific disadvantaged race or class. During the 1930s, the exploited, disadvantaged, and demeaned could not be so clearly identified; they were ubiquitous. Some suffered more than others, and, in retrospect, those who endured the greatest hardships could still be defined by class and race, as well as by sex. It did not appear so obvious at the time, since the majority of Americans were experiencing at least some degree of deprivation, and attention centered on unemployed men. The debate over the "new woman" of the previous decade, who combined work and family, was completely subsumed by anxiety over the "forgotten man" who combined no work with a possibly demoralized and disintegrating family.

Writer and ERA proponent Genevieve Parkhurst did single out women as the most unfortunate victims of the Depression. Awareness of the problems of working women and action on their behalf by women's organizations were her solution to the undue suffering.[70] These were the concerns and activities that defined feminism for Parkhurst as well as for the groups she unfairly accused of insensitivity and inaction. But these issues were not only narrow in scope, they were time-bound as well. The discriminatory features of codes, relief measures, and employment of married women passed with the Depression decade. Feminism itself was victimized by national preoccupation with economic collapse and recovery. Like—and to a great extent because of—their contemporaries, women concerned with female status concentrated on economic issues in the public sphere. No one wrote an incisive feminist analysis of the sexual inequality that pervaded social and economic structures. The watchdogs of working women failed to examine the broader implications of their employment. They did not analyze the connections among work, male-female roles and relationships, and economic expectation that lay at the basis of issues and values concerning female work patterns both inside and outside the home.

chapter 7

New Necessities and
Old Traditions

With opposition to working wives so extensive, it was little wonder that some married women experienced confusion and ambivalence over their employment status. One wife wrote to Mary Anderson that she would be the first to complain if fired, yet she believed that the country would benefit if all wives relinquished their jobs. "I sure feel guilty of my job right now," she confessed, "but I wouldn't tell it to no one else, and I wouldn't quit my job unless I was forced to do so."[1] The contracted economy of the 1930s mandated that many women seek gainful employment while the competition for limited jobs reinforced cultural assumptions concerning the proper sexual division of labor within family and society. At the same time women were caught in this dilemma, the nature of family life, needs, and values were altering, further complicating choices and attitudes regarding employment by wife and mother.

Middle-class families adhered closely to the traditional allocation of social roles. "Middletown's business class has stood firm in its deeply grooved habit of thought that the normal thing is for the husband to provide and for the wife to be provided for." But the Lynds conceded that some flexibility in these attitudes occurred during the economic emergency. A sizable group of geographically dispersed families of above-average educational and occupational attainments, who had been surveyed in 1927, were questioned again six years later. Over that period of time, half of the families had suffered income reductions, but the sample generally remained well above the national level in terms of economic comfort. Although there were few working wives in the group at either time, husbands' attitudes toward the employment of married women had relaxed. In 1927, one-third stated that they would oppose their spouses' working under any conditions; the proportion was one-sixth by 1933.[2]

Married black women, whose high work rates all along the range of income levels suggests some immunity from traditional attitudes, did not always escape patriarchal values, especially upon achieving some semblance of middle-class status. A black social worker from Arkansas remembered, "My mother was a teacher. She never did teach, because my father never did want her to work. He was the person to wear the pants in the family. He wanted to be the strong one."[3]

Male hostility to married women workers crossed class lines; men were conscious that status within the family was closely linked to earning capacity. This situation even prevailed in working-class families, where inadequate or unstable income often required financial supplements by wives. Industrial employment had been irregular long before the 1930s, and brief periods of wage earning by married women were not uncommon. The Depression forced a continuation of established practices. But family members tried to preserve the semblance of patriarchal organization during crises, for wives as well as husbands accepted conventional familial patterns. The employment of married women was justified in terms of absolute economic necessity or as the result of circumstances, such as ill health, which were beyond anyone's control. The temporary nature of the wife's job was constantly emphasized. "The wife as an intermittent source of family income" adhered closely to her role as helpmate, representing less of a threat to her husband's authority and self-esteem and contributing to a more philosophical acceptance of the family's difficulties.[4] The fiction of the temporary expedient was occasionally impossible to maintain in the face of long-term male unemployment. One young couple, both of whom were opposed to working wives, had difficulty coping with her six-year history as sole wage earner. The wife wanted to retire, and her husband had to endure her parents' "throwing it up to him."[5]

Yet, instances were frequent in which no attempt to rationalize the necessity of a wife's employment succeeded. The degree to which many men internalized their roles as breadwinners and endured loss of self-respect when unemployment undermined their ability to support their families was dramatic. The psychological impact of enforced idleness was often as emotionally debilitating as the loss of income was economically disruptive. One jobless working-class husband insisted that "the women's place is in the home. I would rather starve than let my wife work." Another felt that accepting relief was the ultimate degradation, but having allowed his wife to work was close behind. Few statements were more revealing about the effect of unemployment and the toll traditional role expectations exacted from men than the reaction of one who insisted, "I would rather turn on the gas and put an end to the whole family than let my wife support me."[6]

Acting upon these sentiments, some unemployed or underemployed men did forbid their willing wives to seek work. One young mother wanted to "get us out of the hole" and resume the job she had held prior to her marriage. Her former employer did not object to the employment of married women, but her husband did. He was adamant in his belief that wives were assuming the jobs of men who should always have preference. He vetoed his wife's desire to supplement the family income. Wives willing to work sometimes resented the intransigence of their spouses. One married woman remembered that her husband was too proud to let her work, so, in her view, they suffered unnecessary deprivation.[7]

Even the possibility of sizable increments in family income did not sway many men. Gallup asked married men their opinion of their wives' obtaining employment, and approximately 80 percent indicated their disapproval. When those who answered negatively were asked if they would alter their view if their wives could earn $25 per week, only 17 percent replied positively; at $50 per week, 27 percent would reconsider.[8] In the midst of economic deprivation, when the median income was little more than $1,000 per year, the fact that the possibility of large additions to family income influenced men's attitudes to such a limited extent was one more indication of the intensity with which they adhered to traditional values.

In middle-class families caught in the economic maelstrom of the 1930s "the effort to meet the situation included the employment of the mother not previously employed," but as in the case of working-class families, the temporary and emergency nature of her efforts was stressed. Those families with some financial reserves fell back on savings or reduced expenditures before resorting to the employment of wives. Robert Angell's study of the adaptation by fifty families of college students who had suffered sudden and long-term income decreases revealed seven cases in which the wife engaged in wage earning. This proportion is the same as the national figure of 15 percent in 1940, but the percentage of wives at paid work in the Angell sample and in the census are not really comparable: The former were all white, middle-class women, the latter included significant numbers of blacks and foreign-born who crowded the lower rungs of the occupational ladder. A study of Berkeley, California, families found almost 40 percent of mothers (including 18 percent of women classified as middle-class and nondeprived and twice that proportion of deprived middle-class women) worked at some time during the 1930s. Decennial counts missed significant numbers of wives and mothers for whom employment was a short-term adaptation to the Depression but a work experience nonetheless.[9]

Like other investigators of Depression-decade family adjustment, Angell concluded that the ability of individual families to weather the hardships and dislocations of the period, including the entrance of wife and mother into the labor force, was determined by the degree of strength and stability the family displayed prior to the economic collapse. If families became disorganized under the pressure of economic conditions, deprivation and role adjustments exacerbated but did not cause tensions already present. The sociologists also agreed that husbands were most severely affected by their changed positions because of the demands society placed on them as breadwinners; but the investigators accepted this role orientation and its relationship to the familial power structure. The extent to which the position of authority of the unemployed man changed and the degree to which idle men accepted new functions within the family were important parameters used by sociologists to describe and measure the adaptation of the families to economic dislocation. But these studies also indicated the lengths to which married women, regardless of social class, carried attempts to mitigate the effects of changed status on their husbands. With few exceptions, those wives who assumed new work roles viewed their efforts within the traditional family framework and exhibited little desire to usurp positions of authority.[10]

The facts that working wives sought to perpetuate the male-dominated household and that most men and women alike opposed working wives were related to anxiety over family stability and social order. When pollsters asked opponents of married women workers to explain their attitudes, two-thirds indicated that they adhered to traditional modes of sexual division of labor. They believed either that working wives usurped jobs that rightfully belonged to male breadwinners or that "women's place is in the home." One-fifth of the other respondents stated that "healthier and happier home life [results] if women don't work," a sentiment closely linked to the virtually unanimous replies to an *American Magazine* article, "Should I Take a Job When My Husband Has One Too?" Hundreds of letter writers advised the author to stay home, enjoy the work of developing strong character in her children and of making her husband master of a real home.[11] These prescriptions for domestic bliss and family stability were only a few steps removed from more hyperbolic pleas for social and political order based on traditional family structure and roles. One school superintendent denounced the employment of married teachers as "detrimental to home building and the home is one of the stable institutions upon which the welfare of the future of our government depends." Massachusetts watchdog Florence Birmingham insisted working wives "are deserters from their post of duty, the home, which in the American system of government is the only unit of society on which the country depends for existence." Divorce, juvenile delinquency, and potential matriarchy would vanish if only married women abdicated their jobs to the rightful income earners of families.[12]

Social critics had worried about the instability of the American home and the disorganization of family life for decades, but the extent and intensity of concern varied over time. Sociologist Hornell Hart quantified the approval or disapproval expressed in publications on the subjects of birth, marriage, and divorce rates as well as willingness to accept sexual freedom as criteria of social concern. From approximately 1915 to 1925, he discovered fewer articles and books on these topics and less anxiety expressed over them than earlier in the century. His content analysis of material printed after the mid-1920s, however, revealed a quantitative upsurge in interest in and increased opposition toward birth control information and practice, liberalized divorce laws, and freer sexual morality. He concluded that Americans were experiencing a renewed and heightened concern over the well-being of family life and the home. A survey of periodical literature related to the family, conducted by the AAUW during the 1930s, indicated the continuing nature of these anxieties. But the later study added a topic to "those problems which were being more generally discussed" in relation to the family: the position of the homemaker in a changing society.[13]

The years immediately preceding the Depression witnessed another type of revolt against the industrialization and urbanization that impinged so heavily upon traditional family structure, functions, and roles. Typified by Ralph Borsodi, "back-to-the-land" advocates attacked the pitfalls of urban life and economic interdependency. They suggested physical removal to the countryside and the establishment of self-sufficient households. Mrs. Ralph Borsodi described the personal satisfaction that would accrue to women from direct economic contributions to the family.[14] Critics dismissed these schemes as the "idealizing of a former age and an attempt to re-create a family system maladjusted to our present industrial order," but the movement gained adherents during the 1930s.[15] Economic collapse intensified efforts to come to terms with decades of rapid change. In many respects, attempts to reinforce traditional sex roles and behavior, especially under the impact of the Depression-induced attack on the conventional concept of masculinity, was as great an exercise in nostalgia as the attempt to create a rural, cottage-industry economy.

Most Americans could not envision social order, generally, and family stability, specifically, in any context other than one that included the rigid demarcation of sexual spheres. Testimonial and advice literature reiterated the imperatives of the female role as supportive wife and nurturing mother. The virtues of adhering to idealized roles were explicit in the written testimonials of admitted ex-feminists who renounced their jobs and subsequently enjoyed the thrills of homemaking and child rearing. All of the training and effort expended in pursuit of careers, they insisted, could better be spent at home.[16] Writer Margaret Culkin Banning advised young women to gain good educations, learn independence, carve out careers, and then marry and devote themselves to husbands and children. A husband especially "wants someone to restore his courage every other day, and build up his faith in himself."[17] Most writers of marriage manuals praised young women for the employment that made marriage possible but then encouraged them to relinquish their jobs at the earliest opportunity. Marriage and homemaking should constitute their ultimate careers.[18] Americans even received advice on marital problems by radio. On Sunday evenings, millions of listeners heard the familiar refrain, "Mr. Anthony, I have a problem." To questions concerned with the issue of working wives, John J. Anthony, who was director of a marriage counseling service, answered: "I never advise a woman to work outside the home unless it is financially necessary." To the husband whose spouse was forced to succumb to economic exigencies he had additional advice: "Spare her all the work that you can at home. And redouble your own efforts to find a job."[19]

Not all social observers succumbed to conventional prescriptions when analyzing marriage, family, roles, and status. During the 1920s, growing numbers of sociologists turned their attention to the study of the family and altered the framework within which their analysis took place. Prior to the mid-1920s, almost half the material dealt with the subject matter from an anthropological and historical perspective. Texts written after 1926, however, shifted to contemporary social, economic, and psychological concerns.[20] A few sociologists conceived the family as an institution in a state of disintegration or disorganization, but the majority described it as an institution in the process of transition. William Ogburn redefined family functions in order to understand and cope with a vital social unit undergoing perceptible changes within a rapidly shifting environment. The family, he argued, could no longer be pictured as an economic unit producing goods but rather as a social and psychological one producing happiness. Personal interrelationships replaced economic interdependency as the glue that bound smaller, nuclear families together.[21]

Textbooks on the sociology of the family also examined the status of women within the context of changing family structure and social expectations. One of the early studies of the 1920s by Ogburn and Ernest Groves described increasing participation of married women in the labor force and the subsequent difficulties faced by both husbands and wives. They were especially sympathetic to working wives who encountered opposition and scorn from husbands and society. They placed career and marriage advocates in the vanguard of the movement to make the role of wife compatible with changing conditions, permitting "the most complete social expression of human beings who happen to have been born female."[22]

The concentration on the new functions of the family and the relationship of women to the new social order continued to characterize marriage and family textbooks through the Depression decade. In classic examples of textbook lag, sociologists and social psychologists reiterated much of the feminist rhetoric of the previous decade and expressed sympathy and understanding for the working wife who faced the physical burden of two jobs and the emotional conflict over two roles. The Depression exaggerated these problems as more women sought employment and "families were caught during this transition between new necessities and old traditions."[23] Women suffered from severe cases of cultural lag and received little support as "parents, education, religion, and art have only intensified her problems by their conservative refusal to recognize the change or help her to find some way of life compatible with her needs and new responsibilities."[24]

Many of the social scientists recognized that the antagonism against married working women resulted from the assumed association between the changing roles of women and fears over the disruption of family life. Their literature conveyed a sense of optimism, however, that after this period of transition, and in spite of numerous obstacles, an emancipated woman and a new and viable family order would emerge.[25] It was only necessary to accept the family as an agent for the development of personality, an institution based on the strength of affectional bonds. "Readjustment of familial patterns in terms of companionship and mutual affection is necessitated by woman's actual and potential economic independence and by their educational and social equality." Whatever relationship between their new definitions of the family and the changing roles of women, most of the sociologists accepted the alterations with equanimity. Yet, their insistence on the passing of productive economic functions of the family and emphasis on residual emotional ones was too narrow and simple. It allowed sociologists to accept the upheavals wrought by economic transformation and to discuss the family and female roles within that context, but it ignored both persistent and newly developing social and economic functions, ties, and values that better characterized families and influenced the increasing employment of married women.[26]

The experiences and testimony of working wives themselves demonstrated these characteristics of family life. While primarily an urban phenomenon, even married women in rural, nonfarm areas availed themselves of employment opportunities when possible. In one rural county in Rhode Island, 480 wives engaged in 60 different occupations. In one section of rural Mississippi, 64.5 percent of the women in three textile mills, and 44.3 percent of those in two garment factories were married. The BPW surveyed its married members, largely engaged in teaching, clerical work, or trade in smaller cities with populations under 25,000; the Women's Bureau studied a cross section of working wives (excluding domestics); Cecile LaFollette sampled 625 married women workers, primarily native born, half of whom had obtained at least two years of college education; and Vassar College questioned 100 employed married alumnae.[27] Across this wide geographic and occupational range, in answers to these formal investigations as well as in individual pleas for tolerance, economic necessity dominated the stated reason for employment of married women. Regardless of parameters of measurement, family incomes were stretched to the breaking point during the Depression, and emphasis on economic need is hardly surprising. A mid-decade survey of incomes of families and individuals, exclusive of those on relief, revealed that the median income of American families was $1,070. One-third of the families and single individuals earned $780, or less, annually. Average income ranged from $1,175 for wage earners and $1,710 for clerical workers, to $2,485 for salaried business persons and $3,540 for independent professional workers. The first two categories constituted 43 percent of all families; the latter two, 15.7 percent. Only one-fifth of all families had annual incomes over $2,000 per year.[28] In a large number of cases, total family income resulted from contributions of two or more wage earners. Census data from 1930 revealed that approximately one-third of all families had more than one income contributor. In one-quarter of these cases, there were two workers; in the remainder, three or more. From the standpoint of large-scale unemployment during the Depression, these multi-wage earning families served as a buffer between individual joblessness and destitution. The WPA estimated that half of the nation's unemployed belonged to families in which some member retained work.[29]

Supplementary family wage earners, however, were more likely to be unmarried sons and daughters than wives. Unmarried daughters were often the largest additional income contributors, not because their earning capacity was greater than their brothers' but because family values decreed that young women relinquish a greater share of their earnings to the family coffer. Studies revealed that the largest proportional income contributors were wives, but turning over their total paychecks did not compensate for the smaller size of those earnings.

Married women's lower educational attainments and their inexperience in the case of new entrance into gainful employment interrupted work patterns in the instance of those reentering the work force and discriminatory hindrances in many areas all curtailed wives' earning capacity. The combined incomes of fathers and daughters were continually higher than those of husbands and wives. But all supplementary workers appeared to suffer a higher incidence of unemployment during the Depression than male heads of families. Young people, in particular, found fewer occupational opportunities and were discharged more often and more quickly than the principal wage earner.[30]

The economic duress of the decade had little effect on the proportion of multi-income-earning families. At the end of the 1930s, the proportion of families with more than one wage earner remained one-third of all families, and the average number of workers per family remained the same as well. One shift did take place. The likelihood that a supplementary wage earner was a child under eighteen was lower, and that position was generally assumed by the mother. Prolonged compulsory education, child labor legislation embodied in FLSA, and reduced employment opportunities for young people contributed to their decreased participation in the labor force. But the need for income increments to the family remained and, increasingly, the married woman apparently accepted that responsibility.[31]

The impact of additional wage earners on a family's economic status was great. Among the third of all families with incomes below $800 annually, less than 20 percent had a supplementary income contributor. The rate increased to almost 25 percent in families whose annual income fell between the $800 and $1,600-per-year level. But over one-third of all families with annual earnings between $1,600 and $2,500 attained that level with the aid of two or more income contributors. The latter category represented comfortable middle-class status. Only one-fifth of American families fell within that income range at the end of the decade. While wives were most likely to work if their husbands' earnings were low, work force participation rates for urban married women, whose spouses' income fell between $1,500 and $2,000, still approximated the national average of 15 percent. One out of seven wives at this economic level was pushing her family into a comfortable income range.[32]

Case histories of the 1930s read like unceasing litanies of reduced food consumption, mended clothing, foreclosed mortgages on homes, and curtailed social activities. But the extent of economic deprivation varied greatly. Some individuals and families remained virtually untouched, although most Americans experienced some degree of contraction. Most Americans had also experienced new conceptions of desirable living standards prior to the Depression, and they clung as firmly as possible to them in the face of diminishing monetary means by which to satisfy them. Lower price levels prior to mid-decade and increased installment buying afterwards helped close the gap. A working wife could also maintain a desired level of consumption, but not without conflicts. In Middletown, acceptance of "the goodness of a wife's being a homemaker" opposed the pressure of a "skyrocketing psychological standard of living. If the single woman in Middletown works for bread, it appears to be for more than bread alone that its married women leave their home to work." Home economist Hazel Kyrk noted that a wife's income increments might be small, "yet without them the family would be deprived of many things they consider essential. They may be sufficient to move their manner of living from one level to another."[33]

What a family considered essential was personal and varied, but contemporaries realized that the concept of economic necessity was changing, that consumption practices had altered. Income ceilings in proposed state legislation curbing married women workers ranged from $800 to $1,600, demonstrating the difficulty of arbitrarily defining need in monetary terms.[34] Much of the difficulty resulted from changing consumption practices, tentatively described in a study for the Social Science Research Council and confirmed by an extensive government-sponsored survey of spending patterns among several hundred thousand nonrelief families during the mid-1930s. Data collected by the government's Consumer Purchase Study were compared to statistics from a similar Bureau of Labor Statistics study conducted from 1917 to 1919. The later sample included white wage-earning and lower salaried families in the $1,200 to $1,500 income bracket (representing two-thirds of nonrelief families) in thirty-five cities.

In spite of variations in location, definite trends were evident. While total consumption of food changed little, families in two-thirds of the cities spent less proportionately on food than they had during the earlier period, because prices were consistently lower. Expenditures for clothing also decreased, partially as a consequence of style changes as well as deflated cost. Reduced income did not force a reduction in living standards in these areas. The government study discovered increased spending for housing and related items. Rents and mortgage payments varied greatly, but, with the exception of one city, expenditures for fuel, light, and refrigeration increased. The report concluded that there was little doubt that housing standards in urban areas improved greatly. A larger percentage of people assumed the costs and experienced the comforts of electric lighting and modern plumbing than ever before, and spending for miscellaneous items was markedly higher in two-thirds of the cities. Families spent increased proportions of their incomes for items ranging from the services of barbers and hairdressers to the conveniences of automobiles (if not the newest model), gas, and oil. In the midst of the nation's worst economic disaster, investigators concluded that Americans were better fed, clothed, and housed and more mobile than ever before.[35]

Families were willing to sacrifice future security for present consumer satisfaction. The sample in almost half of the cities revealed income deficits, with borrowing most often in the form of installment buying. In those areas that indicated a margin of savings, the amount was lower than in the 1917-19 study. Investigators suggested that these developments reflected renewed optimism over economic recovery and the desire to compensate for considerable belt tightening during the early years of the Depression. But, they also believed that the study revealed more long-term developments: "It would seem that an important change in attitudes toward consumption expenditures had occurred among moderate income urban families. . . . The change in the ideas of these workers as to how they ought to live has resulted in fundamental changes in their expenditure patterns."[36]

These noted changes in consumption patterns and expectations required a closer examination of the meaning of economic need as expressed by working wives. Married working women who belonged to the BPW had median incomes of $1,300 at the end of the 1930s, almost one-third greater than that of half of American families. The wives in the LaFollette study, also business and professional women, averaged about $1,000 in annual income which, when added to their husbands' earnings, gave these families median incomes of $3,082, financial resources three times the national median. At a time when one cost-of-living survey established $1,250 as an adequate income for a couple and estimated that $1,600 to $2,000 was more than adequate for a

family of five, the testimony of these women indicates that their supplements to family income did indeed reflect increases in families'
perceived economic needs.[37]

The constant refrain of economic need raises questions of veracity as
well as definition. Because the employment of married women came
under such pervasive attack and because need was considered a mitigating factor, many wives may have sought refuge under this protective
shield. However, insistence upon the economic imperative of their
employment more likely reflected changing definitions of that concept,
as indicated in the government's study of urban consumption patterns.
The BPW special study recognized that economic need as expressed by
working wives had different meanings. For one group, those in low-
paying jobs, economic necessity retained its conventional definition.
Married women in white-collar occupations, however, work "because
of need to maintain or improve their standard of living or for a career."
The number of the latter was negligible, the report added.[38] The desire,
even determination, on the part of some families to increase their
purchasing power and raise the quality of their living standards with the
added income of employed wives indicated that need had become a
relative term, economic values had altered, and expectations were
decidedly higher.

Two items mentioned most repeatedly by married women (sometimes
as indicators of the necessity of their income contribution and occasionally as separate explanations for their employment) were home
purchase and children's education. Home ownership did increase
dramatically during the 1920s, fulfilling cultural aspirations as well as
physical needs. President Hoover convened a Home Ownership Conference in 1931, and announced that "the sentiment for home ownership
is so embedded in the American heart that millions of people who dwell
in tenements, apartments, and rented rows of solid brick have aspirations
for wider opportunity in the ownership of their own homes."[39] Hazel
Kyrk recognized the growing role of home ownership within the context
of changing living standards and cultural values. A home of one's own
became a symbol of stability, well-being, and security that money income
alone did not convey. "It is a goal that perhaps more frequently than
any other, families have deliberately set up as the one they desire to
attain."[40] During the Depression, controversy arose over the financial
feasibility and social desirability of home ownership, as reduced incomes

and bank foreclosures made a significant dent in the ownership rate.[41] "The little gray home in the West" or East,[42] however, remained a fixed American ideal. The testimony of working wives in numerous studies and in countless letters to editors indicated married working women shared these values and envisioned their employment as a means toward fulfillment.

When working married women claimed that their earnings made education for their children possible, they seldom furnished specifics. Whether added income helped finance college educations or whether a mother's employment permitted a child to prolong secondary schooling was not clear. But increases in school attendance indicated that large numbers of boys and girls and young men and women, who formerly would have been labor force participants, were delaying their entry into gainful occupations. Expectations that associated educational attainments with occupational achievement accompanied legal sanctions that kept children in the schoolroom. The economic dislocations that began in the late 1920s placed some brake on this trend.[43] Among working-class families, the strain of male unemployment forced children under eighteen sometimes, along with their mothers, to assume the burden of family support. When a meat packer in Omaha could find no employment, the mother had to go to work and "now has to take her sixteen-year-old daughter out of school to work."[44] The difficulty many young people experienced in finding employment and the programs initiated by the National Youth Administration made this employment pattern less common. Mothers were more likely to enter or remain in the work force, replacing—rather than joining—young family members as longer periods of formal education became the norm.

An additional explanation for employment given by women, married and single, was their support of dependents. Income contributions to individuals living both within the households of working wives and outside were common. LaFollette's study of comfortable families revealed that almost 30 percent of the women had more than one dependent in their homes, and over one-third of the families made some financial contribution to at least two persons outside the household. The average period of financial support was four and one-half years, indicating that many of these arrangements predated the Depression. Working women over a broad occupational range indicated a high incidence of aid to individuals outside the nuclear family. In Cleveland, over 40 percent, and throughout Utah, half of the working wives surveyed made cash contributions averaging $23 per month to family members living outside their homes. Business and professional women, primarily in smaller communities, related comparable experiences. While the Depression increased the number of their dependents (as women's incomes fell), these familial interrelationships were not products of the economic disaster alone.[45]

Detailed descriptions of the financial responsibilities of New York families, in which wives lost their jobs, illustrated these complex economic networks. Besides their own children, one couple was supporting the wife's "father and mother and helping support a sister with three children whose husband is a chronic invalid. In another case, the couple constituted the source of support of the husband's mother and the three children of a widowed sister."[46] The twenty-eight couples surveyed admitted full or partial financial aid to seventy-one persons, in addition to their children, with parents, nieces, and nephews most often described as dependents. Government workers discharged under the provisions of Section 213 revealed similar situations. Of those who answered questionnaires, 697 reported responsibility for over 500 persons, only half of whom were their own children. The remainder were largely the parents of the couples who suffered income loss because of the wife's dismissal.[47]

The familial responsibilities and the counterproductive effects of discharging some workers, often forcing their dependents onto relief rolls, were arguments advanced to counter restraints on working wives. The evidence not only supports the rationale, it illustrates the complexities of family structure and kinship networks as well. Family historians have demonstrated the shortcomings in equating the household with the family in analyzing familial structure and functions. Residential proximity and financial interdependency form important links among family members who do not necessarily share the same residence. The testimony of working wives enforces the importance of economic ties and indicates that economic interrelationships were not limited to large urban areas or to working-class families or to the early stages of industrialization.[48] The frequency with which married women workers reverted to their support of dependents as a justification for their employment implies familial support was socially acceptable and even anticipated.

These financially based kinship networks contradicted the emphasis placed by sociologists of the 1920s and 1930s on the reduced economic functions of the family, simply because families no longer produced the bulk of their physical needs as an economic unit. Financial responsibilities persisted beyond the boundaries of the nuclear family upon whom the social scientists focused their attention, and those responsibilities often could not be met by one income earner in a family. Together with rising living standards and reduced incidence of child labor, financial obligations to kin thrust married women into the role of supplementary wage earners. As public welfare programs alleviated some of the responsibilities to the extended family, working wives could devote more of their earnings toward fulfilling newly defined economic needs.

Studies of family networks describe mutual exchanges within kinship relationships. Children not only supported their elderly parents and other relatives but often received services in return. This was particularly true in periods of unemployment and in cases of working mothers. Grandparents often looked after children whose parents were income earners. Parents of working women in LaFollette's study, who lived in their homes, contributed to the household in terms of homemaking duties and care of young children. Working mothers with children under school age invariably made arrangements for their supervision, which often meant care by adult relatives, often grandmothers. Forty percent of the female garment workers in a small Mississippi mill town had a grandmother care for the children, and a quarter of the mothers in the textile mills left youngsters in the care of older female parents. In the latter case, there was a much higher rate of husband-wife employment in the same factory, and the possibility that parents could alternate work shifts and child care was greater.[49]

Regardless of geographic location, occupation, or class level, patterns of child care were remarkably similar. Once children reached school age, provision for supervision decreased somewhat, but reliance on the school as surrogate parent was seldom complete. Only one-fifth of mothers in southern textile mills made no arrangements for the care of their school age children after school, and this comparatively high rate can be attributed to the structure of the mill town where proximity of work and home allowed for sporadic supervision. Working mothers usually sent their older children off to school themselves and arranged for a relative or for hired help to prepare meals at the noontime break. These arrangements did not alleviate maternal concerns. Employed mothers admitted great anxiety over poor discipline by surrogate parents, even family members, or over the activities of their unsupervised children after school hours when child-care arrangements were least likely to be made.[50]

Child care by family members, hired help, and primary schools should not mask the marked impediment child-rearing responsibilities placed in the path of the majority of potential working mothers. Labor force participation rates for married women with children under the age of ten dropped precipitously.[51] Children require care, and social norms decree that mothers provide it. When the popular radio soap opera of the period, "Ma Perkins," began in 1933, the announcer asked at the conclusion of the first episode, "Can a woman run a man's business in a man's world and not neglect her family [?]"[52] Almost thirty years later, the program succumbed to the competition of television without providing a solution to the dilemma caused when work is performed in the public "man's world" and children are raised in the private female preserve of the home. Reconciling the conflicts between the physical separation of women's productive and reproductive functions was and remains the crucial issue in the debate over women's roles in contemporary society. While some working mothers often with the aid of kin tried to harmonize roles with alternative child-care provisions, the vast majority of mothers during the 1930s still accepted their prescribed role and willingly engaged in the full-time socialization of their children.

Besides assistance with the supervision of children, family members both inside and outside the household sometimes contributed housekeeping services. In addition, many married women workers testified that they engaged domestic help. Even in rural Mississippi, many textile and garment workers employed household workers. When working wives defended their jobs on the basis of the employment they, in turn, provided for domestic workers and laundresses, they argued from fact. Yet, investigators concluded that regardless of arrangements made, working wives still retained the responsibility for the major share of housekeeping, along with child rearing. When available, the help of older parents was most likely to be considerable, whereas working wives admitted aid from husbands and children was minimal.[53]

In spite of arguments to the contrary, household chores remained time consuming, and married working women found themselves with two jobs. The benefits of the highly vaunted labor-saving devices, which supposedly eased homemaking functions and, for feminists, necessitated out-of-home activities for married women, were more apparent than real. While students of census data attributed the growing numbers of working wives to the spread of household conveniences such as washing machines and vacuum cleaners, social commentators overlooked the higher, more demanding standards of homemaking that accompanied the growing availability of electrical appliances. The washing machine often replaced the hired laundress, added a function to homemaking, and resulted in higher standards of cleanliness as well.[54]

Household technology affected female employment outside the home as well as homemaking within. The washing machine displaced laundresses who often worked in their own homes, thereby escaping enumeration by the census bureau which defined gainful employment as out-of-home work. They represented an additional supply of married women seeking compensatory earnings. Many new entrants into the labor force were not actually new income earners but women who had changed the location of their work. Several other groups of married women fell within this category. The constantly expanding apparel industry replaced numerous home-bound seamstresses. Changing household and residential patterns also undermined the ability of married women to supplement family income within their homes. During the late nineteenth and early twentieth centuries, large numbers of urban migrants eased their entry into industrial society by boarding and lodging in private households. Housing shortages, which had made this arrangement functional, eased during the 1920s, while immigration ceased and rural influx diminished during the Depression.[55] Women were less likely to contribute to family coffers by serving boarders, although in numerous cases when families "doubled up" during the 1930s, homemaking responsibilities may have increased.

While electric appliances, changing consumption patterns, and housing arrangements affected women's work outside the home, new household technology altered but did not reduce their work inside. Time-expenditure studies that compared work weeks of farm and small rural community homemakers with those of wives of business and professional families in urban areas revealed insignificant differences in the amounts of time each group devoted to housekeeping. Urban and supposedly well-equipped homemakers spent twelve hours less per week on household chores than rural wives, but the city-based women received considerably more household assistance. That contribution made the total hours devoted to home care comparable. In addition, urban women spent proportionately more time on child care than their rural counterparts. In all, homemaking still engaged much of a woman's time. While a working wife often cut corners, her responsibilities could not be minimized. Activities associated with meal preparation were especially time consuming. Forty-three percent of the time of farm homemakers and 33 percent of the total homemaking hours expended by urban women was devoted to food purchasing, preparation, and serving. The majority of women interviewed by LaFollette stated that planning and serving meals were their greatest problems, regardless of the aid of kitchen appliances. Whether they had help from family members, hired domestics, or relied totally upon themselves, married women who worked spent less time on housekeeping than did full-time homemakers. But, whereas homemakers averaged fifty-six hours per week on their chores, combined jobs of working wives required time expenditures of at least seventy-five hours per week. It was little wonder that so many married working women admitted that they would prefer to give up their jobs or, if they enjoyed the personal and financial aspects of employment, that they were physically exhausted from their dual responsibilities.[56]

With time studies indicating that homes and young children required over fifty hours of effort each week, proponents of full-time homemaking as a career felt justified in their assertions. The demands of housekeeping were devalued because they received no monetary reward, they argued. But the defenders of domesticity insisted that the unpaid housewife made economic contributions to the family, providing goods and services that would have to be purchased otherwise. The reduced purchase of canned goods, especially early in the 1930s, and the burgeoning of home canning indicated the validity of this premise.[57] The extensive BPW study articulated this economic trade-off. Noting that increasing numbers of families were accepting the wife as supplementary wage earner, the report still concluded that the "majority of middle-class families have decided that it is more economical for the wife to produce a non-money income in the home than to work in the outside world."[58]

Furthermore, the chief of the Federal Bureau of Home Economics argued that homemaking could and should be esteemed because it was the "only occupation engaging a significant number which gives economic security to its workers." None of the nation's 28 million housewives lost their jobs because of the economic crisis. In fact, she wrote that their work load actually increased.[59] Whatever the merits of this reasoning, family case studies demonstrated that homemakers survived the emotional pressures of the decade with much less strain than their unemployed or underemployed husbands. They experienced little threat to their conventional roles.[60] And a wife and mother coping with her domestic responsibilities through this period of stress could provide a positive model for her daughters, a situation with great implications for the next generation of young women and their attitudes toward work and family. Glen Elder has pointed out that mothers with the aid of children, usually daughters, played a prominent role in the family's adaptation to adverse circumstances, indicating that family life and domesticity could bring rewards to women.[61]

Within the context of these cross-currents, contradictions, and complexities, the proportion of married women workers continued to grow. More young women married and remained at work at least until the birth of their first child, while older women entered the labor force in direct response to Depression-induced deprivation or changing patterns of consumer demand. During the decade, women encountered fewer professional opportunities and found more menial jobs in those supposedly desirable white-collar areas where they also encountered the greatest incidence of discrimination. At the same time, uncertainty existed over work roles; domestic and child-rearing functions were occasionally eased by family members or by hired assistance, but seldom was the issue of primary responsibility raised.

The possibility of debate over these questions, first raised during the 1920s, was stifled. In a decade during which economic recovery and social stability monopolized public attention, and intellectuals toyed with economic but not social revolution, feminism retreated. Monitoring women's economic gains outside the home and social obligations within it ceased. Defenders of the position of working wives clung to the status quo and envisioned their employment in terms that emphasized the familial context within which most married women themselves perceived their work. The gap between feminist rhetoric and female employment had narrowed at the expense of feminism. The gulf between the reality of the working wife and the ideal of the married woman as wife and homemaker continued to grow. In accepting dual roles, the married working woman also accepted dual burdens, and the voices of concern and protest were barely whispers.

Epilogue

In 1945, a graduate student at Columbia University sent a copy of her master's degree essay to the Women's Bureau. "Married Women at Work" traced employment trends, described discrimination during the Depression, and concluded married women would retire to their homes with the end of the wartime emergency and the return of prosperity. Her predictions were predicated on the assumptions that the female response to wartime labor shortages was temporary and that only dire economic circumstances drove wives into the work force. The prediction proved false, along with the underlying rationale.[1]

During World War II, industry and government actively recruited female labor, and women responded in unprecedented fashion. The number of working women grew by more than half, while the number of employed wives more than doubled. In five years, the percentage of married women gainfully employed rose from 15 percent to over 24; the proportion of the female labor force that was married increased from one-third to one-half; the median age of a working woman rose to slightly over thirty-five. These dramatic changes were accompanied by attitudinal shifts on the part of the women themselves. In response to numerous polls and surveys, new entrants into jobs indicated that they planned to continue working after the war. In spite of post-1945 demobilization and economic dislocation, women did retain, regain, or discover new areas of employment. Labor force participation by married women soared beyond wartime peaks. The census enumerators of 1950 confirmed this development, and it has continued unabated ever since.

During the national emergency, the white, married, older woman emerged as the typical female worker and has remained so, challenged only by younger married wives and mothers in recent years. Two trends accelerated the pace of these changes in post-war America. In the workplace, white-collar clerical, sales, and service occupations—jobs compatible with middle-class status—burgeoned. Requiring minimal formal training or long-term career commitment, these jobs facilitated the periodic entry and exit of married women, who could adjust work patterns to the needs of individual and family life cycles. In the home, rising price levels and the triumph of consumerism during the postwar boom created pressure for added family income. The social characteristics of women workers, the structure of the female work force, and the economic values and demands of the family all intersected. On the basis of numbers of working women alone, it is difficult to view World War II as anything but a watershed with regard to female employment.[2] However, the configurations of the female labor force were all distinguishable prior to the war, with the Depression playing a major role in reinforcing or enhancing material values and expectations, in necessitating work force participation by married women, and in diminishing the status of the occupations into which they poured.

The principal force propelling married women into the work place—economic need increasingly defined as heightened desire for material goods and services—was both present during and exacerbated by the Depression. The long-term trend in consumerism was accelerated by the deprivation so widely experienced during the 1930s, a psychological legacy influencing the economic aspirations of parents and children in the postwar period. The Depression reinforced familial values generally (the desire for home, marriage, children, and security) while requiring new work roles for many wives as the means to secure desired levels of material comfort and security. For the majority of working wives and their families, gainful employment was perceived as an extension of female-nurturing activity and not just a response to more impersonal forces, such as occupational demand of the labor market and demographic features of supply.[3]

Perceptions of economic necessity had already influenced the number of working wives during the Depression. Whether in response to dire economic emergencies or in order to maintain living standards already achieved, some wives sought and found employment regardless of possible family misgivings and distinct public condemnation. Work was an experience, perhaps a short-term one misssd in a census taken at a given moment in time, shared by a greater number of married women than ever before. The total undoubtedly exceeded the 15 percent recorded in 1940. Had Depression-related discrimination been less prevalent, the ability and desire to find work might have been even greater, the proportion of wives at work higher, and the dramatic leap that marked the wartime period less pronounced.

As for occupational structure, more menial clerical and service jobs already dominated the white-collar category by 1940, gaining at the expense of professional work. Pressure and replacement of women by men in more desirable areas of employment, intense competition among women for existing opportunities in sex-segregated jobs further encouraged by well-intentioned advisors, and technological and economic developments in the work place all contributed to downward mobility. Why this development endured beyond the 1930s is more conjectural. It is difficult to measure the psychological effects of public hostility and personal inability to fulfill occupational expectations on future aspirations, career commitments, and desire for economic progress on the working women who survived the Depression and on the younger women who followed them into the labor force. But a lowering of economic status occurred during the 1930s and continued thereafter.

Frank Stricker suggests that increased jobs as managers and proprietors and continuous literary evidence of dissatisfaction with domesticity indicate that the career impulse of women did not dissipate during the postsuffrage era. Women did not surrender to infatuation with the sexual revolution of the 1920s or to the feminine mystique of the 1950s.[4] By implication, they did not react negatively to the dislocations of the Depression either. The tenacity with which many women clung to their occupational achievements during the 1930s supports his thesis, in part. Post-Depression labor force developments do not. Managerial and proprietary occupations that supposedly compensate for losses in professional categories do not require the investments in time and training for certification associated with careers, nor are real estate agents and beauty-shop owners far removed in status from clerks and salespersons in "pink-collar ghettos." None of these occupations demands the commitment associated with the conventional concept of career and, perhaps most revealing of all, neither do the feminized professions. As for chafing at the constraints of domesticity, at the conscious level this dissatisfaction is not necessarily synonymous with the desire for a career. The most articulate exponent of female discontent with conventional roles in the postwar period labeled the phenomenon "the problem that has no name."[5]

While Stricker insists that educational and economic goals remained high for half a century, he admits they often fell short of expectations. It is to his credit that he blames the burden of double roles on married women workers and economic discrimination for this fact rather than faulting women themselves. And he correctly assesses the need for feminists and intellectuals to interpret and articulate common, if not universal, female discontent at home and work "as collective phenomena, rooted in fundamentally inegalitarian social and economic structures."[6] However, a receptive audience is necessary as well: a large-scale constituency that can relate feminist questions and issues to the reality of their daily lives. During the 1920s, many individuals addressed the issues of women's work and family life, but the proportion of middle-class working wives was small. When these numbers expanded significantly by the mid-1940s, when an ideology that identified the discriminatory practices in the work place, that protested the added burdens of domestic responsibilities experienced by married women workers, and that described the dissatisfactions among homemakers with constricted activities would have found a larger, more receptive audience, the feminist impulse of the 1920s had succumbed to Depression-decade pressures.

Writer and National Woman's Party member Nancy Barr Mavity provided a vivid example of the evaporation of the feminist perspective. During the mid-1920s, she wrote that "the chance to choose one's work as a person instead of a sex being [is] worth the hard and complex struggle to amend our entire social and economic constitution."[7] Unlike many of her contemporaries who advocated marriage and careers, she did not ignore the need to mount an assault on the allocation of sex roles within the family which burdened the working wife or to examine the prejudices that determined employment opportunities and practices outside the home. A quarter-century after the debate over marriage and gainful employment "burned like a roaring fire," Mavity applauded the end of "the revolution that we were so vociferous about." She surveyed the economic scene in 1951 and discovered the burgeoning numbers of working wives who "are not motivated by feminism, but by common sense applied to economic dilemma." Not with condemnation but with admiration and praise, she described "young couples, who care less about abstract justice than they do about the good life for their families, [and] have toppled a good many time-honored prejudices."[8] In effect, she failed to distinguish changes in actual behavior from persistence of cultural ideals.

A new generation of social scientists added theoretical support to the many time-honored prejudices that had not been toppled at all. More concerned with stability and less tolerant of social change, more normative than empirical in their methodology,[9] sociologists like Talcott Parsons incorporated the rigid, century-old, sex-role dichotomy into their postwar writing. Parsons instructed women to stay home and fulfill expressive functions, while their husbands played instrumental roles as breadwinners and determiners of family status. If wives must work, their employment must not be competitive in terms of earnings or status with that of their husbands.[10] Gone was the erroneous equating of gainful employment with female emancipation and equality implicit in Mavity, because female employment, all evidence to the contrary, was an anomaly. Gone was the warning of one sociologist of the family who collaborated on a popular text just prior to the vogue gained by the functional sociologists. Marion Bassett of Wellesley College had insisted that women's progress was not simply a matter of economic activities but a matter of ideology. "The more important question is the ideology or scheme of cultural values which governs the roles and relations of men and women both in and outside the home," she wrote in 1944.[11] Two decades passed before significant numbers of women, most of whom had come of age with no memories of the Depression, addressed the disparity between the reality of women's lives and the social decrees that affect female roles and expectations which Bassett had identified.

The contemporary woman's movement that surfaced in the 1960s has engaged in the most wide-ranging examination of and organized attempts to overcome sexist practices and institutions to date. Feminists have gained legislative and judicial support for anticipated advances in the economic sphere. Yet, in spite of the appearance of gains, occupational progress has been more apparent than real. The Equal Pay Act of 1963, Title VII of the 1964 Civil Rights Act, and affirmative action programs still have failed to overturn all pay differentials between men and women who perform the same work or, more important, to make significant inroads into the rigidly segregated labor force which is what actually accounts for the great—and growing—discrepancies between male and female earnings. Occupational gains made by women remain individual and modest although they are perceived as collective and extensive. Women repair telephone lines, reach middle-management positions in business, and are entering law and medical schools in unprecedented numbers, but the average woman entering the labor force or at work is still most likely to find herself in the kind of job where nine-tenths of all employed women have been and remain. Nontraditional work at higher salary rates remains elusive, affirmative action programs that attempt to compensate for past liabilities are under attack, and though judicial interpretation of Title VII has overturned protective legislation as restrictive, more subtle forms of discrimination continue and even proliferate.[12]

Limitations in occupational progress are compounded by negligible changes in allocation of domestic roles. Husbands and children may be more apt to help with the household chores of the working mother, but mother and family alike believe they are alleviating some of *her* responsibilities. Equalizing household functions remains as remote as equalizing economic opportunities, and even more elusive is equalizing the value and priority women assign to work and family roles. Whether one of myriad typists in a "pink-collar" enclave or an apparently dedicated successful career woman, most wives continue to subordinate their economic roles to familial ones. Sociologist Jessie Bernard, who has written extensively on women, marriage, and the family, concluded from her own studies and those of other researchers that the contemporary well-educated, middle-class woman is most likely to work and marry, most likely to be a "feminist—wittingly or unwittingly," most likely to portend the future contours of family life. And within the context of a dual career-marriage, she will still most likely "contribute more than her husband does to the running of the household. . . and much more to child care. And if there has to be a choice between her husband's career and her own, his will be chosen."[13]

The extent to which women accept and internalize primary commitments to family has led some feminists, past and present, to incisive analyses and condemnations of the family, sometimes in conjunction with the capitalist economic order, as the ultimate oppressor of women.[14] The persistence with which women cling to familial attachments, even as they alter their roles in response to external demands of the economy, internal demands of their families, or personal desire for occupational success, is a fact that must be faced by feminists generally and not only those who would completely overturn social institutions and revolutionize economic systems. The unfinished business of feminism—new style of the 1920s—still remains.

Feminists, moderate or radical, may not find simple answers, but it is essential that they persist in asking the questions and raising the issues for public debate and private consideration. The experience of the 1930s is especially applicable to the contemporary feminist movement, now functioning in a milieu increasingly concerned with inflation, impending energy crises, and the state of the nation's economic health. The Great Depression exacted a special toll from women: intensified labor at home, growing work force participation but diminished economic status, and destruction of an already enfeebled women's movement which tried to protect working women by wrapping them in traditional familial roles and values. How to loosen the emotional, sociological, and ideological bond between women and their families so they can achieve their potential free from constraints is the perennial issue addressed by serious feminists. How feminism can survive "hard times" intact may become an additional concern.

Key to Abbreviations

Publications

ER	*Equal Rights*
ERIFW	*Equal Rights Independent Feminist Weekly*
IndW	*Independent Woman*
JAAUW	*Journal of the American Association of University Women*
JHE	*Journal of Home Economics*
JNEA	*Journal of the National Education Association*
L&L	*Life and Labor Bulletin*
NYT	*New York Times*
S&S	*School and Society*
WP	*Woman's Press*
WW	*Woman Worker*

Women's Organizations

AAUW	American Association of University Women
BPW	National Federation of Business and Professional Women's Clubs
LWV	National League of Women Voters
NWP	National Woman's Party
WTUL	National Women's Trade Union League
YWCA	Young Women's Christian Association

Notes

Introduction

1. *New York Times*, 20 September 1931.

2. Estelle B. Freedman, "The New Woman: Changing Views of Women in the 1920s," *Journal of American History* 61 (September 1974): 372-93, surveys these and more general views of women during the first post-suffrage decade.

3. Joan Kelly-Gadol, "The Social Relation of the Sexes: Methodological Implications of Women's History," *Signs* 1 (Summer 1976): 809-24; Gerda Lerner, "Placing Women in History: A 1975 Perspective," in *Liberating Women's History: Theoretical and Critical Essays*, ed. Berenice A. Carroll (Urbana: University of Illinois Press, 1976), pp. 357-68.

4. Rudolph C. Blitz, "Women in the Professions, 1870-1970," *Monthly Labor Review* 97(May 1974): 34.

5.See the Essay on Sources for titles of critical literature on census employment and occupational data. Two recent studies that focus on racial and ethnic factors on female occupational structure include Julia Kirk Blackwilder, "Women in the Work Force: Atlanta, New Orleans, and San Antonio, 1930-1940," *Journal of Urban History* 4 (May 1978): 331-58; and Dolores Janiewski, "Race, Class, and the Sexual Division of Labor: The Difficulties of Collective Action in Durham during the 1930s" (Paper presented at the Fourth Berkshire Conference on Women's History, August 1978).

6. Robert W. Smuts, *Women and Work in America* (New York: Columbia University Press, 1959), p. 111.

7. Mary Anderson, "The Economic Status of Wage-Earning Homemakers," *Journal of Home Economics* 24 (October 1932): 866; "Pin Money or 'Coupling Pin' "? *Life and Labor Bulletin* 10 (January 1932: 3.

Chapter 1

1. "The Women of To-Day," *North American Review* 157 (October 1893): 423; Lillian W. Betts, "The New Woman," *Outlook* 52 (12 October 1895): 587. For a description of events marking what he refers to as "The Nineties: The First Decade of Modern America," see Carl Degler, *The Age of the Economic Revolution, 1876-1900,* 2nd ed. (Glenview, Ill.: Scott Foresman, 1977), pp. 115-53. For a perceptive study that relates an outburst of energy to a variety of popular and intellectual cultural developments, including women's activities, see John Higham, "The Reorientation of American Culture in the 1890s," in his *Writing American History: Essays in Modern Scholarship* (Bloomington: Indiana University Press, 1972), pp. 73-102. Lois W. Banner describes "The Emergence of the Modern American Woman: The 1890s" in *Women in Modern America: A Brief History* (New York: Harcourt, Brace, Jovanovich, 1974), pp. 1-42.

2. Eleanor Flexner, *Century of Struggle: The Woman's Rights Movement in the United States* (New York: Atheneum, 1973), chaps. 16, 19-23; Aileen Kraditor, *The Ideas of the Woman's Suffrage Movement* (New York: Columbia University Press, 1967), chaps. 3, 4, 5; Sophonisba P. Breckenridge, *Women in the Twentieth Century: A Study of Their Political, Social and Economic Activities* (New York: McGraw-Hill, 1933), pp. 14-22.

3. Breckenridge, *Women in the Twentieth Century,* p. 25; Flexner, *Century of Struggle,* pp. 208-09.

4. Joseph A. Hill, *Women in Gainful Occupations, 1870-1920,* Census Monograph, no. 9 (Washington, D.C. : Government Printing Office, 1929), pp. 19-24, 52; Robert W. Smuts, *Women and Work in America* (New York: Columbia University Press, 1959), p. 38; U.S., Department of Commerce, Bureau of the Census, *Report on Population of the United States at the Eleventh Census, 1890,* part 2, pp. cxix, cxxiii.

5. Elizabeth Faulkner Baker, *Technology and Women's Work* (New York: Columbia University Press, 1964), chaps. 2, 3; Mary P. Ryan, *Womanhood in America: From Colonial Times to the Present* (New York: New Viewpoints, 1975), pp. 197-208; Hill, *Women in Gainful Occupations,* p. 45; Smuts, *Women and Work,* pp. 17-19.

6. William S. Elsbree, *The American Teacher: Evolution of a Profession in a Democracy* (New York: American Book, 1939), pp. 199-206; Baker, *Technology and Women's Work,* pp. 55-60; Smuts, *Women and Work,* pp. 19-20.

7. Elsbree, *American Teacher,* pp. 319-25, 334, 338-51.

8. Lewis M. Chamberlain and L. E. Meece, *Women and Men in the Teaching Profession* (Lexington: University of Kentucky Press, 1937), p. 12; Hill, *Women in Gainful Occupations,* pp. 41, 63.

9. "The College Woman and the Vocations," *Survey* 27 (23 December 1911): 1401; *Vocational Training: A Classified List of Institutions Training Educated*

Women for Occupations Other Than Teaching (Northampton, Mass.: Press of Gazette Printing, 1913).

10. Chase Going Woodhouse, *After College What? A Study of 6665 Land Grant Women, Their Occupations, Earnings, Families and Some Undergraduate and Vocational Problems*, Institute of Women's Professional Relations Bulletin no. 4 (Greensboro: North Carolina College for Women, 1932). Woodhouse, "The Occupations of Members of the American Association of University Women," *Journal of the American Association of University Women* 21 (June 1928): 120.

11. Willystine Goodsell, "The Educational Opportunities of American Women," *Women in the Modern World, Annals of the American Academy of Political and Social Sciences* 143 (May 1929): 8, 12; "Academic Status of Women on University Faculties," *JAAUW* 17 (January-March 1924): 5-11.

12. Mary M. Roberts, *American Nursing: History and Interpretation* (New York: Macmillan, 1954), pp. 9-14, 44-47, 164; Deborah MacLurg Jensen, *History and Trends of Professional Nursing* (St. Louis: C. V. Mosby, 1955), pp. 192-94, 254-55. Smuts, *Women and Work*, p. 20; Baker, *Technology and Women's Work*, pp. 60-63.

13. Hill, *Women in Gainful Occupations*, p. 42.

14. Ernest V. Hollis and Alice L. Taylor, *Social Work Education in the United States: The Report of a Study Made for the National Council of Social Work Education* (New York: Columbia University Press, 1951), p. 519; Roy Lubove, *The Professional Altruist: The Emergence of Social Work As a Career, 1880-1930* (Cambridge: Harvard University Press, 1965), pp. 1-3, 12-16.

15. Hollis and Taylor, *Social Work Education*, pp. 130-31, 151; Lubove, *Professional Altruist*, pp. 47-49; "Is Social Work a Profession?" *Proceedings*, National Conference of Charities and Corrections, 1915.

16. U.S., Department of Commerce, Bureau of the Census, *Thirteenth Census of the United States Taken in the Year 1910*, vol. 5: *Population, 1910, Occupational Statistics*, p. 93; *Fourteenth Census of the United States Taken in the Year 1920*, vol. 4: *Population, 1920, Occupations*, p. 42.

17. Quoted in Sharon B. Wells, "The Feminization of the American Library Profession, 1876-1923" (Master's thesis, University of Chicago, 1967), p. 64. Also see Dee Garrison, "The Tender Technicians: The Feminization of Public Librarianship, 1876-1905," in *Clio's Consciousness Raised: New Perspectives on the History of Women*, eds. Mary Hartman and Lois W. Banner (New York: Harper Torchbooks, 1974), pp. 158-78.

18. "The Origins of Sexism in Librarianship, "*American Libraries* 3 (April 1972): 427.

19. Louis Round Wilson, *Education and Libraries* (Hamden, Conn.: Shoe String Press, 1966), pp. 253-56; *Fourteenth Census*, vol. 4, p. 42.

20. These characteristics of a profession were outlined by Elizabeth Kemper Adams, *Women Professional Workers: A Study Made for the Women's Educa-*

tional and Industrial Union (New York: Macmillan, 1921), pp. 1-2. They are comparable to those of Flexner but with less emphasis on the scientific basis of knowledge obtained and the altruistic purposes to which that knowledge would be put.

21. J. Stanley Lemons, *The Woman Citizen: Social Feminism in the 1920's* (Urbana: University of Illinois Press, 1972), p. 59; Hill, *Women in Gainful Occupations,* p. 41.

22. Baker, *Technology and Women's Work,* p. 212; Margery Davies, "Women's Place Is at the Typewriter: The Feminization of the Clerical Labor Force," *Radical America* 8 (July-August 1974): 5-10.

23. Hill, *Women in Gainful Occupation,* p. 56; Flexner, *Century of Struggle,* p. 208; Smuts, *Women and Work,* pp. 21-22.

24. Hill, *Women in Gainful Occupations,* pp. 52, 85, 94, 101, 111, 117; Ryan, *Womanhood in America,* pp. 195-206. On the native-born, middle-class origins and educational attainments of women entering government clerical jobs during the late nineteenth century, see Cindy S. Aron, "To Barter Their Souls for Gold: Female Clerks in Federal Government Offices, 1862-1890" (Paper presented at the Newberry Library Conference on Women's History and Quantitative Methodology, July 1979).

25. Azel Ames, *Sex in Industry: A Plea for the Working Girl* (Boston: J. R. Osgood, 1875).

26. *Women in Industry: Decision of the United States Supreme Court in Curt Muller vs. State of Oregon . . . and Brief for the State of Oregon by Louis D. Brandeis assisted by Josephine Goldmark* (New York: National Consumer League, 1908), p. 7.

27. U.S., Department of Labor, Bureau of Labor Statistics, *Bulletin No. 175* (Washington, D.C. : Government Printing Office, 1915), summarized a nineteen-volume Senate study of working conditions of women in industry. See Kraditor, *Ideas of the Woman's Suffrage Movement;* Peter Filene, *Him/Herself: Sex Roles in Modern America* (New York: Harcourt, Brace, Jovanovich, 1975), pp. 15-16; Ryan, *Womanhood in America,* pp. 225-30, on the preoccupation with motherhood imagery across the social spectrum during the early twentieth century.

28. "Women in the Business World," *Outlook* 51 (11 May 1895): 778; Edward Bok, "The Return of the Business Woman," *Ladies' Home Journal* (March 1900): 16.

29. "The Stenographer Plus," *Ladies' Home Journal* (February 1916): 33; "What Every Stenographer Knows," *Office Economist* 4 (March 1922): 12; Justine Mansfield, "Business Girls As 'Office Housekeepers'," *Office Economist* 8 (May 1926): 7, 13-14; Davies, "Women's Place Is at the Typewriter," pp. 15-21.

30. Dorothy Richardson, *The Long Day: The Story of a New York Working Girl As Told By Herself* (New York: Century, 1906), pp. 269-73; final letter in Florence W. Saunders, *Letters to a Business Girl: A Woman in the World*

of Business. . . Relations of Employer to Employee (Chicago: Laird and Lee, Publishers, 1908); Sophonisba P. Breckenridge, "The Activities of Women Outside the Home," in *Recent Social Trends in the United States: Report of the President's Research Committee on Social Trends,* vol.1 (New York: McGraw-Hill, 1933), p. 722; Charles H. Judd, "Education," in *Recent Social Trends,* vol. 1, p. 333; Davies, "Women's Place Is at the Typewriter," pp. 10-16; Smuts, *Women and Work,* chap. 3.

31. Saunders, *Letters to a Business Girl;* [G.G. de Aquirre], *Women in the Business World or Hints and Helps to Prosperity* (Boston: Arena, 1894); Ruth Ashmore, *The Business Girl in Every Phase of Her Life* (Philadelphia: Curtis, 1895).

32. *Woman's Home Companion* 32 (February 1905): 22; Ibid. 32 (June 1905): 26.

33. Donald Robin Makosky, "The Portrayal of Women in Wide Circulation Magazine Short Stories" (Ph.D. diss., University of Pennsylvania, 1966), pp. 28-38, 50-65.

34. Judd, "Education," p. 331.

35. Anna L. Burdick, "The Wage-Earning Girl and Home Economics," *Journal of Home Economics* 11 (August 1919): 329.

36. *Good Housekeeping* 61 (August 1915): 168-74; Ibid. (July 1915): 60-66; Ibid. (October 1915): 470-77; Ibid. (November 1915): 615-20. Also see Mary A. Laselle and Katherine E. Wiley, *Vocations for Girls* (New York: Houghton Mifflin, 1913); Eli Witner Weaver, ed., *Vocations for Girls* (New York: A. S. Barnes, 1913); Catherine Filene, ed., *Careers for Women: New Ideas, New Methods, New Opportunities to Fit a New World* (New York: Houghton Mifflin, 1920); Adams, *Women Professional Workers.*

37. Quoted in Lemons, *Woman Citizen,* p. 44.

38. Hill, *Women in Gainful Occupations,* pp. 258-62. These figures, unlike most compiled by Hill, include women in agricultural pursuits. Whereas the censuses of 1900 and 1910 were taken in the spring when farming is active, the 1920 count took place in January. As a result, agricultural workers were under-counted. Had agricultural labor been excluded in the 1900 and 1920 figures, the relative growth in the employment of native-born white women in this age group would have been even more dramatic.

39. Hill, *Women in Gainful Occupations,* pp. 78-79.

40. Ibid., p. 83; U.S., Department of Labor, Women's Bureau, *Women in Industry,* Bulletin no. 91 (Washington, D.C.: Government Printing Office, 1931), pp. 17-18.

41. John Martin, "Women's Work Before Marriage," *Survey* 35 (4 March 1916): 670.

42. Florence Kelley, "Married Women in Industry," *Proceedings of the Academy of Political Science* (October 1910): 90-96. Katherine S. Anthony, *Mothers Who Must Earn* (New York: Russell Sage Foundation, 1914); *Summary*

of the Report on the Conditions of Women and Child Wage Earners in the United States, especially summary of vol. 13; U.S., Department of Labor, Children's Bureau, *Infant Mortality: Results of a Field Study. . . On Births in One Year,* Bureau Publications, nos. 9, 20, 29, 37, 52, 68, 72 (Washington, D.C.: Government Printing Office, 1915-20), focused narrowly on the possible relationships among working women, infant mortality, and child neglect; Gwendolyn Hughes, *Mothers in Industry: Wage Earning By Mothers in Philadelphia* (New York: New Republic, 1925), was one study made from a broader perspective.

43. Filene, *Him/Herself,* p. 43.

44. Edward H. Clarke, *Sex in Education; or a Fair Chance for the Girls* (Boston: J. R. Osgood, 1873). For developments in higher education for women, see Thomas Woody, *A History of Women's Education in the United States,* vol. 2 (New York: Science Press, 1929); Flexner, *Century of Struggle,* chap. 8.

45. Filene, *Him/Herself,* pp. 27-28; Flora MacDonald Thompson, "The Truth About Women in Industry," *North American Review* 178 (May 1904): 751-60.

46. Charlotte Perkins Gilman, *Women and Economics: A Study of the Economic Relations Between Men and Women As a Factor in Social Evolution* (1898; reptd. New York: Harper & Row, 1966); Carl Degler, "Charlotte Perkins Gilman on the Theory and Practice of Feminism," *American Quarterly* 8 (Spring 1956): 21-39. For an incisive analysis of early twentieth-century feminism, see Daniel Rodgers, *The Work Ethic in Industrial America, 1850-1920* (Chicago: University of Chicago Press, 1978), chap. 7.

47. Olive Schreiner, *Woman and Labor* (New York: Frederick A. Stokes, 1911), pp. 65, 110, 272, passim; June Sochen, *The New Woman: Feminism in Greenwich Village, 1910-1920* (New York: Quadrangle Books, 1972), chap. 1.

48. Sochen, *The New Woman,* pp. 47-52; Russell Lynes, *The Domesticated Americans* (New York: Harper & Row, 1957), pp. 51-52.

49. Thompson, "Truth About Women in Industry," p. 751.

50. Comment by Rubinow, in Charles Zueblin, "The Effect on Women of Economic Dependence," *American Journal of Sociology* 14 (March 1909): 614-19.

51. J. E. Cutler, "Durable Monogamous Wedlock," *American Journal of Sociology* 22 (September 1916): 250.

52. Simon N. Patten, "Some New Adjustments for Women," *Independent* 61 (20 September 1906): 674-81; Helen M. Bennett, *Women and Work: The Economic Value of College Training* (New York: D. Appleton, 1917); Scott Nearing and Nellie M. S. Nearing, *Woman and Social Progress: A Discussion of the Biologic, Domestic, Industrial, and Social Possibilities of American Women* (New York: Macmillan, 1912), p. 276.

53. For a generational analysis of sex roles and feminism, see Filene, *Him/Herself;* for the shift in feminist focus, see Carl Degler, "Revolution Without

Ideology: The Changing Place of Women in America," in *The Woman in America*, ed. Robert Jay Lifton (Boston: Beacon Press, 1964), pp. 193-210.

Chapter 2

1. For a historiographic review, see Estelle B. Freedman, "The New Woman: Changing Views of Women in the 1920's, *"Journal of American History* 61 (September 1974): 372-93. James McGovern predated the flapper phenomenon in "The American Woman's Pre-World War I Freedom in Manners and Morals," *Journal of American History* 55 (September 1968): 315-33; and William Chafe stressed persistence of traditional goals in *The American Woman: Her Changing Political, Social, and Economic Roles, 1920-1970* (New York: Oxford University Press, 1972), pp. 94-96. For reform activities during the 1920s, see Clarke Chambers, *Seedtime of Reform: American Social Service and Social Action, 1918-1933* (Minneapolis: University of Minnesota Press, 1963), pp. 61-83; and J. Stanley Lemons, *The Woman Citizen: Social Feminism in the 1920's* (Urbana: University of Illinois Press, 1973). William O'Neill made the original distinction between social and hard-core feminism and indicated the shortcomings of each in "Feminism As a Radical Ideology," in *Dissent: Explorations in the History of American Radicalism*, ed. Alfred F. Young (De Kalb: Northern Illinois University Press, 1968), pp. 275-300, while Lemons sympathized with the social feminists in *Woman Citizen*, chap. 7.

2. Emilie J. Hutchinson, "The Economic Problems of Women," *Women in the Modern World, Annals of the American Academy of Political and Social Sciences* 143 (May 1929): 130. Peter Filene describes work and marriage feminism, which he labels "revised feminism," in *Him/Herself: Sex Roles in Modern America* (New York: Harcourt, Brace, Jovanovich, 1975), pp. 144-52. Elaine Showalter discusses the importance attributed to combining career, marriage, and motherhood and the related problems experienced by seventeen feminists who contributed to a series, "These Modern Women," published by *Nation* in 1926 and 1927. Pruette was one of the contributors; Hinkle was one of three psychiatrists invited to respond to the anonymously published biographical sketches. Showalter describes the feminists as "[m]iddle class, highly educated, and white" professional women. See *These Modern Women: Autobiographical Essays from the Twenties* (Old Westbury, N.Y.: Feminist Press, 1978), intro.

3. Dorothy Dunbar Bromely, "Feminist—New Style," *Harper's Magazine* 155 (October 1927): 552-60; Mary Ross, "Shall We Join the Gentlemen?" *Survey* 57 (1 December 1926): 263.

4. For broad definitions of feminism, see Gerda Lerner, "Women's Rights and American Feminism," *American Scholar* 40 (Spring 1971): 236; *The Female*

Experience: An American Documentary (Indianapolis: Bobbs-Merrill, 1977), pp. 391-94.

5. Grace L. Coyle, *Jobs and Marriage? Outlines for the Discussion of the Married Woman in Business* (New York: Woman's Press, 1928); "The Work of the Committee on the Economic and Legal Status of Women," *Journal of the American Association of University Women* 20 (October 1926): 8; "The Home and Job Problem," *Woman Citizen* 10 (June 1926): 15-16; *Cleveland Plain Dealer*, 27 February 1928.

6. Amey E. Watson, "Employer-Employee Relationships in the Home," *Women in the Modern World, Annals of the American Academy of Political and Social Sciences* 143 (May 1929): 51; Beatrice M. Hinkle, "Changing Marriage: A By Product of Industrialism," *Survey* 57 (1 December 1926): 286-89; Alice Beal Parsons, *Woman's Dilemma* (New York: Thomas Y. Crowell, 1926), pp. 191-93; Sophonisba Breckenridge, *Women in the Twentieth Century: A Study of Their Political, Social and Economic Activities* (New York: McGraw-Hill, 1933), pp. 99-100.

7. Viva Booth, foreword to *Annals* (May 1929): vii.

8. Elizabeth H. Pleck criticized the recent reliance on the thesis stressing the separation of home from work in "Two Worlds in One: Work and Family," *Journal of Social History* 10 (Winter 1976):178-95. The feminists of the 1920s, however, never questioned the development of separate workplace and home or its centrality to the discussion of women's declining status. On the sense of status loss among women during the nineteenth century, see Gerda Lerner, "The Lady and the Mill Girl," *Midcontinent American Studies Journal* 10 (Spring 1969): 5-14; Gail Parker, ed., *The Oven Birds: American Women on Womanhood 1820-1920* (Garden City, N.Y.: Anchor Books, 1972), introduction; Daniel T. Rogers, *The Work Ethic in Industrial America 1850-1920* (Chicago: University of Chicago Press, 1978), pp. 184-89.

9. Ross, "Shall We Join the Gentlemen?" p. 266.

10. Robert V. Wells, "Demographic Change and the Life Cycle of American Families," in *The Family in History,* Theodore K. Rabb and Robert I. Rotberg, eds. (New York: Harper & Row, 1973), pp. 85-94.

11. Margaret H. Speer, "Education, Business and Babies," *Independent Woman* 7 (June 1928): 245, 284-85; Lena Madesin Phillips, "The Two-Job Wife Debate," Ibid. 6 (May 1927): 4-5; "Should Married Women Work?" Ibid. 5 (October 1922): 20; Virginia MacMakin Collier, *Marriage and Careers: A Study of One Hundred Women Who Are Wives, Mothers, Homemakers and Professional Workers* (New York: Channel Bookshop, 1926), pp. 14-24; "This Wife Gets a Paycheck," *Collier's* 76 (19 December 1925): 30.

12. Ann D. Wood, "The Fashionable Diseases: Women's Complaints and Their Treatment in Nineteenth-Century America," *Journal of Interdisciplinary History* 4 (Summer 1973): 25-52; Abraham Myerson, *The Nervous Housewife* (Boston: Little, Brown, 1920), pp. 75, 245-67.

13. Hutchinson, "The Economic Problems of Women," pp. 132-36. Anne Steese Richardson, "When Mother Goes to Business," *Woman's Home Companion* 57 (December 1930): 22; Parsons, *Woman's Dilemma*, pp. 292-94; Ethel Puffer Howes, "Continuity for Women," *Atlantic Monthly* 130 (December 1922): 735; "This Wife Gets a Paycheck," p. 30.

14. Bromley, "Feminist—New Style," p. 553; Anna Garlin Spencer, *The Family and Its Members* (Philadelphia: J. B. Lippincott, 1923), p. 8; Editorial, *Equal Rights* 14 (31 December 1927): 368.

15. Editorial, *IndW* 9 (February 1925): 16.

16. Louis I. Dublin, "Homemaking and Careers," *Atlantic Monthly* 138 (September 1926): 337, 340; Collier, *Marriage and Careers*, pp. 4-5; Parsons, *Woman's Dilemma;* Anna Garlin Spencer, *Woman's Share in Social Culture*, 2nd ed. (Philadelphia: J. B. Lippincott, 1925), p. xxix.

17. Ann Hark, "Side by Side with Their Husbands," *Ladies' Home Journal* 47 (February 1930): 14, 161.

18. Ross, "Shall We Join the Gentlemen?" p. 267.

19. Mary Margaret McBride, "Marriage on a Fifty-Fifty Basis," *Scribner's Magazine* 86 (December 1929): 661.

20. Nancy Barr Mavity, "The Wife, the Home, and the Job," *Harper's Magazine* 153 (July 1926): 197.

21. Graphologist to Emma Hirth, November 17, 1924, Bureau of Vocational Information Collection, box 28, folder 350, Schlesinger Library, Radcliffe College (hereafter SL).

22. "The Home-Plus-Job Women," *Woman Citizen* 10 (March 1926): 15-16; Jane Littell, "Meditations of a Wage-Earning Wife," *Atlantic Monthly* 134 (December 1924): 723; "We Both Had Jobs," *Woman's Home Companion* 52 (August 1925): 34; Anne Byrd Kennon, "College Wives Who Work," *JAAUW* 20 (June 1927): 103; Collier, *Marriage and Careers*, p. 74.

23. "Friend-Husband: The Story of An Independent Woman," *Saturday Evening Post* 197 (25 April 1925): 112.

24. "We Both Had Jobs," p. 34; McBride, "Marriage on a Fifty-Fifty Basis," p. 662; Mavity, "The Wife, the Home, and the Job," pp. 189-99; Littell, "Meditations of a Wage-Earning Wife," p. 733.

25. *Survey* 49 (15 November 1922): 235; "Should Wives Take Jobs?" *Literary Digest* 84 (24 January 1925): 23; Collier, *Marriage and Careers*, pp. 81-90.

26. "I'm Glad I Married a Business Woman—A Symposium," *IndW* 6 (October 1927): 12-14; "The Fifty-Fifty Husband," *Woman's Home Companion* 55 (April 1928): 31; Robert S. Lynd and Helen Merrell Lynd, *Middletown: A Study in Contemporary American Culture* (New York: Harcourt, Brace, 1929), pp. 7, 26-27; Lorine Pruette, *Women and Leisure: A Study in Social Waste* (New York: E. P. Dutton, 1924), chap 6.

27. Geoffrey H. Steere, "Freudianism and Child Rearing in the Twenties," *American Quarterly* 20 (Winter 1968): 759-67; John B. Watson, *Psychological*

Care of Infant and Child (New York: W. W. Norton, 1928); U.S., Department of Labor, Children's Bureau, *Are You Training Your Child to Be Happy?* (Washington, D.C., 1928).

28. Spencer, *Family and Its Members*, chap. 2; Eva vB. Hansl, "What About the Children?" *Harper's Magazine* 154 (January 1927): 220-27.

29. Jessica G. Cosgrave, "The Recurrent Career," *IndW* 8 (January 1925): 3, 43; Sophie Kerr, "The Married Woman and the Job," *Woman's Home Companion* 54 (March 1927): 137.

30. vB. Hansl, "What About the Children?" p. 224; Emily Newell Blair, "Jobs After Motherhood," *Outlook* 155 (4 June 1930): 167-69; Ethel Puffer Howes, "Accepting the Universe," *Atlantic Monthly* 129 (April 1922): 452; Mary Ross, "Can Mother Come Back?" *Survey* 58 (1 April 1927): 38-39; Virginia Pope, "The Middle Aged Woman in Business," *Woman Citizen* 11 (April 1926): 43. Seventy percent of the feminists who contributed to the *Nation* series married. They solved this dilemma by remaining childless. See Showalter, *These Modern Women*, p. 5.

31. Anna Steese Richardson, "What About the Children?" *Woman's Home Companion* 58 (January 1931): 21-22; Helena Huntington Smith, "The Job Versus the Child," *Outlook* 149 (2 May 1928): 37-38; A. H. B. Peterson, "First Aid for Busy Mothers," *IndW* 7 (July 1928): 302-03, 327; Eunice Fuller Barnard, "The Child Takes a Nurse," *Survey* 57 (1 December 1926): 324-25; Parsons, *Woman's Dilemma*, pp. 249-57.

32. "Both Thanks—Career and Children," *Woman Citizen* 8 (1 December 1923): 15; Cosgrave, "Recurrent Career," p. 3; Smith, "Job Versus the Child," pp. 8-9; Ruth Hale, "Has Modern Woman Disrupted the Home?" *IndW* 8 (January 1929): 6-7; Bromley, "Feminist—New Style," p. 559; Alice Beal Parsons, "How Changing Conditions Change Mothers," *Progressive Education* 3 (October 1926): 295-99; John B. Watson, "Weakness of Woman," *Nation* 125 (6 July 1927): 10.

33. Collier, *Marriage and Careers*, pp. 90-95; Ira Wile, "As Children See It," *Survey* 57 (1 December 1926): 335-36; Angell, "Home and Office," *Survey* 57 (1 December 1926): 320.

34. Kennon, "College Wives Who Work," p. 106.

35. Clark, "Trying to Be Modern," p. 155.

36. Grace R. Foster, *Social Change in Relation to Curricular Development in Collegiate Education for Women* (Waterville, Me.: n.p., 1934), pp. 79-135; Bessie Bunzel, "The Woman Goes to College," *Century Magazine* 117 (November 1928): 28-31. For evaluations of the home economics movement as a revolt against careerism, see Chafe, *The American Woman*, pp. 103-07; and Filene, *Him/Herself*, pp. 146-47.

37. Storm Jameson, "Wages for Wives," *IndW* 8 (March 1929): 99, 141;

"Working Wives," *Survey* 50 (15 June 1923): 318; Emily Newell Blair, "Profits for Wives," *Outlook* 156 (1 Octover 1930): 170-71; Mildred Wood, "Homemaking As a Possible Profession," *Journal of Home Economics* 18 (December 1926): 63-67.

38. Willystine Goodsell, *The Education of Women: Its Social Background and Its Problems* (New York: Macmillan, 1924), p. v; "Social and Economic Problems of the Home," *JHE* 18 (March 1926): 148.

39. Bunzel, "The Woman Goes to College," p. 33.

40. Chase Going Woodhouse, "Modern Homemaking in Relation to the Liberal Arts College for Women," *JAAUW* 19 (October 1925): 7-8; Clara M. Brown, "New Problems and a New Curriculum," *JAAUW* 23 (January 1930): 74-76; Dublin, "Homemaking and Careers," p. 341.

41. Woodhouse, "Modern Homemaking," p. 8.

42. Esther H. Stock, "Cooperative Housekeeping," *IndW* 7 (April 1928): 158-60; Ethel Puffer Howes, "The Smith Institute for the Coordination of Women's Interest," *Annals* (May 1929): 20; Parsons, *Woman's Dilemma.*

43. Virginia M. Collier, "Review of Woman's Dilemma," *IndW* 6 (October 1927): 41.

44. *IndW* 1 (June 1920): 11; Susan D. Becker, "An Intellectual History of the National Woman's Party" (Ph.D. diss., Case Western Reserve University, 1975), chap. 8; Chase Going Woodhouse, "Studies of the Institute of Women's Professional Relations," *JHE* 21 (September 1929): 655-58.

45. For an intellectual history of the work ethic in the United States during the nineteenth and early twentieth centuries, see Rodgers, *The Work Ethic;* Eudora Ramsey Richardson, "From Pram to Office," *JAAUW* 21 (June 1928): 115; Bromley, "Feminist—New Style," p. 559.

46. Lynd and Lynd, *Middletown*, pp. 75-76; Floyd Dell, *Looking at Life* (New York: Alfred A. Knopf, 1924), pp. 14-17; Hutchins Hapgood, *A Victorian in the Modern World* (New York: Harcourt, Brace, 1939), pp. 93, 502-03; Christopher Lasch, *The New Radicalism in America: The Intellectual As a Social Type* (New York: Alfred A. Knopf, 1963), p. 102, on Randolph Bourne.

47. "This Wife Gets a Paycheck," *Collier's* 76 (19 December 1925): 30.

48. Lorine Pruette, "The Married Woman and the Part Time Job," *Annals* (May 1929): 301-14; Katherine Angell, "Home and Office," *Survey* 57 (1 December 1926): 318.

49. U.S., Department of Labor, Women's Bureau, *Family Status of Breadwinning Women in Four Selected Cities*, Bulletin no. 41 (Washington, D.C.: Government Printing Office, 1925).

50. "Four Ways to Support a Family," *Survey* 57 (1 December 1926): 280-85.

51. Collier, *Marriage and Careers*, pp. 14, 22.

52. Lynd and Lynd, *Middletown*, p. 29.

53. Ross, "Shall We Join the Gentlemen?" p. 266.

54. Lynd and Lynd, *Middletown,* pp. 83-85. On the development of the concept of an American standard of living and changing notions of economic need by the 1920s, see Winifred D. Wandersee Bolin, "The Economics of Middle Income Family Life: Working Women During the Great Depression," *Journal of American History* 65 (June 1978): 64-66, entire article, and chap. 7 above for continuing trends during the 1930s.

55. Valerie Kincade Oppenheimer, *The Female Labor Force in the United States* (Berkeley: University of California Press, 1970), chap. 2; Gilbert W. Clemens, "Why the Spectacular Rise of the Electric Refrigerator Is Significant,"*Advertising and Selling* 8 (26 January 1927): 21, 58; Rupert L. Burdick, "Selling Women Their Own Kitchens," *Advertising and Selling* 7 (19 May 1926): 30, 76.

56. Hugh A. Stoddert Kennedy, "The New Plutocrat," *Century Magazine* 116 (August 1928): 461; "Those Wage-Working Wives," *Literary Digest* 98 (15 September 1928): 68.

57. Tree Day Program, 1922, Archives of Case Western Reserve University, Cleveland, Ohio.

58. *New York Times,* 26 December 1927; Phyllis Blanchard and Carlyn Manasses, *New Girls for Old* (New York: Macaulay, 1930), pp. 174-77; Chafe, *The American Woman,* pp. 102-03.

59. Breckenridge, *Women in the Twentieth Century,* p. 115; U.S., Department of Commerce, Bureau of the Census, *Fifteenth Census of the United States, 1930: Population,* vol. 5, pp. 273, 274; Clarence Long, *The Labor Force Under Changing Income and Employment* (Princeton, N.J.: Princeton University Press, 1958), pp. 106-07.

Chapter 3

1. Mary Phlegar Smith, "Legal and Administrative Restrictions Affecting the Rights of Married Women to Work," *Annals* (May 1929): 263; *New York Times,* 22 December 1928; *Independent Woman* 5 (November 1922): 18.

2. Smith, "Legal and Administrative Restrictions," p. 263; "A Railroad Boycotts Women," *Equal Rights* 14 (6 October 1928): 276-77; John F. Stover, *American Railroads* (Chicago: University of Chicago Press, 1961), pp. 197-98; Edith Abbott, *Women in Industry: A Study in American Economic History* (New York: D. Appleton, 1910), pp. 250-55; *ER* 12 (29 August 1925): 226.

3. Solomon Fabricant, *The Trend of Government Activity in the United States Since 1900* (New York: National Bureau of Economic Research, 1952), pp. 29, 71-77; also see Howard W. Odum, "Public Welfare Activities," *Recent Social Trends,* chap. 24; C. H. Wooddy, "The Growth of Governmental Functions," Ibid., chap. 25, and C. E. Merriam, "Government and Society," Ibid., chap. 29.

4. Clarence Heer, "Trends in Taxation and Public Finance," *Recent Social Trends,* p. 1331.

5. See chapter 4 for details on married women teachers.

6. *ER* 12 (5 September 1925): 236; Gladys Oaks, "Should Married Women Work?" *New York World,* 11 January 1931, reprinted in *ER* 16 (24 January 1931): 405; Veterans' preference legislation and employment practices in the U.S. Civil Service expanded greatly after World War I establishing precedents for preferential hiring as well as discriminatory firing. See Paul P. Van Riper, *History of the United States Civil Service* (Evanston, Ill.: Row, Peterson, 1958), pp. 269-71, and U.S. Civil Service Commission, *History of the Federal Civil Service, 1789 to the Present* (Washington, D.C.: Government Printing Office, 1941), pp. 96-102.

7. *ER* 17 (19 December 1931): 367; Alma Lutz, "Penalizing Marriage," *IndW* 11 (February 1932): 76-77; Gladys Oaks, "Should Married Women Work?" *ER* 16 (24 January 1931): 405-06; *ER* 16 (31 January 1931): 414; *NYT,* 3 May 1931, sec. 3, p. 6; "California Women Defeat Bill Against Marriage," *ER* 17 (25 July 1931): 195-96; "Joint Resolution of the Wisconsin Legislature," *ER* 17 (14 March 1931): 42; "Married Couples Employed in State Service" (Study by the University of Wisconsin, 1931), quoted in *Wives Need Their Jobs* (New York: National Federation of Business and Professional Women's Clubs, 1939), p. 5.

8. "Still the Working Wives' Problem,"*ER* 18 (6 February 1932): 6; *ER* 17 (7 November 1931): 316.

9. U.S., Congress, House, *Congressional Record,* 72nd Cong., 1st sess., 1932, 75, pt. 8: 9062ff; Ibid., pt. 9: 9514-20.

10. Ibid., pt. 8: 9062ff; Ibid., pt. 9: 9514-20; Ibid., pt. 13, letter introduced 24 June 1932, p. 13844; Ibid., pt. 11: 9514-20; Ibid., pt. 13: 13849-57; Ibid., pp. 14159-63, 14233; "The History of Section 213," *Equal Rights Independent Feminist Weekly* 1 (30 March 1935): 28-29.

11. "The President and the Bill," *ER* 18 (13 August 1932): 221-22; "Gail Laughlin Condemns Discharge of Married Women," *ER* 18 (23 July 1932): 197-98.

12. "Report of Legislative Chairman Rosa Cunningham," *IndW* 13 (August 1932): 235-36.

13. Quoted in *ER* 18 (13 August 1932): 222.

14. *Washington Herald,* 28 June 1932, reprinted in *ER* 18 (13 August 1932): 223.

15. *Washington Herald,* 14 September 1932, reprinted in *ER* 18 (1 October 1932): 279.

16. "Effects of 213 on Retirement," *Government Standard* 6 (22 March 1934): 4; "The History of Section 213," *ERIFW* 1 (30 March 1935): 28-29. Jessie Decker to Frances Perkins, 11 April 1933; Carlotte S. Tait to Frances Perkins, 24 April 1933; Christine Covell to Frances Perkins, 13 September 1933, Frances Perkins Collection, box 62, Married Women Workers folder, National Archives (hereafter NA). *Government Standard* 7 (21 June 1935): 3.

17. Description of the meeting, 8 May 1933, OF 252 (Government Employees), Franklin D. Roosevelt Library (hereafter FDRL); and in *ER* 19 (22 April 1933). Belle Sherwin to Marvin H. McIntyre, 21 April 1933, OF 252, FDRL; Memorandum, Belle Sherwin to Members of the Department of the Legal Status of Women, League of Women Voters Collection, series 2, box 340, folder 147, Library of Congress (hereafter LC); Dorothy Kenyon to Mary Anderson, 13 March 1934, Women's Bureau Collection, box 878, Dorothy Kenyon and Organization folder, NA.

18. Homer S. Cummings to the President, 24 June 1933, 3-4, OF 95. FDRL; "Attorney General Opinion on 'Married Persons'," *Federal Employee* 18 (August 1933): 8, 27-29.

19. NWP Minutes, Alma Lutz Collection, box 1, folder 5, Schlesinger Library (hereafter SL); *NYT,* 9 July 1933.

20. Louis McH. Howe to Mrs. Mae Wilson Camp, 27 July 1933, OF 252, FDRL.

21. *NYT,* 26 September 1933; "Government Workers Council Meets," *ER* 19 (30 September 1933): 275; *Washington Daily News,* 15 September 1933, reprinted in *ER* 19 (14 October 1933): 295; Memo, H. M. K. to Mr McIntyre, 26 October 1933; Memo, M. H. M. to the President, 4 November 1933; Memo, L. Douglas to Mr. McIntyre, 29 December 1933, OF 252, FDRL; Memo, J. S. Spelman to Mr. Lowery, 2 December 1933; F. D. R. to E. R., 9 January 1934, OF 252, FDRL.

22. *League News* 7 (December 1933): 11; *NYT,* 25 April 1934; Annual Report of the Committee on Dismissal of Married Persons in the Civil Service of the WJCC, 3 December 1934, Selma Borschardt Collection, box 158, folder 17, Labor History Archives, Detroit; *NYT,* 23 March 1935; Celler described the fate of bills in his testimony before the House Committee on the Civil Service on H.R. 5051, 8 April 1935, p. 5.

23. U.S., Congress, House, *Congressional Record,* 75th Cong., 1st sess., 1937, 81, pt. 6: 6925-28; "From Our Readers to Our Readers," *Literary Digest* 116 (25 November 1933): 30-31; Ibid., 116 (2 December 1933): 48; Ibid. (23 December 1933): 30; *NYT,* 3 March 1936; Letter to the *Philadelphia Evening Bulletin,* reprinted in *ER* 20 (29 December 1934): 381, 383.

24. *Fortune,* October 1936, p. 222; Gallup poll and quote in *National Poll of Public Opinion,* 15 November 1936, in LWV Collection, series 2, box 340, Government and Legal Status of Women folder, LC. See Kay Boals, "Review Essay: Political Science," *Signs* 1 (Autumn 1975): 166-67, on political attitude polling as a process of attitude formation which can be applied to the ubiquitous sampling of sentiment on married women workers during the late 1930s.

25. *Washington Herald,* 27 April 1935.

26. *New York Herald Tribune,* 1 May 1935.

27. Rupert Hughes, "Section 213: A Story behind the Headlines," *New York Herald Tribune*, 19, 26 January, 9, 16, 23 February 1936. *History of the Federal Civil Service*, p. 120.

28. "History of Section 213," *ERIFW* 1 (30 March 1935): 28.

29. Report of Government Workers Council, "The Married Worker Ouster," Employment Discrimination, Married Women folder, SL (mimeographed).

30. Iva Lowther Peters, *Occupational Discrimination Against Women: An Inquiry into the Economic Security of American Business and Professional Women* (New York: BPW, 1935), p. 3; "Report on Committees," *IndW* 14 (August 1935): 254; Henrietta Rollofs, "Women's Freedom of Choice," *Woman's Press* 30 (March 1936): 117.

31. Alma Lutz, "What Price Marriage?" *ER* 20 (9 June 1934): 149; Lorine Pruette, ed., *Women Workers Through the Depression: A Study of White Collar Employment Made by the American Woman's Association* (New York: Macmillan, 1934), p. 155.

32. U.S., Congress, House, *Hearings Before the Committee on the Civil Service on H.R. 5051*, "To Amend the Married Persons' Clause," 74th Cong., 1st sess., 1935, p. 31; Edith Valet Cook, *The Married Woman and Her Job* (Washington, D.C.: LWV, 1936), p. 4.

33. John Garraty, "The New Deal, National Socialism, and the Great Depression," *American Historical Review* 77 (October 1973): 404-39. Garraty compares policies and the political and psychological climate but ignores the similarities in attitude and policy toward women workers. On varied curbs on working women throughout Europe, see Marguerite Thibert, "The Economic Depression and the Employment of Women," *International Labour Review* 27 (April 1933): 443-70; "The Abolition of Women's Employment As a Remedy for Unemployment," *International Labour Review* 27 (May 1933): 620-30; Dennis H. Cooke and E. R. Endow, "Local Residents and Married Women As Teachers," *Review of Education Research* 4 (June 1934): 292.

34. *NYT*, 22 April 1936.

35. Eleanor F. Dolan and Margaret P. Davis, "Antinepotism Rules in American Colleges and Universities," *Educational Record* 41 (October 1960): 285-95; Heather Sigworth, "The Legal Status of Antinepotism Regulations," *American Association of University Professors Bulletin* 58 (March 1972): 31-34; Sophonisba P. Breckenridge, "University Women in the New Order," *Journal of the American Association of University Women* 26 (June 1933): 198.

36. Ware's letter quoted in Janet Fowler Nelson, *Working Wives* (New York: Woman's Press, 1937), p. 37.

37. John D. Biggers, *Final Report on Total and Partial Unemployment*, vol. 4: *The Enumerative Check Census* (Washington, D.C.: Government Printing Office, 1938), pp. 112-13.

38. *NYT*, 9 October 1938.

39. Dorothy D. Crook, *State vs. the Married Woman Worker* (New York: BPW, 1940), p. 30; Louis McH. Howe to Hon. D. W. Bell, 10 December 1934, OF 95, FDRL. This memorandum refers to a letter from Mary F. Rooney, secretary of the Massachusetts Women's Political Club, to Senator Walsh urging President Roosevelt to issue an executive order removing married women yeomen from the veterans' preference list; *Boston Herald*, 22 June 1935; Florence Birmingham to Rep. John Cochran, 8 July 1937, letter inserted into the *Congressional Record*, 75th Cong., 1st sess., 81, pt. 6: 6933; *NYT*, 1 May 1938; "Right of Married Women to Earn Under Attack in Massachusetts," *ER* 24 (1 June 1938): 269, 271; "Can Working Women Marry?" *ER* 24 (1 September 1938): 315.

40. *ER* 24 (15 October 1938): 345; *Employer* 1 (December 1938): 1, 3; Crook, *State vs. Married Woman Worker*, pp. 29-39; "Democracy—for Whom?" *IndW* 18 (March 1939): 68.

41. Correspondence between Birmingham and Roosevelt between 2 June 1939 and 5 July 1939, can be found in the Eleanor Roosevelt Collection, FDRL. Also see *Boston Globe*, 1 July 1939; Crook, *State vs. Married Woman Worker*, p. 20.

42. *Boston Globe*, 1 July 1939; *Boston Herald*, 1 July 1939, clipping in Shepard Notebook, Alma Lutz Collection, SL.

43. Resolutions of the Massachusetts Women's Political Party, 18 July 1939, Eleanor Roosevelt Collection, FDRL; *NYT*, 20 July 1939.

44. "Old Maids and Transients," *ERIFW* 1 (13 April 1935): 42; *NYT*, 20 May 1939; *Life and Labor Bulletin* 6 (November 1939): 4.

45. Dorothy Kenyon to the AAUW convention, *NYT*, 22 June 1939.

46. The folder of the Wage Security Plan is in the Shepard Notebook, Alma Lutz Collection, SL.

47. "On the Firing Line," *IndW* 18 (April 1939): 114; "Marriage—A Bar to Employment?" *JAAUW* 30 (April 1939): 172; "Call the Dishonor Roll," *IndW* 18 (May 1939): 149; *NYT*, 26 February 1939; Ibid., 14 July 1939.

48. *Journal of the Senate of the Ninety-Third General Assembly of the State of Ohio*, vol. 118 (Columbus: F. J. Heer, 1939), pp. 162, 167; *IndW* 18 (March 1939): 68; Minutes of the Ohio League of Women Voters Convention, 23-24 May 1939, Ohio League of Women Voters Collection, box 11, Ohio State Historical Society; "On the Firing Line," p. 114; Crook, *State vs. Married Woman Worker*, pp. 28-31; "Call the Dishonor Roll," p. 149.

49. *NYT*, 18, 21, 25 January 1940. *Official Journal of the Proceedings of the House of Representatives of the State of Louisiana at the Sixteenth Extra Session of the Legislature* (Baton Rouge: Thomas J. Morgan's Sons, 1940), pp. 47-48; *NYT*, 21 February, 17 April, 10 July 1940; *IndW* 19 (July 1940): 210.

50. The papers of the American Federation of State, County and Municipal Employees were being catalogued when this writer examined them. The period

under consideration, however, had been processed and appeared extremely complete. On the attitude of the CIO union, see "Boston Local Fights Ban on Working Wives," *Employee* 1 (December 1938): 1, 3; "Wives Are Citizens in Massachusetts," *Government Guide* 1 July 1939): 5; Wives Are Also People," Ibid., 1 (June 1939): 1, 8, 10.

51. *IndW* 18 (August 1939): 274.

52. "My Day," *Cleveland Press*, 13 July 1939.

53. *NYT*, 7 June 1939; *Should Married Women Work?* pp. 16, 62.

54. Editorial, "Working Wives," *Woman's Home Companion* 66 (October 1939): 1; Margaret Culkin Banning, "Wanted: All Women," *Good Housekeeping* 111 (September 1940): 21; Editorial, "Should Wives Work?" *Ladies' Home Journal* 58 (January 1941): 4, 35.

55. Edith Valet Cook to Chairman, 1 April 1938, LWV Collection, series 2, box 359, circular letter, Government and the Legal Status of Women folder, LC; Bertha MacGregor, "Status of Women," *Zontian* (January 1936): 7.

56. "Effects of Dismissing Married Persons from the Civil Service" (Mimeographed study by the Women's Bureau, March 1936); U.S., Department of Labor, Women's Bureau, *Female Workers in Their Family Environment*, Bulletin no. 183 (1941); *Wives Need Their Jobs* (New York: BPW, 1939), p. 4.

57. "What Price the Career Mother?" *IndW* 16 (February 1937): 42.

58. Ruth Shallcross, *Should Married Women Work?* (Study by BPW published as Public Affairs Pamphlet, no. 49, New York, 1940), p. 12; *Cleveland Plain Dealer*, 3 March 1940; Helen Robbins Bitterman, "Can Working Women Marry?" *ER* 25 (15 March 1939): 44; Clare Belle Thompson and Margaret Lukes Wise, "Shall We Fire the Married Women?" *Liberty* 16 (30 September 1939): 14, 15.

59. Shallcross, *Should Married Women Work?* p. 12.

60. "Should Wives Work?" *Ladies' Home Hournal* 58 (January 1941): 4.

61. "Democracy—for Whom?" *IndW* 18 (March 1939): 68; Helen Pearce, "The Married Woman's Right to Work," *Zontian* (November 1938): 8. Among numerous references to noncompetitive job segregation, see Anna Steese Richardson, "The Right of the Married Woman to Work for Wages," *Woman's Home Companion* 66 (October 1939): 8; Kathleen McLaughlin, "Shall Wives Work?" *NYT Sunday Magazine*, 23 July 1939, p. 19; "Marriage—A Bar to Employment?" *JAAUW* 30 (April 1939): 172.

62. *Harper's Magazine* (September 1927): 551-59; *New York Herald Tribune*, 8 May 1935.

63. Genevieve Parkhurst, "Is Feminism Dead?" *Harper's Magazine* 170 (May 1935): 735-45.

64. Institute of Women's Professional Relations, *Proceedings of the Conference on Women's Work and Their Stake in Public Affairs*, 28-30 March 1935, p. 6.

65. "A Feminist Thinks It Over," *ER* 23 (15 December 1937): 13; E. G.

Beston, "'Discrimination' vs. 'Career' " *Zontian* (April 1937): 13; *NYT*, 12 July 1939; Dora Neum, "Legislation That Limits Women Workers," *Zontian* (September 1939): 4; *IndW* 19 (August 1940): 265-66.

66. *IndW* 18 (August 1939): 260; Almere L. Scott, "The Woman's Centennial Congress,"*Zontian* (February 1939): 8.

67. "Danger to Democracy of Legislation Against Minority Groups," Mary Winslow Collection, box 1, folder 2, SL.

68. *Woman's Press* (October 1939): 414-15.

69. *Should Married Women Be Denied Employment?* pamphlet, LWV, p. 6. "Legislation That Limits Women Workers," p. 5; Valeria Hopkins Parker, "Wedlock, Wages, and Women," *IndW* 18 (June 1939): 169.

70. Roosevelt's "Arsenal of Democracy" speech illustrates the popularity of this perception. On reactions among intellectuals, see Edward A. Purcell, Jr., *The Crisis of Democratic Theory: Scientific Naturalism and the Problem of Value* (Lexington: University of Kentucky Press, 1973), pt. 3.

Chapter 4

1. U.S., Department of Commerce, Bureau of the Census, *Fifteenth Census of the United States: 1930, Population,* vol. 5: *General Report on Occupations,* p. 47.

2. Charles H. Judd, "Education," in *Recent Social Trends in the United States: Report of the President's Research Committee on Social Trends,* vol. 1 (New York: McGraw-Hill, 1933), chap. 7; U.S., Department of the Interior, Bureau of Education, *Biennal Survey of Education, 1924-26* (Washington, D.C.: Government Printing Office, 1928), chap. 12; Edward S. Evenden, Guy C. Gamble, and Harold G. Blue, "Teacher Personnel in the United States," Bulletin no. 10 (Washington, D.C.: Government Printing Office, 1935), pp. 26-27, 100-01.

3. Judd, "Education," pp. 342-50; Charl Williams, "The Position of Women in the Public Schools," *Annals* (May 1929), 156; "Teachers' Salaries and the Cost of Living," *School and Society* 39 (17 March 1934) : 336-37.

4. *Research Memorandum on Education in the Depression* (New York: Social Science Research Council, 1937), pp. 52-68, 123-24; Judd, "Education," pp. 371-73; Robert S. Lynd and Helen Merrell Lynd, *Middletown in Transition: A Study in Cultural Conflicts* (New York: Harcourt, Brace, 1937), pp. 222-24.

5. "Deepening Crisis in Education," *S&S* 38 (25 November 1933): 711-12.

6. William C. Bagley, "The Profession of Teaching," *S&S* 34 (25 July 1931): 105-09; "The Teachers' Turn to Be Helped," Ibid. (8 August 1931): 201.

7. "The Maintenance of School Services During the Period of Economic Depression," *S&S* 36 (6 August 1932): 161-64; "Starving the Schools," Ibid. 35 (12 March 1932): 359-60; "The School Crisis," Ibid., 37 (25 February 1933): 243; "The Economy Program of the New York Board of Education and Unemployed

Teachers," Ibid., 36 (30 July 1932): 141-42; "Opening of the New York City Schools," Ibid. (17 September 1932): 367; Ibid., 38 (14 October 1933): 495-96.

8. "The Economy Program of the New York Board," p. 142; "Opening the New York City Schools," p. 367.

9. "The Depression and the Schoools," *S&S* 36 (13 August 1932): 213; "Deepening Crisis in Education," pp. 711-12; *S&S* 36 (27 October 1932): 569; Ibid., 37 (11 February 1933): 183; Ibid., 38 (14 October 1933): 495; National Education Association, *The Status of the Teaching Profession*, Research Bulletin, vol. 18 (March 1940): 61.

10. Walter H. Gaumnitz, "Salary Trends in Rural Schools," *School Life* 22 (June 1937): 301.

11. "Economies in Secondary Education," *S&S* 37 (14 January 1933): 41; Ibid., 38 (23 September 1933): 407-08; "Many Cities Report Salary Increases," *School Life* 20 (June 1935): 230.

12. "Deepening Crisis in Education," p. 712.

13. "The Plight of the Chicago Schools," *S&S* 37 (6 June 1933): 578; "The Chicago School Situation," Ibid., 38 (29 July 1933): 153-54; Ibid. (12 August 1933): 222; Studs Terkel, *Hard Times: An Oral History of the Great Depression* (New York: Pantheon Books, 1970), p. 388.

14. Terkel, *Hard Times*, pp. 388-89.

15. "Blank Pay Days," *Saturday Evening Post* 206 (1 July 1933): 70; Eunice Langdon, "The Teacher Faces the Depression," *Nation* 137 (16 August 1933): 182-84.

16. *Journal of the National Education Association* 25 (May 1936): 76; Lynd and Lynd, *Middletown in Transition*, p. 229; *Status of the Teaching Profession*, p. 61.

17. "Many Cities Report Salary Increases," p. 230; Lynd and Lynd, *Middletown in Transition*, p. 229 n.; *Status of the Teaching Profession*, p. 61.

18. *Status of the Teaching Profession*, p. 63; "The Depression and the Classroom Teacher," *JNEA* 22 (December 1933): 263-64; Lynd and Lynd, *Middletown in Transition*, p. 228.

19. Judd, "Education," pp. 329, 342.

20. "Opening of the New York City Schools," p. 367; *S&S* 38 (16 September 1933): 377-78; Ibid. (14 October 1933): 496; Ibid., 36 (29 October 1932): 569; "Depression and the Classroom Teacher," p. 264; Lynd and Lynd, *Middletown in Transition*, pp. 206-07. For rates of growth in secondary school attendance from 1919 to 1936, adjusted to actual size of age cohort during that period, see *Research Memorandum on Education in the Depression*, pp. 65-66.

21. "Post-Grad High-School Students," *S&S* 36 (19 November 1932): 655; Ibid., 38 (16 September 1933): 377-78.

22. "Malnutrition of the School Children of New York City," *S&S* 36 (12

November 1932): 624; "The New York City Relief Fund," Ibid., 35 (6 February 1932): 174, 181-82; "Blank Pay Days," p. 69.

23. Willard S. Elsbree, *The American Teacher: Evolution of a Profession in a Democracy* (New York: American Book, 1939), p. 535.

24. Elsbree, *The American Teacher*, chap. 34; Howard K. Beale, *Are American Teachers Free?* (New York: Charles Scribner's Sons, 1936), p. 375; Jeane Westin, *Making Do: How Women Survived the '30s* (Chicago: Follett, 1976), p. 213; *JNEA* 21 (January 1932): 14.

25. Beale, *Are American Teachers Free?* pp. 59-67, 583-84; *Research Memorandum on Education in the Depression*, pp. 90-91; Lynd and Lynd, *Middletown in Transition*, p. 235; *Status of the Teaching Profession*, pp. 72-3; "Teachers at the Battle of Oaths," *School Life* 20 (June 1935): 234-35; "The Teachers' Oath of Allegiance," *JNEA* 24 (May 1935): 138.

26. Beale, *Are American Teachers Free?* pp. 497-99, 504-14.

27. David Wilbur Peters, *The Status of the Married Woman Teacher* (New York: Teachers College, Columbia University, 1934), p. 34; Earl William Anderson, *The Teacher's Contract and Other Legal Phases of Teacher Status* (New York: Teachers College, Columbia University, 1927), pp. 43-45; Paul N. Garver, "Legal Status of Married Women Teachers," *S&S* 34 (24 October 1931): 571-73; I. N. Edwards, "Marriage As a Legal Cause for Dismissal of Women Teachers," *Elementary School Journal* 25 (May 1925): 692-95.

28. Charles E. Reeves, "Why Discriminate Against Married Teachers?" *Nation's Schools* 2 (September 1928): 53, 55; *ER* 13 (24 July 1926); Anderson, *The Teacher's Contract*, pp. 44-45; T.C. Holy, *Cleveland Teachers' Salaries: A Study Sponsored by the Cleveland Teachers' Federation in Cooperation with the Cleveland Board of Education* (Cleveland: Cleveland Teachers' Federation, 1932), pp. 162-63.

29. Anderson, *The Teacher's Contract*, pp. 43-44, 117-18.

30. "Requirements Affecting Appointment, Retention and Promotion of Teachers," *Research Bulletin of the National Education Association* 6 (September 1928): 221.

31. U.S., Department of Commerce, Bureau of the Census, *Fourteenth Census of the United States Taken in the Year 1920*, vol. 4, pp. 142, 698; *Fifteenth Census of the United States, 1930*, vol. 5: *General Report on Occupations*, p. 47.

32. "Employment of Married Women as Teachers," *Research Bulletin of the National Education Association* 10 (January 1932): 20.

33. Logan A. Waits, "Board Rules Affecting the Status of Married Women Teachers in Ohio," *S&S* 33 (27 June 1931): 867-71; "Training Rural Teachers," Ibid., 35 (30 January 1932): 158-59; National Education Association of the United States, Committee on the Economic Status of the Rural Teacher (Untitled report) (Washington, D.C.: National Education Association, 1938).

34. Holy, *Cleveland Teachers' Salaries*, p. 163; Leo M. Chamberlain and Leonard E. Meece, *Woman and Men in the Teaching Profession* (Lexington: University of Kentucky Press, 1937), section 1, on wage differentials.

35. "Women Are Asked to Pay the Bill for the Depression," *JAAUW* 38 (April 1935): 167.

36. National Education Association Committee on Tenure, *Married Women Gainfully Employed* (Washington, D.C.: National Education Association, 1940), p. 12; "Can Married Women Legally Be Discriminated Against in Salary Scheduling?" *S&S* 52 (17 August 1940): 111-12.

37. "Three Approaches to the Married Woman Teacher Problem," *American School Board Journal* 82 (February 1931): 64; National Education Association, "Employment of Married Women as Teachers" (1932), pp. 14-15; Chamberlain and Meece, *Women and Men*, p. 54; *NYT*, 2 February 1932; *Cleveland Plain Dealer*, 18 February 1933; Ibid., 15 April 1933; "Teacher Personnel Procedures: Selection and Appointment," p. 61; Peters, *Status of Married Woman Teacher*, p. 52.

38. "When Wives Teach School Should Eugenicists Demure?" *Eugenics* 4 (February 1931): 60-61; *National Education Association Research Bulletin* 10 (January 1932): 14; Chamberlain and Meece, *Women and Men*, p. 54; Peters, *Status of Married Woman Teacher*, p. 49; W. C. McGinnis, "The Married Woman Teacher," *School Executives Magazine* 50 (June 1931): 453; David Snedden, "Personnel Problems in Educational Administration: Married Women as Public School Teachers," *Teachers College Record* 36 (April 1935): 614.

39. "Teacher Personnel Procedures: Employment Conditions in Service," *National Education Association Research Bulletin* 20 (March 1942): 107; "Teacher Personnel: Selection and Appointment," Ibid., 20 (May 1942): 60; T.V. Goodrich, "Should Married Teachers Be Fired?" *School Executives Magazine* 52 (September 1932): 6-8.

40. Elsbree, *The American Teacher*, pp. 549-53; *Status of the Teaching Profession*, p. 55.

41. See chapter 5 for incidence of discrimination against married women workers in other occupational categories.

42. *ER* 16 (30 August 1930): 239-40; Alma Lutz to School Board, Everett, Mass., 25 January 1934, Alma Lutz Collection, box 45, Massachusetts Branch Correspondence folder, SL; "Teachers' Troubles," *Time* 26 (29 July 1936): 26.

43. *Research Memorandum on Education in the Depression*, p. 146n.; National Education Association of the United States, *Proceedings of the Seventy-First Annual Meeting*, vol. 71 (Washington, D.C.: National Education Association, 1933), p. 221; "Teacher Personnel: Selection and Appointment," p. 60; McGinnis, "The Married Woman Teacher," p. 452.

44. *American Teacher* 14 (February 1931): 7; Ibid., 26 (May 1942): 38; "Sum-

mary and Conclusions of M.A. Thesis of Aileen W. Robinson," *American Teacher* 19 (May-June 1935): 8-9.

45. Clara G. Roe, "Should Married Women Work?" *American Teacher* 24 (January 1940): 28–29; G. B. Peubl to Board of Directors, AFT, n.d., Toledo Federation of Teachers Collection, box 18, Married Teachers 1934-38 folder, Archives of Labor History.

46. National Education Association of the United States, Committee on Tenure and Academic Freedom, *Court Decisions under Teacher Tenure Laws, 1932-1946* (Washington, D.C.: National Education Association, 1947), p. 110; *ER*, n.s. 2 (18 April 1936): 50.

47. National Education Association, *Status of the Married Teacher* (1938), p. 8.

48. Elsbree, *The American Teacher*, p. 478.

49. M. M. Chambers, "Enforced Celibacy in Schools," *Nation's Schools* 18 (August 1936): 31; Chamberlain and Meece, *Women and Men*, p. 57; "Sauce for the Gander," *S&S* 31 (19 April 1930): 537-39; "Legal Status of the Married Woman Teacher," Ibid., 34 (24 October 1931): 571; Walter A. Terpenning, "The Educational Veil," *Forum* 83 (October 1932): 232; Logan Abner Waits, "A Study of the Comparative Efficiency of Single and Married Women as Teachers," *Educational Administration and Supervision* 8 (November 1932): 630-33; Dennis H. Cooke and William A. Shanks, "Relative Efficiency of Married and Single Women Teachers," *The Peabody Reflector and Alumni News* (November 1932): 320-24; "Evidence on the Efficiency of Married Women. Teachers," *Elementary School Journal* 35 (October 1934): 89-91.

50. Reath Osborne, "Marriage and the School Teacher," *Plain Talk* 10 (October 1934): 4; "Three Approaches to the Married Woman Teacher Problem," p. 64; Mary Finch Hoerner, "The Married Woman as a Teacher of Home Economics," *Journal of Home Economics* 24 (February 1932): 110.

51. Terpenning, "The Educational Veil," p. 233; Naomi White, "Let Them Eat Cake," *Education Digest* 4 (January 1939): 42; Frances Donovan, *The Schoolma'am* (New York: F. A. Stokes, 1938), pp. 35-36; Lorine Pruette, *Women Workers Through the Depression: A Study of White Collar Employment Made by the American Woman's Association* (New York: Macmillan, 1934), p. 109.

52. Chamberlain and Meece, *Women and Men*, p. 57; Anne O'Hagan, "Married Women Teachers: 1930 Model," *Woman's Journal* 16 (January 1931): 46; "Can Working Women Marry?" *ER* 24 (1 September 1938): 315; *Cleveland Plain Dealer*, 15 May 1931, p. 1.

53. Virginia Cocheron Gildersleeve, *Many a Good Crusade* (New York: Macmillan, 1954), pp. 108, 179-80. She could have been referring to Freudians like Helena Deutsch, who stressed female erotic passivity in and fulfillment through marriage, and to a Jungian, M. Esther Harding, who was even more explicit in

equating careers with rejection of femininity, the latter being manifested in marriage and motherhood. See Ruth Waterbury, "Do Career Women Wreck Their Men?" *Liberty* 16 (11 November 1939): 51-52, popularizing vicarious career gratification through sexual satisfaction: "What I want is to die while some man is kissing me and declaring I have inspired him to the heights. And I challenge you to show me any career woman who does not wish the same thing— or who has failed at getting it."

54. Chamberlain and Meece, *Women and Men,* pp. 26-37; *Fortune* 16 (July 1937): 103; Ralph F. Strebel, "Education: A Profession for Men," *JNEA* 21 (February 1932): 56.

55. Beale, *Are American Teachers Free?* p. 406.

56. Strebel, "Education: A Profession for Men," p. 55; "The Young Educator and the Depression," *S&S* 35 (12 March 1932): 346.

57. Westin, *Making Do,* p. 183.

58. U.S., Department of the Interior, Office of Education, *Biennial Survey of Education in the United States,* "Statistical Summary of Education, 1939-40," vol. 2 (Washington, D.C.: Government Printing Office, 1943), p. 34.

Chapter 5

1. U.S., Department of Labor, Women's Bureau, *Women's Occupations Through Seven Decades,* pp. 160, 162, 165, 169.

2. Jay F. Otis, "Will Librarians Live?" *Wilson Bulletin* 10 (September 1935): 25-29; Ibid., 9 (June 1935): 582; "The Question of Salaries," *Library Journal* 59 (15 September 1934): 712-13; Constance Auer, "I Became a Librarian," *Nation* 132 (25 February 1931): 213-14.

3. Gertrude Springer, "Social-Work Salaries," *Survey* 67 (15 December 1931): 299-301; "Salary Cuts Among Social Workers" *New Republic* 70 (17 February 1932): 22; "Social Workers on the Spot," *Survey* 71 (April 1935): 111.

4. Springer, "Social-Work Salaries," p. 300; Jeane Westin, *Making Do: How Women Survived the '30s* (Chicago: Follett, 1976), pp. 184-85, 194-95.

5. "We Live on Relief," *Scribner's Magazine* 95 (April 1934): 285.

6. Westin, *Making Do,* pp. 183, 193-94.

7. Ibid., p. 194.

8. Carolyn Conant Van Blarcom, "The Trained Nurse and the Depression," *Nation* 137 (11 October 1933): 406-07.

9. Jo Ann Ashley, *Hospitals, Paternalism, and the Role of the Nurse* (New York: Teachers College Press, 1976), pp. 30, 59-68, 90; Janet M. Geister, "Nurses Out of Work," *Survey* 65 (15 December 1930): 320-31.

10. Quoted in Ashley, *Hospitals, Paternalism, and the Role of the Nurse,* p. 70.

11. Virginia McCormick, "Are There Too Many Nurses?" *Survey* 64 (15 July 1930): 349-50; "Nurses and the Eight-Hour Day," *Survey* 70 (March 1934): 86; *Survey* 73 (November 1937): 358.

12. Lillian D. Wald, "What Keeps the Nurses Going?" *Survey* 68 (15 November 1932): 590-91.

13. Data computed by Alba M. Edward from U.S., Department of Commerce, Bureau of the Census, *Sixteenth Census of the United States: 1940, Population: Comparative Occupation Statistics for the United States, 1870-1940* (Washington, D.C.: Government Printing Office, 1943), p. 49; U.S., Department of the Interior, Office of Education, *Biennial Survey of Education in the United States*, "Statistical Summary of Education, 1939-40," vol. 2 (Washington, D.C.: Government Printing Office, 1947), p. 34; U.S., Department of Commerce, Bureau of the Census, *Fifteenth Census of the United States: 1930, Population*, vol. 5: *General Report on Occupations*, p. 48; *Sixteenth Census of the United States, 1940*, vol. 3: *The Labor Force*, pp. 88, 90.

14. Ashley, *Hospitals, Paternalism, and the Role of the Nurse;* Grace A. Abbott, *From Relief to Social Security: The Development of the New Public Welfare Services and Their Administration* (Chicago: University of Chicago Press, 1941), pp. 361-62.

15. Robert S. Lynd and Helen Merrell Lynd, *Middletown in Transition: A Study in Cultural Conflicts* (New York: Harcourt, Brace, 1937), p. 57.

16. Lorine Pruette, "Women Workers Have Come Through," *American Scholar* 5 (Summer 1936): 328-36; Helen Field, "Are Women Losing Ground?" *Survey* 67 (1 January 1932): 352-54.

17. *Sixteenth Census of the United States, 1940, Population: Comparative Occupation Statistics for the United States, 1870-1940*, p. 49; Jesse Bernard, *Academic Women* (University Park: Pennsylvania State University Press, 1964), p. 40; Caroline D. Smiley, "Are Women Being Educated to a Dead End?" *Equal Rights Independent Feminist Weekly* 1 (15 March 1937): 35.

18. Bernard, *Academic Women*, pp. 54-55; George Martin, *Madame Secretary: Frances Perkins* (Boston: Houghton Mifflin, 1976), p. 370.

19. William Chafe, *The American Woman: Her Changing Political, Social, and Economic Roles, 1920-1970* (New York: Oxford University Press, 1972), p. 91.

20. Margaret W. Rossiter, "The 1930's: Expansion or Withdrawal?" (Paper presented at the Berkshire Conference on Women's History, Bryn Mawr, 11 June 1976).

21. Miriam Simons Leuck, *Fields of Work for Women*, 3rd ed. (New York: Appleton-Century, 1938), pp. 9, 355-58; Adah Peirce, *Vocations for Women* (New York: Macmillan, 1933), pp. 8-11; Frank Stricker stresses discrimination and the dual burden of work and home rather than diminished career aspirations as important factors in women's occupational attainments in "Cookbooks and

Law Books: The Hidden History of Career Women in Twentieth Century America," *Journal of Social History* 10 (Fall 1976): 1-19.

22. Virginia Britton, "Gainfully Employed Homemakers," *Journal of Home Economics* 30 (September 1938): 468.

23. International Association of Altrusa Clubs, Inc., "Non-Partisan Public Affairs Committee Study Outline No. 6," Married Women, Employment Discrimination folder, SL; Grace Nies Fletcher, "He Wants My Job!" *Independent Woman* 14 (May 1935): 154.

24. Mabel O. Moran, "Unemployed Woman," *Woman's Press* 26 (June 1932): 349-51; Promotion Pamphlet, 1937, Case Western Reserve University Archives, box 22A-21, Cleveland.

25. Edna C. McNight, "Jobs—for Men Only? Shall We Send Women Workers Home?" *Outlook* 159 (2 September 1931): 12.

26. Lorine Pruette, *Women Workers Through the Depression: A Study of White Collar Employment Made by the American Woman's Association* (New York: Macmillan, 1934), pp. 21-22.

27. Ibid., pp. 4-5, 29; Lorine Pruette, "Why Women Fail," in *Woman Coming of Age*, ed. V. F. Calverton and Samuel Schmulhausen (New York: Horace Liveright, 1931), pp. 240-59.

28. Chase Going Woodhouse, "Some Trends in Women's Work," *Social Forces* 16 (May 1938): 552; "Women's Work and Economic Change," *JAAUW* 30 (January 1938): 83-87; "The Education and Position of Women in a Democracy" (Report of the Conference at Keuka College, 7 November 1938), Institute of Women's Professional Relations Collection, box 4, SL; Chase Going Woodhouse, "Some Trends in Women's Work Today," *JAAUW* 29 (April 1936): 136-37; *New York Times*, 14 May 1939: Chase Going Woodhouse, *Opportunities for the Home Economist: New Jobs in Consumer Service* (New York: Mc Graw-Hill, 1938), pp. 5, 48.

29. Pruette, *Women Workers Through the Depression*, p. 109; Chase Going Woodhouse, "The Dental Hygienist," *Occupations* 14 (April 1936): 651; "Opportunities in Hospital Dietetics," Ibid., 16 (December 1937): 276-77; Helen S. Willard, "Occupational Therapy— A New Profession," Ibid., 17 (January 1939): 293.

30. Estelle Hamburger, *It's a Woman's World* (New York: Vanguard Press, 1939); Hortense Odlum, *A Woman's Place* (New York: Charles Scribner's Sons, 1939); *NYT*, 8 December 1938; Catherine Oglesby, *Business Opportunities for Women* (New York: Harper & Brothers, 1937), pp. 45-54.

31. Eugenia Wallace, "Office Work and the Ladder of Success," *IndW* 6 (October 1927): 16-18; "Women in Business II," *Fortune* 12 (August 1935): 55.

32. "Women in Business II," p. 86; "Women in Business III," *Fortune* 12 (September 1935): 81.

33. Benjamin R. Andrews, "The Budgeteers," *WP* 26 (September 1932): 540-41; Orlee Pell, "Two Million in Offices," *WP* 33 (June 1939): 256.

34. Grace Coyle, "Women in the Clerical Occupations," *Annals* (May 1929): 180-87; Elizabeth Gregg MacGibbon, "Exit—The Private Secretary," *Occupations* 15 (January 1937): 295-300.

35. "A Central Stenographic and Typing Department," *Office Economist* 12 (August-September 1930): 3-4, 12; J. George Frederick, "The Secretary-less Business Man," Ibid., 14 (July-August 1932): 3-4, 12; "A Successfully-Operated Stenographic Division," Ibid., 18 (September-October 1936): 9.

36. U.S., Department of Labor, Women's Bureau, *Employment of Women in Offices*, Bulletin no. 120, p. 17; Caroline F. Ware, "The 1939 Job of the White-Collar Girl," *WP* 33 (June 1939): 254-55; *WP* 27 (September 1933): 394; *WP* 29 (November 1935): 506; Marian H. Barbour, "The Business Girl Looks at Her Job," *WP* 30 (January 1936): 18-19; Wilma Noyes, "Conflicts in the Business Girl's Mind," *WP* 32 (October 1938): 451, 456.

37. Gladys L. Palmer, "Occupational Trends in Women's Employment," *WP* 28 (October 1934): 465; Field, "Are Women Losing Ground?" p. 393; "Trends in Occupations for Women," *Occupations* 16 (November 1937): 175; Meridel LeSueur, "Women on the Breadlines," in *The American Writer and the Great Depression*, ed. Harvey Swados (Indianapolis: Bobbs Merrill, 1966), p. 183; "The Older Woman Worker," *Woman Worker* 18 (March 1938): 6-7. Age was a factor in judging women in industry just as it has been for men since the turn of the century. In other occupations, qualifications based on youth were more apt to apply to women only.

38. Mary Rebecca Lingenfelter and Harry Dexter Kitson, *Vocations for Girls* (New York: Harcourt, Brace, 1939), contents, pp. 311, 324.

39. Rosalie Carter, "Dentistry Is a Woman's Job," *IndW* 17 (October 1938): 318-20; "Women in Banking," *American Banking Association Journal* 26 (September 1933): 69; *Women's Work and Education* 8 (October 1937); Edith Harper, "Office Management Is a Woman's Job," *IndW* 19 (March 1940): 78-79.

40. Rose C. Feld, "Back to the Kitchen? Women Say 'No,' " *NYT Magazine*, 9 June 1935, p.8.

41. Jean Lipman-Blumen, "Toward a Homosocial Theory of Sex Roles: An Explanation of the Sex Segregation of Social Institutions," *Signs* 1, pt. 2 (Spring 1976): 15. This entire issue of *Signs* is devoted to an interdisciplinary examination of occupational segregation.

42. Two attempts to measure the extent of occupational segregation conclude that during the 1930s little shift occurred. However, the methods of calculation mask one or both of the deleterious occupational development of the Depression decade: the entrance of men into feminized fields and loss by women of non-traditional professional and managerial jobs. Both trends meant serious decline

in women's status as long as unencumbered access to all occupations did not exist. See Oppenheimer, *The Female Labor Force*, pp. 68-69, 71; Edward Gross, "Plus Ça Change . . .? The Sexual Structure of Occupations Over Time," *Social Problems* 16 (Fall 1968): 201-02.

43. Rossiter, "The 1930's: Expansion or Withdrawal?"; U.S., Department of Labor, Women's Bureau, *Economic Status of the University Woman in the U.S.A., Report of the Committee on Economic and Legal Status of Women, AAUW in Cooperation with the Women's Bureau*, Bulletin no. 170 (Washington, D.C.: Government Printing Office, 1939), pp. 8, 20, 26, 44-45.

44. "The Post," *Bulletin of the American Library Association* 32 (June 1938): 402; Clara W. Herbert, *Personnel Administration in Public Libraries* (Chicago: American Library Association, 1939), p. 50; *Sixteenth Census of the United States, 1940, Population*, vol.3: *The Labor Force*, p. 115.

45. Genevieve Parkhurst, "Is Feminism Dead?" *Harper's Magazine* 170 (May 1935): 742; "Matrimony and the Job," *Survey* 65 (15 February 1931): 532.

46. U.S., Department of Labor, Women's Bureau, "Effects of Dismissing Married Persons from the Civil Service" (mimeographed, March 1936); Doris Best, "Employment of Wives Increasing," *Personnel Journal* 17 (December 1938): 212-19; "Employment of Women After Marriage," *Conference Board Management Record* 1 (October 1939): 151.

47. "Store Attitudes on the Married Woman," *Department Store Economist* 2 (10 August 1939): 3; Frances R. Donovan, *The Saleslady* (Chicago: University of Chicago Press, 1929), p. 177; U.S., Department of Labor, Women's Bureau, *Employment Conditions in Department Stores in 1932-33: A Study in Selected Cities in Five States*, Bulletin no. 125 (Washington, D.C.: Government Printing Office, 1936).

48. Westin, *Making Do*, p. 201.

49. "Store Attitudes on the Married Woman," p. 3; " 'An Issue Not to Be Overlooked,' " *Department Store Economist* 2 (25 August 1939): 2, 22; Ruth Shallcross, *Should Married Women Work?* (New York: National Federation of Business and Professional Clubs, 1940), p. 9; "Legislatively Speaking," *IndW* 19 (May 1940): 147; *IndW* 20 (August 1940): 252. Combating discrimination in the private sector of the economy was seldom successful. Local BPW clubs were encouraged to ferret out instances of such practices, to investigate the situation thoroughly, and to apply to the state and national federation for aid. Local groups were also encouraged to write letters to offending firms but were cautioned to use publicity with care. Alma Lutz of the NWP conducted a one-woman letter-writing campaign against Massachusetts firms that banned married women but with no success. The problem was so diffuse and public sentiment so strong that effective action among private employers was largely futile. See *Procedure in Cases of Discrimination*, pamphlet of the NFBPWC, Inc., 1936, pp. 3, 6-7.

50. Best, "Employed Wives Increasing," p. 216; "Employment of Women

After Marriage," p. 151; U.S., Department of Labor, Women's Bureau, *Women Workers in Their Family Environment,* Bulletin no. 183 (Washington, D.C.: Government Printing Office, 1941), p. 24.

51. Frances Maule, *She Strives to Conquer: Business Behavior Opportunities and Job Requirements for Women* (New York: Funk & Wagnalls, 1934), p. 166.

52. Frances Maule, *Girl With a Paycheck: How She Lands It—Holds It—Makes It Grow* (New York: Harper & Brothers, 1941), p. 255.

53. Elizabeth Gregg MacGibbon, *Manners in Business* (New York: Macmillan, 1936), pp. 149, 151-52. Sympathy for the employer is expressed by Loire Brophy in *If Women Must Work* (New York: D. Appleton-Century, 1936), p. 110.

54. *NYT,* 14 November 1936.

55. U.S., Department of Labor, Women's Bureau, *Women's Occupations Through Seven Decades,* Bulletin no. 218 (Washington, D.C.: Government Printing Office, 1947), pp. 42-43.

56. Gertrude Bancroft, *The American Labor Force: Its Growth and Changing Composition* (New York: John Wiley & Sons, 1958), p. 207; Franklin E. Frazier, "Some Effects of the Depression on the Negro in Northern Cities," *Science and Society* 2 (Fall 1938): 492; Clarence D. Long, *The Labor Force Under Changing Income and Employment* (Princeton, N.J.: Princeton University Press, 1958), pp. 293-94; Valerie Kincade Oppenheimer, *The Female Labor Force in the United States: Demographic and Economic Factors Governing Its Growth and Changing Composition* (Berkeley, Calif.: Institute of International Studies, 1970), p. 21.

57. *IndW* 19 (January 1940): 31.

58. Pruette, *Women Workers Through the Depression,* pp. 5, 6.

59. Ibid., p. 6.

Chapter 6

1. "Resolution on Unemployment and Working Women," Frances Perkins Papers, box 82, Women General folder, National Archives.

2. Genevieve Parkhurst, "Is Feminism Dead?" *Harper's Magazine* 170 (May 1935): 735-45; William Chafe, *The American Woman: Her Changing Social, Economic, and Political Role, 1920-1970* (New York: Oxford University Press, 1974), p. 130.

3. Anita Pollitzer, "Equal Pay and the N.R.A. Codes, *"Equal Rights* 19 (2 September 1933): 243; *New York Times,* 16 July 1933; Summary of Biennial Report, April 1932-1934, Department of the Legal Status of Women, National League of Women Voters Papers, series 2, box 323, Circular Letters, Government and Legal Status of Women Department folder, LC; Geline Bowman to General Johnson, 10 August 1933, Frances Perkins Papers, box 81, Women General folder, N.A.; *NYT,* 9 August 1933.

4. Lois MacDonald, Gladys L. Palmer, and Theresa Wolfson, *Labor and the N.R.A.* (New York: Affiliated Schools for Workers, 1934), pp. 10, 30.

5. U.S., Department of Labor, Women's Bureau, *Employed Women Under N.R.A. Codes*, Bulletin no. 122 (Washington, D.C.: Government Printing Office, 1934), pp. 24-25; Elisabeth Christman to Gen. Hugh S. Johnson, 28 February 1934, Women's Trade Union League Papers, box 6, Headquarters records, January to April 1934 folder, LC.

6. *Life and Labor Bulletin*, August 1933; Elisabeth Christman to Hugh S. Johnson, 21 February 1934, Women's Trade Union League Papers, box 6, Headquarters Records, January to April 1934, LC; *NYT*, 29 August 1934; Helena Hill Weed, "The New Deal That Women Want," *Current History* 41 (November 1934): 181-82; *Independent Woman* 13 (August 1934): 269; *NYT*, 11 October 1934; Women's Bureau memo to Eleanor Roosevelt, 19 February 1934, Marian Anderson Papers, box 1, folder 14, SL; unpublished history of the Labor Advisory Board, Rose Schneiderman Papers, box 3, folder 2, Tamiment Library, New York University.

7. Lorine Pruette, *Women Workers Through the Depression: A Study of White Collar Employment Made by the American Woman's Association* (New York: Macmillan, 1934), p. 107; *Employed Women Under N.R.A. Codes*, pp. 13, 21; Angus McDonald, "Labor Provisions of the N.R.A. Codes" (Master's thesis, University of Oklahoma, 1934), p. 158.

8. U.S., Department of Labor, Women's Bureau, *Wage Earning Women and the Industrial Conditions of 1930*, Bulletin no. 92 (Washington, D.C.: Government Printing Office, 1932), p. 5; Grace L. Coyle, "Shrinking Pay Envelopes," *Woman's Press* 25 (August 1931): 481-82; "Emma, Gladys, Concetta!" *Life and Labor Bulletin* 9 (June 1931): 1-2.

9. " 'Relief' in Sight," *WP* 27 (January 1933): 34; "Chicago's Industrial Information Service," *WP* 25 (March 1931):154-55; "Study and Action on Unemployment," *WP* 24 (April 1930): 256-57; U.S., Department of Labor, Women's Bureau, *Women Workers in the Third Year of the Depression*, Bulletin no. 103 (Washington, D.C.: Government Printing Office, 1933), p. 8.

10. Vera Buch Weisbord, *A Radical Life* (Bloomington: Indiana University Press, 1977), pp. 302-03.

11. Elsie D. Harper, "Back to the Sweatshops," *WP* 27 (February 1933): 89; Elsie D. Harper, "Labor Standards," *WP* 29 (February 1935): 78-79; "Homework Banned in Artificial Flowers," *WP* 18 (March 1938): 14-15. Homework had not disappeared during the 1920s, especially in the highly seasonal needle trades. See U.S., Department of Labor, Women's Bureau, *Industrial Homework*, Bulletin no. 79 (Washington, D.C.: Government Printing Office, 1930).

12. Quoted in *America's Working Women: A Documentary History—1600 to the Present*, ed. Rosalyn Baxandall, Linda Gordon, and Susan Reverby (New York: Vintage Books, 1976), p. 248.

13. "Concerning Codes," *WP* 27 (September 1933): 395; *WP* 27 (October 1933): 441.

14. "Ethics for Homemakers," *WP* 24 (August 1930): 555-56; Benjamin R. Andrews, "Household Employment: Its Background and Prospects," *WP* 25 (July 1931): 424-26; David M. Katzman, *Seven Days a Week: Women and Domestic Service in Industrializing America* (New York: Oxford University Press, 1978).

15. Margaret T. Applegate, "Is the Lady of the House at Home?" *WP* 27 (November 1933): 472-74; Jean Collier Brown, "Labor Relationships in the Home," *WP* 34 (October 1940): 417-18; Evelyn Seeley, "Our Feudal House-wives,"*Nation* 146 (28 May 1938): 613-14; *These Are Our Lives* (New York: Norton Library, 1967), pp. 324-34.

16. "The Negro Woman Worker," *WP* 24 (June 1930): 405; Ira De. A. Reid, "The Negro Woman Worker," *WP* 26 (April 1932): 204-06. Classified advertisements for and by household help have long been an index of American nativism and racism. During the nineteenth century, "Protestant American girl" informed a prospective employer that the job-seeking cook, laundress, or chambermaid was not Irish Catholic. At the turn of the century, "English-speaking" was the euphemism for non-Eastern European, and by 1920 the less subtle phrase "white only" appeared more often. Black women's problems were compounded by employer preference for live-in arrangements, which were more appealing to single, white domestic servants but not to black women, a majority of whom were married. See U.S., Department of Labor, Women's Bureau, *Household Employment in Chicago,* Bulletin no. 106 (Washington, D.C.: Government Printing Office, n.d.), pp. 5-8.

17. Elmer Anderson Carter, "The Negro Household Employee," *WP* 28 (July-August 1934): 350-51; Seeley, "Our Feudal Housewives," p. 614; Federal Writers' Project, *The Depression in Harlem,* excerpt in *Hitting Home: The Great Depression in Town and Country,* intro. and ed. Bernard Sternsher (Chicago: Quadrangle Books, 1970), pp. 109-10.

18. "Concerning Codes," *WP* 27 (October 1933): 452; Elizabeth Eastman, "This Capital Letter," *WP* 28 (January 1934): 52.

19. *WP* 28 (April 1934): 213; Amy Hewes, "Women Wage Earners and the N.R.A.," *American Federationist* 41 (February 1935): 159-60; *I Am a Woman Worker,* ed. Andria Taylor Hourwich and Gladys L. Palmer (New York: Affiliated Schools for Workers, 1936), pp. 77, 78.

20. *Employed Women Under N.R.A. Codes,* p. 7, 31; Margaret Williamson, "Y.W.C.A. Members and Codes," *WP* 27 (November 1933): 496-97.

21. Irving Bernstein, *The Lean Years: A History of the American Worker, 1920-1933* (Boston: Houghton Mifflin, 1960); *I Am a Woman Worker,* pp. 122-32; *L&L* 7 (November 1929); *L&L* 8 (February 1930); Vera Buch Weisbord, *A*

Radical Life, chaps. 8-12; "Relief for Danville Strikers," *WP* 24 (December 1930): 858; "A Letter from Danville," *WP* 25 (January 1931): 24.

22. *I Am a Woman Worker,* pp. 71-72, 74, 77.

23. Ibid., pp. 103-04, 119-20.

24. Rose Schneiderman to Eleanor Roosevelt, 17 May 1935, Schneiderman Papers, box 3, Tamiment Library, New York; Rose Schneiderman, "Women in Industry Under the National Recovery Act," mimeographed, Schneiderman Papers, Tamiment Library. She ignores sex differentials in her autobiography written with Lucy Goldwaite, *All for One* (New York: Paul S. Erikson, 1967). Amy Hewes agrees with the more positive evaluation of Section 7a and its support for unionizing in "Women Workers Under the N.R.A.," *American Federationist* 41 (February 1935).

25. *The Trained Woman and the Economic Crisis: Employment and Unemployment among a Selected Group of Business and Professional Women in New York City* (New York: American Woman's Association, 1931), pp. 11-22; Pruette, *Women Workers Through the Depression,* p. 197; U.S., Department of Labor, Women's Bureau, *Women in the Economy of the United States,* Bulletin no. 155 (Washington, D.C.: Government Printing Office, 1937), pp. 35-36; Gladys L. Palmer, *Depression Jobs: A Study of Job Openings in the Philadelphia Employment Office, 1932-1933,* Special Report A-a (Philadelphia: Wharton School of Finance and Commerce, 1934), pp. 1, 8; Gladys L. Palmer, *Trends in the Philadelphia Labor Market in 1934,* Special Report A-5 (Philadelphia: Wharton School of Finance and Commerce, 1935), p. 7; *Census of Partial Employment, Unemployment, and Occupations: 1937,* vol. 1: *United States Summary, Geographic Divisions, and States from Alabama to Indiana* (Washington, D.C.: Government Printing Office, 1938), pp. 1, 5, 7; vol. 4: *The Enumerative Check Census,* p. 15. In a brief footnote to "Labor Force, Employment, and Unemployment, 1929-39: Estimating Methods," *Monthly Labor Review* 67 (July 1948): 50-53, Stanley Lebergott dismissed this census because of its methodological inconsistencies and its unusually high rates of female employment (and implicitly unemployment). The collection of information whereby mail carriers distributed questionnaire cards, President Roosevelt appeared on movie screens encouraging the public to fill them out and return them, and the Census Bureau findings based on demographic probabilities was certainly unorthodox. But indications that women are more honest about their employment status in public, official surveys suggest that the 1937 count should not be dismissed out-of-hand where female labor force rates are concerned.

26. "Action on Unemployment," *WP* 25 (January 1931): 10-14; "Tackling Unemployment," *WP* 25 (February 1931): 97-100; *WP* (March 1931): 179-80; Winifred Frost, " 'No Help Wanted,' " *WP* 26 (June 1932): 348, 354.

27. "The Girl Is Our Responsibility," *WP* 25 (November 1931): 676-77;

Josephine S. Emerson, "In This Time of Unemployment," *WP* 26 (November 1932): 672; *Cleveland Plain Dealer,* 7 January 1934, magazine p. 6; Meridel LeSueur, "Women on the Breadlines," reprinted in *The American Writer and the Great Depression,* ed. Harvey Swados (Indianapolis: Bobbs-Merrill, 1966), pp. 181-90; Ruth L. Porterfield, "Women Available," *American Mercury* 34 (April 1935): 473-75.

28. "How It Feels,"*Survey* 67 (15 February 1932): 530; *Women Workers in the Third Year of the Depression,* pp. 9, 13. John Garraty summarized many of those studies in "Unemployment During the Great Depression," *Labor History* 17 (Spring 1976): 149.

29. LeSueur, "Women on the Breadlines," p. 185.

30. "The Girl Is Our Responsibility," p. 677; "Pin Money or 'Coupling Pin,' " *L&L* 10 (January 1932): 13; *IndW* 10 (March 1931): 141; "Women Must Live," *Survey* 66 (April 1931): 97.

31. William E. Leuchtenberg, *Franklin D. Roosevelt and the New Deal, 1932-1940* (New York: Harper & Row, 1963), p. 133; Weed, "The New Deal That Women Want," p. 183.

32. Leuchtenberg, *FDR and the New Deal,* pp. 120-21; Paul A. Kurzman, *Harry Hopkins and the New Deal* (Fair Lawn, N.J.: R.E. Burdick, 1974), pp. 11-12; *NYT,* 9 November, 5, 26 December 1933; Tamara K. Hareven, *Eleanor Roosevelt: An American Conscience* (Chicago: Quadrangle Books, 1968), p. 64.

33. Ellen S. Woodward, "This Federal Relief," *IndW* 13 (April 1934): 126-27; Weed, "The New Deal That Women Want," p. 183; *NYT,* 28 August, 23 September 1934.

34. Donald S. Howard, *The W.P.A. and Federal Relief Policy* (New York: Russell Sage Foundation, 1943), pp. 269, 278-82, 376, 481; Lewis Meriam, *Relief and Social Security* (Washington, D.C.: Brookings Institution, 1946), pp. 12-13; "Report of the Division of Women's and Professional Projects, July 1, 1935 to January 1, 1937," pt. 3, Works Progress Administration Collection, NA.

35. Howard, *The W.P.A.,* p. 279; Jeanne Westin, *Making Do: How Women Survived the '30s* (Chicago: Follette, 1976), p. 185; Gerda Lerner, ed., *Black Woman in White America: A Documentary History* (New York: Vintage Books, 1972), p. 404; also see Baxandall, Gordon and Reverby, eds., *America's Working Women,* pp. 249-51.

36. Howard, *The W.P.A.,* pp. 278, 281; *NYT,* 12 August 1936; "Assigned Occupations of Persons on W.P.A. Projects," November 1937 (Washington, D.C., 1937), pp. 2, 4. See Ellen S. Woodward, "Women's and Professional Work in the W.P.A.,"*Journal of Home Economics* 28 (November 1936): 617; Marie Dresden Lane and Frances Steegmuller, *Americans on Relief* (New York: Harcourt, Brace, 1938), p. 81.

37. "All Women, Here's Work," *Equal Rights Independent Feminist Weekly* 1 (20 July 1935):154; *National League of Women Voters Newsletter* 1 (23 May 1935); *League News* 7 (October 1933): 3.

38. Meriam, *Relief and Social Security*, p. 418; *Urban Workers on Relief*, W.P.A. Research Monograph, no. 4, pt. 1: *The Occupational Characteristics of Workers on Relief in Urban Areas*, May 1934 (Washington, 1936), p. 24; U.S., Department of Labor, Women's Bureau, *Women Who Work in Offices*, Bulletin no. 132 (Washington, D.C.: Government Printing Office, 1935), pp. 21-22.

39. "Women and the W.P.A.," *Woman Worker* 18 (September 1938): 6; Harry L. Hopkins, "Education Under the W.P.A. Program," *WP* 31 (July-August 1937): 318-19.

40. Quoted in Jerre Mangione, *The Dream and the Deal: The Federal Writers' Project, 1935-1943* (Boston: Little, Brown, 1972), p. 156.

41. Jane Dehart Mathews, *The Federal Theatre 1935-1939: Plays, Relief and Politics* (Princeton, N.J.: Princeton University Press, 1967); Mangione, *The Dream and the Deal*, esp. chaps. 4, 5, 7; Richard D. McKinzie, *The New Deal for Artists* (Princeton, N.J.: Princeton University Press, 1973), pp. 77-78, 93-104.

42. Howard, *The W.P.A.,*, pp. 278, 279, 283; H. O. Anson to Frances Perkins, 3 February 1940, Frances Perkins Papers, box 62, Married Women Workers folder, NA; Memorandum, Ellen S. Woodward to directors, 8 December 1936, Works Progress Administration Collection, box 231, October 1936 to June 1937 folder, NA; Press release, 15 October 1938, Ellen Woodward Collection, box 1, folder 16, SL.

43. Ellen S. Woodward, "This Federal Relief," *IndW* 13 (April 1934): 104, 126-27; "Jobs for Jobless Women," *ERIFW*, n.s. 1 (20 July 1935): 155-56; "Women's and Professional Work in the W.P.A.," *JHE* 28 (November 1936): 617; "Making Housework a Skilled Occupation," *Journal of the American Association of University Women* 30 (October 1936): 23-25.

44. *Statutes at Large of the United States of America from January, 1935 to June, 1936*, vol. 49, pt. 1 (Washington, D.C.: Government Printing Office, 1936), pp. 625-39; Joseph A. Peckman et al., *Social Security: Perspectives for Reform* (Washington, D.C.: Brookings Institution, 1968), p. 255.

45. *WP* 30 (November 1936): 504; *WP* 31 (January 1937): 38.

46. Editorial, *ERIFW* 1 (31 August 1935): 202.

47. Evaline M. Burns, "Amending the Social Security Act," *IndW* 16 (April 1937): 108; Robert B. Stevens, *Statutory History of the United States: Income Security* (New York: McGraw-Hill, 1970), pp. 117-19, 141, 144.

48. *United States Statutes at Large, 1939*, vol. 53, pt. 2: *Public Laws and Reorganization Plans* (Washington, D.C.: Government Printing Office, 1939), pp. 1364-76; Peckman et al., *Social Security*, pp. 80, 256-57; Meriam, *Relief and Social Security*, pp. 116, 117, 123-25, 707-08; Arthur J. Altmeyer, *The Formative*

Years of Social Security (Madison: University of Wisconsin Press, 1966), p. 102.

49. Walter Matscheck and Raymond C. Atkinson, *Problems and Procedures of Unemployment Compensation in the States* (Chicago: Public Administration Service, 1939), p. 10; *ER* 27 (May 1941): 43.

50. Lane and Steegmuller, *Americans on Relief*, pp. 62-66; *NYT*, 8 March 1937; Howard, *The W.P.A.*, p. 278; Nels Anderson, *The Right to Work* (New York: Modern Age Books, 1938), p. 39.

51. Theresa Wolfson, *The Woman Worker and the Trade Unions* (New York: International, 1926), pp. 213-14; Elisabeth Christman to James Myers, 9 May 1939, Women's Trade Union League Papers, box 20, Trade Union Women 1913-42 folder, LC; Women's Bureau to Elizabeth Eastman, 8 June 1939, Ibid.; Alfred G. Trembly, *The Distinct Problem of Women Employees,* Industrial Commentaries (Chicago: n.p., 1940), pp. 20-21.

52. Irving Bernstein, *Turbulent Years: A History of the American Worker, 1933-1941* (Boston: Houghton Mifflin, 1970), pp. 617-19; "Women in Unions," *WW* 18 (November 1938): 11; *WW* 19 (November 1939): 18.

53. Trembly, *Problem of Women Employees*, p. 17; "Position of Married Women in the Economic World" (Report of Special Research Project, National Federation of Business and Professional Women's Clubs, Inc., July 1940), 35-36.

54. "Women in Strikes," *WW* 18 (May 1938): 11; "Women in Unions," *WW* 19 (November 1939): 10-11; James J. Kenneally, *Women and American Trade Unions* (St Albans, Vt.: Eden Press Women's Publications, 1978), p. 166; Westin, *Making Do*, pp. 310-18; *Cleveland Plain Dealer*, 4 April 1937, p. 24.

55. Interview with Pauline Newman, 12 April 1978; Rae Bronstein, "Rose Pesotta of the I.L.G.W.U.," *WP* 31 (September 1937): 383-84; Kenneally, *Women and American Trade Unions*, p. 165.

56. Vivian Gornick, *The Romance of American Communism* (New York: Basic Books, 1977), pp. 40, 50-51; Staughton Lynd and Alice Lynd, *Rank and File: Personal Histories by Working Class Organizers* (Boston: Beacon Press, 1973), pp. 69-88.

57. *ER* 26 (April 1940): 16; "Women in Unions," *WW* 18 (November 1938): 7; Lynd and Lynd, *Rank and File*, pp. 83-84, 88; Gornick, *Romance of American Communism*, p. 40. On the multifaceted conflicts experienced by women organizers among their union activities, traditional social role expectations, male union leadership, and mercurial middle-class female allies, see Alice Kessler–Harris, "Organizing the Unorganizable: Three Jewish Women and Their Union," *Labor History* 17 (Winter 1976): 5-23.

58. Trembly, *Problem of Women Employees*, p. 42; Leuchtenburg, *FDR and the New Deal*, p. 263.

59. Jean Collier Brown, "Legal Measures Pass Us By," *WP* 33 (April 1939):

164-65. State as well as federal legislation ignored domestics. By 1939 only one of 43 states with maximum hour laws and one of 25 states with minimum wage regulations covered domestics. No workmen's compensation laws applied.

60. *WW* (July 1938): 3. Chafe surveys the basic ideological differences among women's groups in *The American Woman*, chap. 5.

61. J. Stanley Lemons, *The Woman Citizen: Social Feminism in the 1920s* (Urbana: University of Illinois Press, 1975), p. 199.

62. *NYT*, 28 August 1934.

63. Claire-Howe (Claire Sifton and Ruth Howe), "Return of the Lady," *New Outlook* 164 (October 1934): 34; *ER* 25 (December 1939): 139; Juanita Tanner, "Selling Femininity Short," *IndW* 16 (July 1937): 201, 222-24; "The Feminine Slant," *IndW* 17 (February 1938): 38, 58-59.

64. Becker, "Intellectual History of the National Woman's Party," chaps. 2, 8.

65. Hareven, *Eleanor Roosevelt;* Joseph Lash, *Eleanor and Franklin* (New York: Norton, 1971), p. 513; James T. Patterson, "Mary Dewson and the American Minimum Wage Movement," *Labor History* 5 (Spring 1964): 134-52. The Women's Bureau head, Mary Anderson, is harsh on Perkins in her *Woman at Work: The Autobiography of Mary Anderson as Told to Mary Winslow* (Minneapolis: University of Minnesota Press, 1951), pp. 238-43. George Martin places the conflict on a more personal level in *Madame Secretary: Frances Perkins*, p. 295.

66. Otis Graham, *Encore to Reform: The Old Progressives and the New Deal* (Cambridge: Oxford University Press, 1967), p. 169.

67. Gerda Lerner, "Women's Rights and American Feminism," *American Scholar* 40 (Spring 1971): 248; "The Lady and the Mill Girl," *Midcontinent American Studies Journal* 10 (Spring 1969): 5-14; Jill Conway, "Jane Addams: An American Heroine," in *The Woman in America*, ed. Robert Jay Lifton (Boston: Beacon Press, 1964), pp. 247-59; Christopher Lasch, *The New Radicalism in America: The Intellectual As a Social Type, 1889-1963* (New York: Alfred A. Knopf, 1965); chap. 2. William Chafe attributes contemporary feminism to the untenable gap between cultural norms and social reality, in *Women and Equality: Changing Patterns in American Culture* (New York: Oxford University Press, 1977), chap. 5.

68. Edna C. McNight, "Jobs—for Men Only? Shall We Send Women Workers Home?" *Outlook* 159 (2 September 1931): 13.

69. See Sidney Ditzion, *Marriage, Morals and Sex in America: A History of Ideas* (New York: Bookman Associates, 1953), p. 384, and Daniel Aaron, *Writers on the Left: Episodes in American Literary Communism* (New York: Harcourt, Brace & World, 1961), p. 167, for altered focus of intellectuals and writers.

70. Genevieve Parkhurst, "Is Feminism Dead?" *Harper's Magazine* 170 (May 1935): 745.

Chapter 7

1. Mrs. G.K. Powers to Mary Anderson, n.d., Women's Bureau Collection, box 1560, Married Women's Employment folder.

2. Robert S. Lynd and Helen Merrell Lynd, *Middletown in Transition* (New York: Harcourt, Brace, 1937), pp. 182, 185-86; Winoma L. Morgan, *The Family Meets the Depression: A Study of a Group of Highly Selected Families* (Minneapolis: University of Minnesota Press, 1939), pp. 18, 86-87.

3. Studs Terkel, *Hard Times: An Oral History of the Great Depression* (New York: Avon Books, 1970), p. 112.

4. E. Wright Bakke, *The Unemployed Worker: A Study of the Task of Making a Living without a Job* (New Haven: Yale University Press, 1940), pp. 118-19; Katherine Dupre Lumpkin, *The Family: A Study of Member Roles* (Chapel Hill: University of North Carolina Press, 1933), pp. 96-97, 115-16.

5. W.P.A., Division of Research, *The Personal Side,* by Jessica A. Bloodworth and Elizabeth J. Greenwood, Special Report (Washington, D.C.: Government Printing Office, n.d.), pp. 349-54.

6. Mirra Komarovsky, *The Unemployed Man and His Family: The Effect of Unemployment upon the Status of the Man in Fifty-nine Families* (New York: Dryden Press, 1940), pp. 61, 76.

7. W.P.A., Division of Research, *The Personal Side,* p. 77; Jeane Westin, *Making Do: How Women Survived the '30s* (Chicago: Follette, 1976), p. 77.

8. Hadley Cantril, ed., *Public Opinion, 1935-1946* (Princeton, N.J.: Princeton University Press, 1951), p. 1045.

9. Robert Cooley Angell, *The Family Encounters the Depression* (New York: Charles Scribner's Sons, 1936); Glen H. Elder, Jr. and Sheila Kishler Bennett, "Women's Work in the Family Economy: A Study of Depression Hardship in Women's Lives,"paper presented to Armington Seminar, Case Western Reserve University, February 1979.

10. Angell, *The Family Encounters the Depression;* Komarovsky, *The Unemployed Man,* p. 12; Ernest R. Groves, "Adaptations of Family Life,"*American Journal of Sociology* 41 (May 1936): 772-79.

11. *Fortune* (October 1936): 222-24; "Should I Take a Job When My Husband Has One Too?" *American Magazine* 115 (February 1933): 134; "Contest Results," *American Magazine* 115 (May 1933): 103.

12. T.V.Goodrich, "Should Married Teachers Be Fired?" *School Executive Magazine* 52 (September 1932): 6; *NYT,* 4 June 1939; Mrs. Edwin S. Fuller to Frances Perkins, 17 April 1933, Frances Perkins Collection, box 62, Married Women Workers folder, NA.

13. Hornell Hart, "Changing Social Attitudes and Interest," in *Recent Social Trends: Report on the President's Research Committee on Social Trends,* vol. 1 (New

York: McGraw-Hill, 1933), pp. 414-23; Harriet Ahlers Houdette, *The American Family in a Changing Society: A Guide to Study and Research* (Washington, D.C.: American Association of University Women, 1939), p. 1.

14. Ralph Borsodi, *This Ugly Civilization* (New York: Harper & Brothers, 1929); Ralph Borsodi, *Flight from the City: An Experiment in Creative Living on the Land* (New York: Harper & Brothers, 1933); Charlie May Simon, "Retreat to the Land," *Scribner's Magazine* 93 (May 1933): 309-12; Philip Curtis, "They Are Moving to the Country," *Harper's Magazine* 171 (June 1935): 67-79; Mrs. Ralph Borsodi, "The New WomanGoes Home," *Scribner's Magazine* 101 (February 1937): 52-56, 76-77; "Working Wives and Others' Bread," *Literary Digest* 123 (15 May 1937): 25-26.

15. J. Stewart Burgess, "The Dilemma of the Modern Family," *Sociology and Social Research* 20 (November-December 1933): 131-34.

16. Margaret Collins, "Careers, Limited," *Scribner's Magazine* 102 (October 1937): 45-48. Also see Jane Allen, "You May Have My Job: A Feminist Discovers Her Home," *Forum* 87 (April 1932): 228-31; Judith Lambert, "I Quit My Job: Mother Goes Back to the Kitchen,"*Forum* 98 (July 1937): 9-15. These "confessions" form a literary genre that predates the Depression. See Eleanor Gilbert, "Why I Hate My Independence," *Ladies' Home Journal* 37 (March 1920): 139-40; "Confessions of an Ex-Feminist," *New Republic* 46 (14 April 1926): 218-20. On the veracity versus the marketability of this "ex-feminist" genre, see Elaine Showalter, ed., *These Modern Women: Autobiographies from the Twenties* (Old Westbury, N.Y.: Feminist Press, 1978), pp. 20-21.

17. Margaret Culkin Banning, *Letters to Susan* (New York: Harper & Brothers, 1936), pp. 93-94.

18. Paul Popenoe, *Modern Marriage: A Handbook for Men*, 2nd ed. (New York: Macmillan, 1940), pp. 25-27, 193-96, 218-19; Leland Foster Wood with the help of Robert Latore Dickenson, *Harmony in Marriage* (New York: Round Table Press, 1939), p. 38.

19. John J. Anthony, *Marriage and Family Problems and How to Solve Them* (New York: Doubleday, Doran, 1939), pp. 154, 155.

20. Hornell Hart and Ella B. Hart, *Personality and the Family* (New York: D. C. Heath, 1935), p. 6; Ernest M. Mowrer, "Recent Trends in Family Research," *American Sociological Review* 6 (August 1946): 499-511.

21. William F. Ogburn, "The Family and Its Functions," in *Recent Social Trends*, pp. 661-708.

22. Ernest Rutherford Groves and William Fielding Ogburn, *American Marriage and Family Relations* (New York: Henry Holt, 1928), pp. 37, 46-57, 76.

23. John Levy and Ruth Monroe, *The Happy Family* (New York: Alfred A. Knopf, 1938), pp. 223-26.

24. Lawrence K. Frank, "Social Change and the Family," in *The Modern American Family*, ed. Donald Young, *Annals of the American Academy of Political and Social Sciences* 160 (March 1932): 101.

25. Una Bernard Sait, *New Horizons for the Family* (New York: Macmillan, 1938), chaps. 14, 15; Ray E. Baber, *Marriage and the Family* (New York: McGraw-Hill, 1939), chaps. 12, 13; Joseph Kirk Folsom, *The Family: Its Sociology and Social Psychiatry* (New York: John Wiley & Sons, 1934).

26. Ernest W. Burgess and Harvey J. Locke, *The Family: From Institution to Companionship* (New York: American Book, 1945), p. 504. For a critical appraisal of the sociologists of the family during this period, see Christopher Lasch, *Haven in a Heartless World: The Family Besieged* (New York: Basic Books, 1977), chap. 2.

27. Margaret Wittemore, "The Wage Earning Homemaker and the Family Income," *Journal of Home Economics* 23 (November 1931): 998-1001; Dorothy Dickens, "Some Contrasts in Women's Employment in Two Types of Industries in Mississippi," *Social Forces* 19 (May 1941): 522-32; U.S., Department of Labor, Women's Bureau, *Female Workers in Their Family Environment*, Bulletin no. 183 (Washington, D.C.: Government Printing Office, 1941), p. 44; Cecile Tipton LaFollette, *A Study of the Problems of 652 Gainfully Employed Married Women Homemakers* (New York: Teachers College, Columbia University, 1934); Mary Shattuck Fisher, "Work of College Women," *Vassar Alumnae Magazine* 24 (January 1939): 7-8.

28. "Income of Families and Single Persons, 1935-36," *Monthly Labor Review* 47 (October 1938): 728-29, 735.

29. W.P.A., Federal Works Agency, *Family Unemployment: An Analysis of Unemployment in Terms of Family Units* (Washington, D.C.: Government Printing Office, 1940), pp. 7-8

30. *Female Workers in Their Family Environment*, pp. 6-8, 45; W.P.A., *Family Unemployment*, p. 9; Samuel A. Stouffer and Paul F. Lazarfield, *Research Memorandum on the Family in the Depression* (New York: Social Science Research Council, 1937), pp. 29-35.

31. U.S., Department of Commerce, Bureau of the Census, *Sixteenth Census of the United States, 1940. Population: The Labor Force, Employment and Family Characteristics of Women* (Washington, D.C.: Government Printing Office, 1943), p. 55; Lynd and Lynd, *Middletown in Transition*, pp. 48-49, 206-12.

32. U.S., Department of Commerce, Bureau of the Census, *Sixteenth Census of the United States, 1940. Population: Families, Family Wage or Salary Income in 1939* (Washington, D.C.: Government Printing Office, 1943), pp. 32, 152; *Employment and Family Characteristics of Women*, pp. 134-35. Winifred D. Wandersee Bolin uses the term "middle income," instead of the ill-defined "middle class," in "The Economics of Middle-Income Family Life: Working Women During the Great Depression," *Journal of American History* 65 (June 1978): 60-74. Bolin's

article describes the concepts of standard of living, economic need, and the impact of changing values on the propensity of married women to enter the labor force during this period; on the earlier relationship between female employment and the achievement or maintenance of middle class status, see Cindy S. Aron, "To Barter Their Souls for Gold: Female Clerks in Federal Government Offices, 1862-1890"(Paper presented at the Newberry Library Conference on Women's History and Quantitative Methodology, July 1979).

33. Lynd and Lynd, *Middletown in Transition*, p. 181; Hazel Kyrk, *Economic Problems of the Family* (New York: Harper & Brothers, 1933), pp. 144-46.

34. See chapter 4 of this volume.

35. Roland S. Vaile, *Research Memorandum on Social Aspects of Consumption in the Depression* (New York: Social Science Research Council, 1937), pp. 19-20; Faith M. Williams, "Changes in Family Expenditures in the Post-War Period," *Monthly Labor Review* 47 (November 1938): 972-76, 977, 979.

36. Williams, "Changes in Family Expenditures, " pp. 977, 979.

37. "The Position of Married Women in the Economic World," mimeographed (Report of Special Research Project of the Business and Professional Women's Clubs, Inc., July 1940), p.6; LaFollette, *Gainfully Employed Homemakers*, p. 31; Frank L. Hopkins, "Should Wives Work?" *American Mercury* 39 (December 1936): 413.

38. "Position of Married Women," p. ii.

39. Quoted in Houdette, *The American Family in a Changing Society*, p. 36.

40. Kyrk, *Economic Problems of the Family*, p. 133.

41. "The Folly of Home Owning," *Forum* 90 (November 1933): 270-74; Stuart Chase, "The Case Against Home Ownership," *Survey* (May 1939): 261-67; Mitchell Dawson, "Home Sweet Home," *Harper's Magazine* (April 1933): 564-74; Charles Stevenson, "Housing—A National Disgrace," *Atlantic Monthly* (December 1938): 835-45; Nathan Straus, "Housing—A National Achievement," *Atlantic Monthly* (February 1939): 204-10.

42. Houdette, *American Family in a Changing Society*, p. 35.

43. Lynd and Lynd, *Middletown in Transition*, p. 206.

44. U.S., Department of Labor, Women's Bureau, *Female Employment in Slaughtering and Meat Packing*, Bulletin no. 88 (Washington, D.C.: Government Printing Office, 1932), p. 117.

45. LaFollette, *Gainfully Employed Homemakers*, pp. 69, 170; *Female Workers in Their Family Environment*, pp. 44-45; "Economic Position of Married Business and Professional Women," *Monthly Labor Review* 51 (December 1940): 1373-74; several studies on support of dependents and supplementary contributions to family income are summarized in "Position of Married Women," pp. 43-47.

46. U.S., Department of Labor, Women's Bureau, "Gainful Employment of Married Women," mimeographed, August 1936, p. 14.

47. Ibid.; "Effects of Dismissing Married Persons from the Civil Service," mimeographed, March 1936.

48. Arlene Skolnick, "The Family Revisited: Themes in Recent Social Science Research," *Journal of Interdisciplinary History* 5 (Spring 1975): 704-19, on changing concepts of the family, as opposed to the household. Michael Anderson describes and analyzes instrumental kinship relations in nineteenth-century industrializing Lancaster, England, especially with regard to working-class poverty and specific critical life situations, in *Family Structure in Nineteenth Century Lancashire* (Cambridge at the University Press, 1971), chaps. 10, 11.

49. Anderson, *Family Structure*, chaps. 10, 11; LaFollette, *Gainfully Employed Homemakers*, p. 76; *Female Workers in Their Family Environment*, p. 10.

50. Dickens, "Two Types of Industries," pp. 527-28; *Female Workers in Their Family Environment*, p. 68.

51. *The Labor Force, Employment and Family Characteristics of Women*, pp. 17-35.

52. Westin, *Making Do*, p. 229.

53. Dickens, "Two Types of Industries," p. 530; La Follette, *Gainfully Employed Homemakers*, p. 110; *Female Workers in Their Family Environment*, p. 9.

54. Ruth Schwartz Cowan, "A Case Study of Technology and Social Change: The Washing Machine and the Working Wife," in *Clio's Consciousness Raised: New Perspectives on the History of Women*, ed. Mary Hartman and Lois W. Banner (New York: Harper Torchbooks, 1974), pp. 245-53; Cowan describes the advent and numerous ramifications of household technology in "Two Washes in the Morning and a Bridge Party at Night: The American Housewife between the Wars," *Women's Studies* 3 (1976): 147-72. However, she does not make the connection between the possible need for wives' income and these desired expenditures.

55. John Modell and Tamara K. Hareven, "Urbanization and the Malleable Household: An Examination of Boarding and Lodging in American Families," *Journal of Marriage and the Family* (August 1972).

56. Hildegarde Kneeland, "A Woman's Economic Contribution in the Home," *Annals* 143 (May 1929): 33-40; Kyrk, *Economic Problems of the Family*, pp. 51, 93; LaFollette, *Gainfully Employed Homemakers*, pp. 110, 138; Virginia Britton, "Gainfully Employed Homemakers," *JHE* 30 (September 1938): 467-69.

57. Robert S. Lynd, "The People as Consumers," in *Recent Social Trends*, p. 907; *The Personal Side* contains countless descriptions of home canning.

58. "Position of Married Women," pp. 28-29. Ruth Milkman describes the important unpaid economic work of women in their homes, in "Women's Work and Economic Crisis: Some Lessons of the Great Depression," *Review of Radical Political Economics* 8 (Spring 1976): 81-85.

59. Hildegarde Kneeland, "Homemaking in This Modern Age: A Challenge to the College Woman," *JAAUW* 27 (January 1937): 76, 78-79.

60. Komarovsky, *The Unemployed Man*, passim.

61. Glen H. Elder, Jr., *Children of the Great Depression: Social Change in Life Experience* (Chicago: University of Chicago Press, 1974), chap. 8.

Epilogue

1. Lillian Shipley, "Married Women at Work" (Master's thesis, Columbia University, 1945), in Women's Bureau Collection, box 1560, NA.

2. William Chafe stresses the crucial role of World War II in women's changing roles and still provides the best overview of postwar developments, in *The American Woman: Her Changing Social, Economic, and Political Role, 1920-1970* (New York: Oxford University Press, 1972), pts. 2,3.

3. Valarie Kincade Oppenheimer focuses on economic and demographic forces in the post-1945 period, in *The Female Labor Force in the United States* (Berkeley: University of California Press, 1970).

4. Frank Stricker, "Cookbooks and Law Books: The Hidden History of Career Women in Twentieth Century America," *Journal of Social History* 10 (Fall 1976): 1-19.

5. Betty Friedan, *The Feminine Mystique* (New York: W. W. Norton, 1963), chap. 1.

6. Stricker, "Cookbooks and Law Books," p. 11.

7. Nancy Barr Mavity, "The Wife, the Home, and the Job," *Harper's Magazine* 153 (July 1926): 198-99.

8. Nancy Barr Mavity, "The Two-Income Family," *Harper's Magazine* 203 (December 1951): 57, 63.

9. Edward A. Purcell, Jr., *The Crisis of Democratic Theory: Naturalism and the Problem of Value* (Lexington: University of Kentucky Press, 1973), pp.261-62.

10. Talcott Parsons and Robert Bales, *Family, Socialization and Interaction Process* (New York: Free Press, 1955).

11. Joseph Kirk Folsom, *The Family and Democratic Society* (New York: John Wiley & Sons, 1944), pp. 619-20.

12. Jane Bryant Quinn, "A Woman's Place,"*Newsweek* (26 February 1979): 73; Judith A. Baer, *The Chains of Protection: The Judicial Response to Women's Labor Legislation* (Westport, Conn.: Greenwood Press, 1978), chap. 5.

13. Jessie Bernard, "The Family," *Radcliffe Quarterly* 65 (June 1979): 6.

14. Juliet Mitchell combines a Marxist perspective with a critique of the family, in *Woman's Estate* (New York: Vintage Books, 1971). For a blatant attack on the family, see Shulamith Firestone, *The Dialectic of Sex: The Case for Feminist Revolution* (New York: William Morrow, 1970). Ruth Milkman applies a socialist-feminist perspective to the 1930s, in "Women's Work and Economic Crisis: Some Lessons of the Great Depression," *Review of Radical Political Economics* 8 (Spring 1976): 73-97.

Essay on Sources

Primary Sources

GOVERNMENT PUBLICATIONS

Census data and related monographs, bulletins of the Women's Bureau of the Department of Labor, and research publications of various New Deal agencies were essential source materials for this study. As mentioned in the Introduction, census reports are as treacherous as they are useful in attempts at long-term comparisons. Changing definitions and categories even make comparisons between 1930 and 1940 difficult. With all the shortcomings, however, the census volumes are central. Joseph Hill's monograph, *Women in Gainful Occupations, 1870-1920*, summarizes important trends from the time sex and vocation became concerns of the Bureau of the Census to the 1920 enumeration. For analysis after that period, *The Fourteenth Census of the United States Taken in the Year 1920*, vol. 4: *Population 1920, Occupations; The Fifteenth Census of the United States, 1930, General Report on Occupations;* and *The Sixteenth Census of the United States, 1940, Population,* vol. 3: *The Labor Force* must be consulted.

Questions asked or deleted at ten-year intervals are often as indicative of social trends, perceptions, and concerns as the figures are of demographic and occupational changes. Concern over female employment and family characteristics is reflected in the Hill monograph and in a series of special reports based on the 1940 census, including: *Family Wage or Salary Income in 1939; Population and Housing, Families, Gen-*

eral Characteristics; and *Employment and Family Characteristics of Women.* The introduction to *Population 1940, Comparative Occupation Statistics for the United States, 1870-1940,* by Alba M. Edwards, describes changes in classifications and definitions as well as the changing concept of gainful employment as opposed to labor force participation. Stanley Lebergott tries to evaluate and correlate 1930 and 1940 census data with other surveys made during the Depression in "Labor Force, Employment, and Unemployment, 1929-39: Estimating Methods," *Monthly Labor Review* 67 (July 1948): 50-53.

Women's employment, particularly women in industry, is well documented by the bulletins of the Women's Bureau. Because the bureau and its director, Mary Anderson, were especially concerned with working conditions and protective legislation for women workers and also in educating the public on the subject of the economic necessity of women's work, the investigations and bulletins reflect these interests. Trends and conditions of female employment are recorded in *The Occupational Progress of Women, 1910 to 1930,* Bulletin no. 104 (1933); *Women in the Economy of the United States,* Bulletin no. 155 (1937); and *Women's Occupations Through Seven Decades,* by Janet M. Hooks, Bulletin no. 218 1947). The latter was very helpful for isolating Depression-decade trends.

The economic contributions of working women, including wives, are described in *Married Women in Industry,* Bulletin no. 38 (1924); *The Employed Woman Homemaker in the United States: Her Responsibility for Family Support,* Bulletin no. 148 (1936); *The Family Responsibilities of Employed Women in Three Cities,* Bulletin no. 168 (1939); and *Female Workers in Their Family Environment,* Bulletin no. 183 (1941). Special mimeographed reports supplemented this data: "Effects of Dismissing Married Persons from the Civil Service" (1936); "Gainful Employment of Married Women" (1936); and "Supplement to Gainful Employment of Married Women" (1939). Additional concerns of the Women's Bureau are reflected in *The Employment of Women in Offices,* Bulletin no. 120 (1934); *Employment Conditions in Department Stores in 1932-1933,* Bulletin no. 125 (1936); and *Employed Women Under N.R.A. Codes,* Bulletin no. 122 (1935). Bureau studies described the effects of the Depression on working women in *Wage-Earning Women and the Industrial Conditions of 1930,* Bulletin no. 92 (1932); *Women Workers in the Third Year of the Depression,* Bulletin no. 103 (1933); *Employment Fluctuations and Unemployment of Women: Certain Indications from*

Various Sources, 1928-1931, Bulletin no. 113 (1933); *The Woman Wage-Earner: Her Situation Today,* Bulletin no. 172 (1939). Many of the bulletin findings, along with other material on the conditions of the female labor force, were summarized in articles in *Monthly Labor Review.* In addition, the Women's Bureau published the monthly *Woman Worker* containing articles on various aspects of women's employment.

Descriptions of the incidence of unemployment and government relief policies and programs can be found in the research reports of the Federal Emergency Relief Agency: *Occupational and Sex Distribution of Gainful Workers on Urban Relief Rolls, May, 1934; Proportions of White Collar, Unskilled Labor, Building Workers, Servant Classes and Females on Relief Varies Markedly from City to City* (1935). The Works Progress Administration later published *Urban Workers on Relief,* part 1: *The Occupational Characteristics of Workers on Relief in Urban Areas* (1936); *Assigned Occupations of Persons Employed on W.P.A. Projects, November, 1937* (1939); *Family Employment: An Analysis of Unemployment in Terms of Family Units* (1940). The mimeographed study, "The Personal Side," by Jessie A. Bloodworth and Elizabeth J. Greenwood, is a W.P.A. collection of case histories which humanizes statistical data, along with the publication *These Are Our Lives,* a Federal Writers Project first printed in 1939 and later reissued (New York: Norton, 1975).

The *Final Report on Total and Partial Unemployment,* vol. 1: *U.S. Summary* contains statistics on female unemployment, and vol. 4: *The Enumerative Check Census* includes the estimated figures of this voluntary enumeration, as well as the conclusions of the director of the project, John D. Biggers, on the relationship between unemployment levels and the entrance of women into the labor force.

Biennial surveys of the Office of Education of the Department of the Interior reveal important trends in school and college enrollments. Two reports of this office deal specifically with teachers: *Teacher Personnel in the United States,* by Edward S. Evenden, Guy C. Gamle, and Harold G. Blue (1935), and *The Legal Status of Married Women Teachers,* by Ward W. Keesecher (1934).

The *Congressional Record,* vols. 75, 78, 79, and 81, contains debates over the Economy Act of 1932 and its eventual repeal. The testimony concerning repeal is recorded in *To Amend Married Persons' Clause, Hearings Before the Commitee on Civil Service on H.R. 5051* (1935). The journals of the Ohio House of Representatives and of the Ohio Senate.

(1935, 1939, 1941) are useful in following continuing efforts by one state to enact legislation inimical to married women in public employment, while the official journal of the Louisiana House of Representatives (1940) relates the only successful passage and subsequent repeal of discriminatory legislation at the state level.

The federal government studies *Consumer Incomes in the United States: Their Distribution in 1935-1936* and *Family Expenditures in Selected Cities, 1935-1936* are summarized in "Income of Families and Single Persons, 1935-36," *Monthly Labor Review* 47 (October 1938); and in Faith Williams, "Changes in Family Expenditures in the Post-War Period," *Monthly Labor Review* 47 (November 1938).

PERIODICALS AND PUBLICATIONS OF WOMEN'S ORGANIZATIONS

The debate over marriage and careers during the 1920s, the reaction of women's organizations to explicit discrimination against working wives during the Depression, and varied conditions of female employment received much coverage in the periodicals of the women's groups. *Equal Rights* (1921-40), the weekly journal of the National Woman's Party, is a mine of information. The material is biased in terms of the organization's self-styled feminism and its support for the Equal Rights Amendment, but the editions are invaluable for documenting restraints against women and, especially, against married women workers during the Depression. *Equal Rights Independent Feminist Weekly* (1935-36) was published by a splinter group during the NWP schism. The format remained that of *Equal Rights,* while the original was greatly reduced in size and content for two years.

Independent Woman (1920-40) is the monthly periodical of the National Federation of Business and Professional Women's Clubs and is an excellent source on the married woman worker issue as well as on the general attitudes toward occupational opportunities of women. The National League of Women Voters published *Woman Citizen* (1921-28), *Woman's Journal* (1928-31), *League News* (1931-40), and *League Quarterly* (1935-38). The latter carried reports on the activities of the League's Department on Government and the Legal Status of Women at the national and state levels. Reflecting their waning fortunes, the Women's Trade Union League published sporadic issues of the *Life and Labor Bulletin* from 1925 to 1940. Contents included conditions of women in industry, union organizing, strike activity, and status of protective legislation, as well as information on married women workers. The monthly *Journal of the American Association of University Women* (1920-40) was useful for its frequent articles on women's education and its relationship to work and marriage. Zonta, a service organization of women executives, expressed their concern over working wives in issues of *Zontian*. *Women's Work and Education* (1935-40) was published by the Institute of Women's Professional Relations and was good on vocational advice and trends during the 1930s.

Woman's Press, published monthly by the YWCA, was valuable because of the organization's activities with and for women along the entire occupational scale. While the concerns of the national office were not also duplicated at local branches, headquarters still conveyed a degree of interest in the plight of blacks and domestic workers that was unusual during this period.

In addition to their regular periodicals, women's organizations published special reports and pamphlets in defense of married women workers and on the relationship between their employment and family life. *The Married Woman and Her Job,* by Edith Valet Cook, and *Should Married Women Be Denied Employment?* were LWV pamphlets. The BPW sponsored *Occupational Discrimination Against Women* (1935), *The Position of Married Women in the Economic World* (1940), *State vs. the Married Woman Worker* by Dorothy D. Crook (1940), and *Should Married Women Work?* (1940) by Ruth Shallcross, which was published as a Public Affairs bulletin. *The American Family in a Changing Society: A Guide to Study and Research,* by Harriet Ahlers Houdette, published by the AAUW, contained a section on working wives.

PUBLICATIONS OF PROFESSIONAL AND LABOR ORGANIZATIONS

The periodicals of professional organization that employed significant numbers of women or that dealt with related issues were surveyed. The publications of the National Education Association, especially its research reports, *School and Society, Elementary School Journal, School Executives Magazine,* and the *American School Board Journal,* all identified the problems of teachers during the 1930s and debated the status of married women teachers. Problems encountered by married librarians were referred to occasionally in the *American Library Association Bulletin;*

discrimination, if any, was ignored in the *American Journal of Nursing*. A variety of issues related to female employment are discussed, and useful information can be found in the *Journal of Home Economics*.

American Federationist, of the American Federation of Labor, has little to say about working wives and not much more about women workers generally. Its affiliate, the American Federation of Government Employees, related its opposition activities concerning Section 213 in *Government Standard.* The rival National Federation of Federal Employees did the same, to a lesser extent, in *Federal Employee.* The short-lived attempt of the Congress for Industrial Organization to unionize government workers below the federal level and its concern with discrimination against wives working at the state level can be found in the equally short-lived *Government Guide* published in 1939 and 1940. Teachers are discussed by the weak, faction-ridden, but vocal, American Federation of Teachers in *American Teacher.*

MANUSCRIPT COLLECTIONS

Several manuscript collections of individuals and organizations as well as unpublished government records were consulted to supplement materials noted above. The Schlesinger Library at Radcliffe College has several collections of varying usefulness. For the pre-Depression period, the Bureau of Vocational Information Papers (1919-26) contains correspondence, clippings, and questionnaires on many aspects of female employment, including one folder on marriage and careers. A much smaller collection from the Institute of Women's Professional Relations, established by the AAUW, was of little use. Several collections of members of the NWP were helpful, especially the papers of Alma Lutz, who was active in Massachusetts and at the national level. Some items in the Emma Guffey Miller papers, particularly those dealing with her opposition to Section 213, and a limited number of items in the Jean Norman Smith collection were helpful. The papers of Mary Anderson, director of the Women's Bureau, are as illustrative of her hostility toward the NWP as of her opposition to discrimination against working women. The library also has two folders of miscellaneous clippings, pamphlets, and reports pertaining to married women workers and the problems they encountered.

A small collection of press releases, speeches, and correspondence of Ellen Woodward, head of the Woman's Division of FERA and WPA, is also located at the Schlesinger Library but was of little use. More valuable is her correspondence with Eleanor Roosevelt, in the Eleanor Roosevelt papers in the Franklin D. Roosevelt Library at Hyde Park. Mrs. Roosevelt's correspondence with Frances Perkins and Mary Anderson, with whom she agreed on matters concerning working women, and with Florence Birmingham, with whom she did not, are also among her papers. The Franklin D. Roosevelt collection includes official papers dealing with government employees, veterans, attorney general decisions, and memoranda relating to Section 213. A small collection of Rose Schneiderman's papers at the Tamiment Library, New York University, is more instructive on the NRA Labor Advisory Board than on Schneiderman herself.

The records of the National League of Women Voters (a huge collection in which the papers of its Committee on Government and the Legal Status of Women were surveyed) and the Women's Trade Union League in the Library of Congress added, in limited ways, to the information found in their official but sporadically published periodicals. The papers of the Women's Joint Congressional Committee are a meager collection of membership lists of issue-oriented subcommittees and some scattered minutes. These records are supplemented by the Selma Borschardt Papers at the Archives of Labor History and Urban Affairs, at Wayne State University, Detroit. Borschardt represented the American Federation of Teachers on the WJCC. The Labor Archives also contains the extensive collections of the American Federation of Teachers and of the Toledo Federation of Teachers that are of some use. More valuable, in a negative fashion, are the records of the American Federation of State, County, and Municipal Employees, which contain large amounts of material on the organization and constitution writing of this newly formed union at the end of the 1930s but not one word on the subject of married women in state employ during this period of widespread opposition. A closer examination of the holdings in the Labor History Archives, Tamiment Library, Wisconsin State Historical Society, and other repositories with strong labor holdings will undoubtedly reveal a richer, more extensive portrait of the female industrial worker inside and outside of unions than is found in this study.

Government records at the National Archives are voluminous and useful. The Frances Perkins papers contain some helpful correspondence, especially one folder on Married Women Workers. An index to the Perkins collection is located at the Department of Labor. The Wom-

en's Bureau collection contains information in departmental correspondence and reports, as well as in additional correspondence of
Mary Anderson. The records of the Works Progress Administration
constitute a huge collection of national, regional, and local projects
and reports. A sampling of correspondence and reports of the Department
of Professional and Women's Projects was informative. Along with the
records of the NRA, these collections still await a much more detailed
survey for a fuller understanding of the New Deal and women workers
than this study furnishes.

PERIODICALS

Numerous periodicals carried articles on the debate over marriage
and careers during the 1920s and on all developments related to women
and work during the Depression. Individual titles can be found in chapter
notes. Women's magazines surveyed include *Ladies' Home Journal, Woman's Home Companion*, and *Good Housekeeping*. More opinion-oriented
and literary magazines that also contain useful articles are: *Nation, New
Republic, Survey, Outlook, Scribner's Magazine, Forum, Century, Harper's
Magazine*, and *Atlantic Monthly*. Somewhere between these two categories, in terms of quality of content and quantity of material, are *Cosmo-
politan, Saturday Evening Post*, and *Literary Digest*.

In the summer of 1935, *Fortune* magazine carried a revealing three-
part series on "Women in Business," in which businesswomen are
equated with secretaries. Attitudes concerning working women can
be found in periodicals published for segments of the business community: *Personnel Journal, Office Economist*, and *Department Store
Economist*. Short studies such as *The Distinct Problem of Women Employees, Industrial Commentaries*, vol. 1 (Chicago, 1940); *Women Workers
and the Labor Supply*, by the National Industrial Conference Board
(New York, 1936); and "Employment of Women After Marriage," in
Conference Board Management Record (October 1939) fall within this
category.

The *New York Times* covers many of the events and developments
with which this study is concerned. The index heading "Women—
Employment" is a helpful guide. The *New York Herald Tribune* serialized
Rupert Hughes's story, "Section 213: A Study Behind the Headlines,"
during February 1936. During July 1936, the *Boston Globe* covered the
Massachusetts debates over discriminatory legislation and the actions

and reactions of Florence Birmingham. The problems of married teachers in Cleveland, Ohio, were reported in the *Cleveland Plain Dealer* and the *Cleveland Press,* along with letters from an Ohio senator promoting his restraining legislative proposals.

BOOKS

Many books published during the years between the world wars deal with economic aspirations and attainments of women. They often reflect the hopes or misgivings of their authors and run the gamut from popular literature to feminist polemic to scholarly study. *Women in the Modern World,* the May 1929 volume of the *Annals of the American Academy of Political and Social Sciences,* and *Woman's Coming of Age,* edited by Samuel D. Schmalhausen and V. F. Calverton (New York, 1931) both contain numerous and varied evaluations of the status of women on the eve of the Depression. Lorine Pruette's *Women and Leisure: A Study of Social Waste* (New York, 1924), and Alice Beal Parsons's *Woman's Dilemma* (New York, 1926) are feminist in perspective. *New Girls for Old,* by Phyllis Blanchard and Carlyn Manassas (New York, 1930), assures readers that the "new woman" still prefers traditional roles. A scholarly monograph is *Women in the Twentieth Century: A Study of Their Political, Social and Economic Activities,* by Sophonisba P. Breckenridge (New York, 1933). Her article on women's activities outside the home, in *Recent Social Trends in the United States: Report of the President's Research Committee on Social Trends* (New York, 1933), summarizes some of the material. *Recent Social Trends* also contains useful articles on education, population, family, government, and attitudes by noted contributors and was helpful in providing a broader historical context in which to place the subject of female employment.

Two studies of members of the American Woman's Association surveyed the impact of the Depression on a select group of New York business and professional women: *The Trained Woman and the Economic Crisis: Employment and Unemployment Among a Selected Group of Business and Professional Women in New York City* (New York, 1931), and *Women Workers Through the Depression: A Study of White Collar Employment Made By the American Woman's Association,* by Lorine Pruette (New York, 1934). The latter has been unfairly criticized for its methodology which is no better or worse than the case study approach that dominates the literature. Nor does it deserve the critical annotation of a recent feminist bibliography which cites the neglect of women in industry. Pruette's sample was limited to New York City, but the white-collar workers she studied represented 45 percent of the female labor force in the 1930s.

Books concerned specifically with working wives, in addition to publications of the Women's Bureau and of women's organizations, include the early study by Katherine Anthony, *Mothers Who Must Earn* (New York, 1914), followed by *Mothers in Industry: Earnings By Mothers in Philadelphia*, by Gwendolyn Hughes. The women surveyed for these studies include the widowed and divorced. More helpful for this writer were *Marriage and Careers: A Study of One Hundred Women Who Are Wives, Mothers, Homemakers and Professional Workers*, by Virginia MacMakin Collier (New York, 1926); *Jobs and Marriage? Outlines for the Discussion of the Married Woman in Business*, by Grace Coyle (New York, 1928); *A Study of the Problems of 652 Gainfully Employed Married Women Homemakers*, by Cecile Tipton LaFollette (New York, 1934); *Working Wives*, by Janet Fowler Nelson (New York, 1937); and *Marriages Are Not Made in Heaven*, by the same author (New York, 1939).

The relationship among women's higher education, female roles, and employment is close and complex and is described and discussed in numerous books over this period of time. An early analysis is *Women and Work: The Economic Value of College Training* (New York, 1917). *The Education of Women: Its Social Background and Its Problems*, by Willystine Goodsell (New York, 1924), reflects pre-1920 developments, while changes that occurred during the 1920s are described in *Social Change in Relation to Curricular Developments in Collegiate Education for Women*, by Grace R. Foster (Waterville, Me., 1934). The extent to which women translated their educational attainments into gainful employment is studied by Emilie J. Hutchinson in *Women and the Ph.D.: Facts From the Experiences of 1,025 Women Who Have Taken the Degree of Doctor of Philosophy Since 1877* (Greensboro, N.C., 1929), and by Chase Going Woodhouse, in *After College—What? A Study of 6665 Landgrant College Women, Their Occupations, Earnings, Families, and Some Undergraduate and Vocational Problems* (Greensboro, N.C., 1932). Constance Warren, *A New Design for Women's Education* (New York, 1940), and Robert G. Foster, *Women After College: A Study of the Effectiveness of Their Education* (New York, 1942), reflect Depression-related attitudes.

In addition to National Educational Association research reports, the status of teachers is well surveyed, often under the auspices of the Teachers College, Columbia University. Studies include *The Teacher's Contractual Status: As Revealed By an Analysis of American Court Decisions*, by Ira Madison Allen (New York, 1928); *The Teacher's Contract and Other Legal Phases of Teacher Status*, by Earl William Anderson (New York, 1927); *Are American Teachers Free?* by Howard K. Beale (New York, 1936); *Women and Men in the Teaching Profession*, by Lewis M. Chamberlain and L. E. Meece (Lexington, Ky., 1937); and *The Status of the Married Woman Teacher*, by David Wilbur Peters (New York, 1934). The problems encountered by educators and school systems generally during the 1930s are summarized in the Social Science Research Council Bulletin, *Research Memorandum on Education in the Depression* (New York, 1937).

Advice literature is popular and valuable source material for historians, but vocational advice books have seldom been surveyed. These books reveal the changing range of occupational opportunities for women, as well as which jobs are considered socially and economically acceptable for them. Publications fall into two major categories, those which list and describe occupations for women of various ages and educational levels and those which focus on self-help advice concerning how to apply for and work on the job. Among the former, for relatively unskilled young women, are *Vocations for Girls*, by Mary A. Laselle and Katherine E. Wiley (New York, 1913); *Vocations for Girls*, edited by Eli Witner Weaver (New York, 1913); *What Girls Can Do*, by Ruth Wanger (New York, 1926); *Occupations for Women: Being the Practical Information Obtained by a Study Made for the Southern Woman's Educational Alliance*, by O. Latham Hatcher (Richmond, Va., 1927); and *Jobs for Girls*, by Hazel Rawson Cades (New York, 1930). For advice to more highly trained women, see *Women Professional Workers: A Study Made for the Women's Educational and Industrial Union*, by Elizabeth Kemper Adams (New York, 1921); *Careers for Women: New Ideas, New Methods, New Opportunities to Fit a New World*, edited by Catherine Filene (New York, 1920); *Vocations for Women*, by Adah Peirce (New York, 1933); *Business Opportunities for Women*, by Catherine Oglesby (New York, 1937) *Business Opportunities for the Home Economist: New Jobs in Consumer Service*, by Chases Going Woodhouse (New York and London, 1938); and the ultimate statement on sex segregation in occupations, *Vocations for*

Girls, by Mary Rebecca Lingenfilter and Harry Dexter Kitson (New York, 1939).

Advice on getting and holding a job, usually clerical in nature, begins with [G.G. deAquire], *Women in the Business World or Hints and Helps to Prosperity* (Boston, 1894); and Ruth Ashmore, *The Business Girl in Every Phase of Her Life* (Philadelphia, 1895). This literary genre became particularly popular during the Depression and included *Letters to Susan*, by Margaret Culkin Banning (New York, 1936); *If Women Must Work*, by Loire Brophy (New York, 1936); *Manners in Business*, by Elizabeth Gregg MacGibbon (New York, 1936); and *Girl with a Paycheck: How She Lands It—Holds It— Makes It Grow*, by Frances Maule (New York, 1941). Maule combined both techniques in *She Strives to Conquer: Business Behavior, Opportunities and Job Requirements for Women* (New York, 1934). By the 1930s, virtually all of these books made some reference to working wives or to women who marry while employed. Trends and new job developments can also be culled from the pages of the journal, *Vocational Guidance*, later renamed *Occupations*.

Marriage manuals also reflect the increased labor force participation of married women. In the case of most books for popular consumption, the message was clearly a prescriptive one that encouraged wives to follow conventional roles, except in cases of extreme economic emergency. Paul Popenoe's *Modern Marriage: A Handbook for Men*, 2nd ed. (New York, 1940) is most traditional in this respect, but *Marriage and Family Problems and How to Solve Them*, by John J. Anthony (New York, 1939); *Love at the Threshold*, by Frances Bruce Strain (New York, 1942); and *Harmony in Marriage: How to Make a Marriage Successful*, by Leland Foster Wood (New York, 1939), were not far behind. Specific encouragement in this direction came from the intellectual community by way of the psychoanalytic writings of Helene Deutsch in *The Psychology of Women: A Psychoanalytic Interpretation* (New York, 1944), and M. Esther Harding in *The Way of All Women* (New York, 1939). Olga Knopf takes exception from a somewhat feminist perspective in *The Art of Being a Woman* (Boston, 1932), and in *Women on Their Own* (Boston, 1935).

Much greater tolerance for the employment of married women is displayed by the sociologists of the period whose textbooks on the family begin to appear in the mid-1920s. While several focus on family disorganization and problems, the general consensus lay in the view that changes in family functions and member roles reflected a society in transition and that a new equilibrium could be reached. To greater or lesser degrees, texts reflect sympathy with changing roles of women within the economy and note the need to alter both the sexual distribution of familial responsibilities and the underlying attitudes that determine them. See *American Marriage and Family Relationships,* by Ernest R. Groves and William Fielding Ogburn (New York, 1928); *Marriage and the Family,* by Ray E. Baber (New York, 1939); *The Family: Its Sociology and Social Psychiatry* (New York, 1934) and *The Family and Democratic Society* (New York, 1944), both by Joseph Kirk Folsom; *Personality and the Family,* by Ella B. Hart and Hornell Hart (New York, 1935); *The Family: Its Organization and Disorganization,* by Ernest R. Mowrer (Chicago, 1932); and *New Horizons for the Family,* by Una Bernard Sait (New York, 1938). Although the author is a home economist and the focus is on income and expenditure, Hazel Kyrk's very insightful and useful *Economic Problems of the Family* (New York, 1933) can be included among these texts.

Sociologists used their case study methodology to produce several studies on the impact of the Depression on family organization and especially on male roles. *The Family Encounters the Depression,* by Robert Cooley Angell (New York, 1936); *The Family: A Study of Member Roles,* by Katherine Dupre Lumpkin (Chapel Hill, N.C., 1933); *The Family and the Depression: A Study of One Hundred Chicago Families,* by Ruth Shoule Cavan and Katherine Howland Ranck (Chicago, 1938); *The Unemployed Man and His Family: The Effect of Unemployment upon the Status of the Man in Fifty-Nine Families,* by Mirra Komarovsky (New York, 1949); and *The Unemployed Worker: A Study of the Task of Making a Living Without a Job* and *Citizens Without Work: A Study of the Effects of Unemployment upon the Workers and Social Relations and Practices,* both by E. Wright Bakke (New Haven, 1940), all make predictable generalizations without questioning the sex-role assumptions underlying their theses, but they all provide poignant insight into Depression hardship. *The Family Meets the Depression: A Study of a Group of Highly Selected Families,* by Winoma L. Morgan (Minneapolis, 1939), surveys families whose life styles were less affected by economic dislocation. Numerous books and articles supplement these studies' descriptions of the social impact of unemployment and deprivation: Lillian Brandt, *An Impressionistic View of the Winter of 1930-31 in New*

York City (New York, 1932); *Cases Studies of Unemployment* (Philadelphia, 1931); Ewan Clague and Webster Powell, *Ten Thousand Out of Work* (Philadelphia, 1933); Jane Addams, "Social Consequences of the Depression," *Survey* 67 (1 January 1932); "Middle-Class Misery," *Survey* 68 (1 September 1932); Pauline V. Young, "The New Poor," *Sociology and Social Research* 17 (January-February 1933), and "Human Cost of Unemployment," in the March-April 1933 issue of the same journal.

In *Research Memorandum on the Family in the Depression* (New York, 1937), Samuel A. Stouffer and Paul F. Lazarsfeld suggest areas for investigation and also present descriptive information. The Social Science Research Council published other useful research-oriented volumes. R. Clyde White and Mary K. White discuss relief in *Research Memorandum on Social Aspects of Relief Policies in the Depression* (New York, 1937), and Roland S. Vaile anticipates many of the trends verified in the more extensive government survey in *Research Memorandum on Social Aspects of Consumption in the Depression* (New York, 1937). Two volumes by Helen Merrell Lynd and Robert S. Lynd, *Middletown* (New York, 1929), and *Middletown in Transition* (New York, 1937), remain classics in coverage and analysis. This writer found few trends or interpretations of trends that are not examined or at least anticipated in these studies.

With the advent of public opinion sampling during the mid-1930s, two volumes are useful for quickly locating relevant polls: *The Gallup Poll: Public Opinion, 1935-1971*, vol. 1: *1935-1948* (New York, 1972); and *Public Opinion, 1935-1946*, edited by Hadley Cantril (Princeton, N.J., 1951). Books written during the Depression on economic problems and public policy capture contemporary flavor and are occasionally helpful. Among them are *The Right to Work*, by Nels Anderson (New York, 1938); *Spending to Save: The Complete Story of Relief*, by Harry L. Hopkins (Seattle, 1938); and *Americans on Relief*, by Frances Steigmuller and Marie Dresden Lane (New York, 1938). *The W.P.A. and Federal Relief Policy*, by Donald S. Howard (New York, 1943), and *Relief and Social Security*, by Lewis Meriam (Washington, 1946), are virtually contemporary, critical analyses of policies. Also, see *Labor and the N.R.A.*, by Lois MacDonald, Gladys L. Palmer, and Theresa Wolfson (New York, 1934); a series of published studies on unemployment in Philadelphia by Gladys Palmer for the Wharton School of Finance and

Commerce 1934 and 1935; and *Problems and Procedures of Unemployment Compensation in the States,* by Walter Matscheck and Raymond Atkinson (Chicago, 1939).

The autobiographies of Mary Anderson, *Woman at Work* (Minneapolis, 1951), and Rose Schneiderman, *All For One* (New York, 1967), if used with care, reveal the functioning of the Women's Bureau and the Labor Advisory Board of the N.R.A., respectively. Lucy R. Mason recounts unionizing activities in *To Win These Rights: A Personal Story of the CIO in the South* (Westport, Conn., 1952). A rich, personal memoir of labor organizing in the South and of Communist activities earlier in the decade can be found in Vera Bush Weisbord's autobiography, *A Rebel Life* (Bloomington, Ind., 1977). Difficult to classify but valuable is the collection of personal accounts, *I Am a Woman Worker,* written by activist working women who participated in the summer schools for potential union leaders conducted at Bryn Mawr and the University of Wisconsin. These selections are often undated, but context easily identifies Depression-decade accounts.

Secondary Sources

DEPRESSION DECADE

Among surveys and monographs of political, economic, and cultural developments of the 1930s are: *Franklin D. Roosevelt, 1932-1940,* by William E. Leuchtenberg (New York, 1964); *Depression Decade: From New Era Through New Deal, 1929-1941,* by Broadus Mitchell (New York, 1947); *Franklin D. Roosevelt and the Launching of the New Deal,* the fourth volume of Frank Freidel's multivolume study of the president (Boston, 1973); the second and third volumes of *The Age of Roosevelt,* by Arthur M. Schlesinger, Jr. (Boston, 1958, 1960); *The Lean Years: A History of The American Worker, 1920-1933* (Boston, 1960) and *The Turbulent Years: A History of the American Worker, 1933-1941* (Boston, 1970), both by Irving Bernstein; *The Formative Years of Social Security,* by Arthur J. Altmeyer (Madison, Wisc., 1966); *The Strenuous Decade: A Social and Intellectual Record of the Nineteen-Thirties,* edited by Daniel Aaron and Robert Bendener (New York, 1970); *Writers on the Left: Episodes in American Literary Communism,* by Daniel Aaron (New York, 1961); and *The Age of the Great Depression,* by Dixon Wechter (New York, 1948). Only the last volume refers to women to any degree.

Women receive more attention in popular histories of the decade: Frederick Lewis Allen, *Since Yesterday: The Nineteen-Thirties in America* (New York, 1939), and Caroline Bird, *The Invisible Scar* (New York, 1966). Collections of oral histories by Studs Terkel, *Hard Times* (New York, 1970), Jeane Westin, *Making Do: How Women Survived the 30's* (Chicago, 1976), Alice Lynd and Staughton Lynd, editors of *Rank and File: Personal Histories by Working-Class Organizers* (Boston, 1973), and Vivian Gornick's *The Romance of American Communism* (New York, 1977), contain personal reminiscences that help humanize the material covered, along with some documents included in *Black Women in White America: A Documentary History*, edited by Gerda Lerner (New York, 1972).

WOMEN'S HISTORY

Books that survey events and developments to the passage of the Nineteenth Amendment include the ground-breaking *Century of Struggle: The Women's Rights Movement in the United States*, by Eleanor Flexner (New York, 1959), and the intellectual history by Aileen Kraditor, *The Ideas of the Woman's Suffrage Movement* (New York, 1967). J. Stanley Lemons covers social reform by women's organizations during the decade following suffrage in *The Woman Citizen: Social Feminism in the 1920s* (Urbana, Ill., 1972). Clarke A. Chambers describes reform (and, implicitly, women's activities) more broadly in *Seedtime of Reform: American Social Service and Social Action, 1918-1933* (Minneapolis, 1963). For a good historiographic review, see Estelle B. Friedman, "The New Woman: Changing Views of Women in the 1920s," *Journal of American History* 61 (September 1974).

No monograph dealing exclusively with women during the 1930s exists, but several studies of women over longer periods describe their activities and experiences during the Depression decade. *The American Woman: Her Changing Social, Economic, and Political Roles, 1920-1970*, by William Chafe, is an incisive survey that begins where Breckenridge, cited above, concludes. *Women in Modern America: A Brief History*, by Lois Banner (New York, 1974), has a textbook format but excellent coverage. William O'Neill's article, "Feminism As a Radical Ideology," in *Dissent: Explorations in the History of American Radicalism*, edited by

Alfred F. Young (DeKalb, Ill., 1968), and *Everyone Was Brave: The Rise and Fall of Feminism in America* (Chicago, 1969), cover this period and stress the decline of feminism after 1920 because of the ideological ineptitude of women and their internecine disputes. Peter Filene describes the marriage and career debate of the 1920s and discrimination during the 1930s and briefly alludes to the reactions of the Business and Professional Women's Clubs in *Him/Herself: Sex Roles in Modern America* (New York, 1974).

THE LABOR FORCE AND WOMEN'S WORK

Several works in addition to Census Bureau monographs and other government publications study work force trends. These include Gertrude Bancroft, *The American Labor Force: Its Growth and Changing Composition* (New York, 1958), and Clarence D. Long, *The Labor Force under Changing Income and Employment* (Princeton, N.J., 1958). The best survey of female labor force trends remains Valerie Kincaid Oppenheimer's *The Female Labor Force in the United States: Demographic and Economic Factors Governing Its Growth and Changing Composition* (Berkeley, Calif., 1970), supplemented by her article, "Demographic Influence on Female Employment and the Status of Women," *American Journal of Sociology* 78 (January 1973). On the debate over changes in the rates of female labor force participation and use of census data, see A. J. Jaffe, "Trends in the Participation of Women in the Working Force," *Monthly Labor Review* 79 (May 1956), and Robert W. Smuts, "The Female Labor Force: A Case Study in the Interpretation of Historical Statistics," *Journal of the American Statistical Association* 55 (May 1960). For an excellent critique of the 1910 census and the critical literature on that count, see Oppenheimer, *The Female Labor Force*, pp. 2-6. On women workers generally, see Sheldon Haber, "Trends in Work Rates of White Females, 1890 to 1950," *Industrial and Labor Relations Review* 26 (July 1973), and for professional women specifically, Rudolph C. Blitz, "Women in the Professions, 1890-1970," *Monthly Labor Review* 97 (May 1974).

Broader aspects of women's work are described by Elizabeth Faulkner Baker, in *Technology and Woman's Work* (New York, 1965), and by

Robert W. Smuts, in *Women and Work in America* (New York, 1959). Two excellent collections of documents are *America's Working Women: A Documentary History, 1600 to the Present*, edited by Rosalyn Baxandall, Linda Gordon, and Susan Reverby (New York, 1976); and *Women in the American Economy: A Documentary History, 1615-1929*, edited by W. Elliot Brownlee and Mary M. Brownlee (New Haven, 1976). The contents of the latter extend only to the eve of the Depression, but the editors include a good introduction. A perennial problem is described in Robert Tsuchigane and Norton Dodge, *Economic Discrimination Against Women in the United States* (Lexington, Mass., 1974), with emphasis on the present. Oppenheimer has devised a formula for computing the extent of sex segregation in the work force in *The Female Labor Force*, as has Edward Gross in "Plus Ça Change. . . ? The Sexual Structure of Occupations over Time," *Social Problems* 16 (Fall 1968). The entire issue of *Signs* 1, part 2 (Spring 1976) is devoted to an interdisciplinary examination of occupational segregation.

Several books and articles are helpful in describing the growth and feminization of professional and clerical work from 1890 to the onset of the Depression, although that is not always their intent. For teaching, see Willard Elsbree, *The American Teacher: Evolution of a Profession in a Democracy* (New York, 1939), and the recent *Motherteacher: The Feminization of American Education*, by Redding S. Sugg, Jr. (Charlottesville, Va., 1978). *The Schoolma'am* (New York, 1938), by Frances K. Donovan, is not as perceptive and valuable as her earlier account as a waitress in *The Woman Who Waits* (Boston, 1920), and *The Saleslady* (Chicago, 1929). For women in higher education, see Jesse Bernard, *Academic Women* (University Park, Pa., 1964); for nursing, Deborah Maclurg Jensen, *History and Trends in Professional Nursing* (St. Louis, 1955), and Mary M. Roberts, *American Nursing: History and Interpretation* (New York, 1954); and, from a contemporary perspective, JoAnn Ashley, *Hospitals, Paternalism, and the Role of the Nurse* (New York, 1976); for librarianship, Dee Garrison, "The Tender Technicians: The Feminization of Public Librarianship, 1876-1905," in *Clio's Consciousness Raised: New Perspectives on Women's History*, edited by Lois Banner and Mary Hartman (New York, 1974), and the master's thesis from the University of Chicago, 1967, "The Feminization of the American Library Profession, 1876-1923," by Sharon B. Wells; for social work, Roy Lubove, *The Professional Altruist: The Emergence of Social Work As a Career, 1880-1930* (Cambridge, Mass., 1965), and Ernest V. Hollis and Alice L. Taylor, *Social Work Education in the United States* (New York, 1951). The growth and identification of clerical occupations as women's work is described by Margery Davies, "Woman's Place is at the Typewriter: The Feminization of the Clerical Work Force," *Radical America* 8 (July-August 1974); and "The 'New Woman' Knows How to Type: Some Connections between Sexual Ideology and Clerical Work, 1900-1930," by Judith Smith (paper presented at the Berkshire Conference on Women's History, October 1974). Grace Coyle was an acute observer of trends in clerical work in her article in the May 1929 *Annals* issue.

Two recent monographs deal with opposite ends of the female occupational spectrum. David M. Katzman discusses domestic servants to the onset of the Depression in *Seven Days a Week: Women and Domestic Service in Industrializing America* (New York, 1978). In *Doctors Wanted: No Women Need Apply* (New Haven, 1977), Mary Roth Walsh focuses on the zenith reached by female physicians in New England around the turn of the century and the downward slide thereafter. The difficulty encountered by professional women is supported by evidence of problems encountered by female scientists in "The 1930's: Expansion or Withdrawal?" (paper presented by Margaret Rossiter at the Berkshire Conference on Women's History, June 1976). Frank Stricker disputes the contention that the career impulse dissipated after 1920 in "Cookbooks and Law Books: The Hidden History of Career Women in Twentieth Century America," *Journal of Social History* 10 (Fall 1976).

The complex influences of economic forces and cultural values on work roles of ethnic women is examined by Barbara Klaczynska in "Why Women Work: A Comparison of Various Groups—Philadelphia, 1910-1930," *Labor History* 17 (Winter 1976). The factors are considered in different urban areas during the Depression by Julia Kirk Blackwilder, "Women in the Work Force: Atlanta, New Orleans, and San Antonio, 1930-1940," *Journal of Urban History* 4 (May 1978). James J. Kenneally has tried, without great success, to fill a major gap in the historical literature in *Women and American Trade Unions* (St. Albans, Vt., 1978), in which chapters 10 and 11 cover the Depression and New Deal. Dolores Janiewski demonstrates the complexity of demographic variables, sexism, and union activities in "Race, Class, and the Sexual Division of Labor: The Difficulties of Collective Action in Durham during the 1930's" (paper read at the Berkshire Conference on Women's History, August 1978).

OTHER SECONDARY SOURCES

For recent studies on changes (or the lack thereof) in family economics and the household responsibilities of women, see Winifred D. Bolin, "The Economics of Family Life: Working Women in the Depression," *Journal of American History* 65 (June 1978); Ruth Schwartz Cowan, "A Case Study in Technological and Social Change: The Washing Machine and the Working Wife," in *Clio's Consciousness Raised;* and Jean Warren, "Time: Resource or Utility," *Journal of Home Economics* 49 (January 1957). A survey of sociological journals—*American Journal of Sociology, American Sociological Review, Social Problems,* and *Sociology and Social Research*—both during and since the Depression has led to the discovery of articles on working women, sex roles, and the family during the 1930s.

Speculation surrounding the impact of the Depression experience on subsequent family values, attitudes, roles and perceptions, is one of the legacies of the Depression itself. Glen H. Elder, Jr. engaged in a longitudinal analysis of generational influence in *Children of the Great Depression: Social Change in Life Experience* (Chicago, 1974). He and Sheila Kishler Bennett, using a different cohort sample, deal with women's work roles and the 1930s' deprivation experience on postwar values and roles in "Women's Work in the Family Economy: A Study of Depression Hardship in Women's Lives" (Paper presented to Armington Seminar, Case Western Reserve University, February 1979).

Two excellent biographies, *Eleanor and Franklin,* by Joseph Lash (New York, 1971), and *Madame Secretary: Frances Perkins,* by George Martin (Boston, 1976), and an article by James T. Patterson, "Mary Dewson and the American Minimum Wage Movement," *Labor History* 5 (Spring 1964), concern women active in the Roosevelt administration who dealt with the problems of working women in various ways. Monographs on WPA projects cited in notes on chapter 6 reveal the incidence of women in administrative positions as well as the relief experience of some women on Federal One projects.

Ph. D. dissertations on women's organizations were helpful: Dorothy Elizabeth Johnson, "Organized Women and National Legislation, 1920-1940," Western Reserve University, 1960; and Susan Becker, "An Intellectual History of the National Woman's Party, 1920-1940," Case Western Reserve University, 1975. For a contemporary misconception of why married women work, the master's thesis of Lillian Shipley,

"Married Women at Work," Columbia University, 1945 (in Women's Bureau Records, National Archives) is interesting. Sylvia Slavin Schram is more accurate in her analysis of the gap between public perception and economic reality in "Women Overboard: Section 213 of the National Economy Act of 1932" (Paper presented at the Berkshire Conference on Women's History, October 1974). On the fictional images of working women, Donald Robin Makosky's Ph.D. dissertation, "The Portrayal of Women in Wide-Circulation Magazine Short Stories," University of Pennsylvania, 1966; and B. June West's "Attitudes toward American Women As Reflected in American Literature between the Two World Wars," University of Denver, 1954, were helpful. Winifred Bolin elaborates on women as workers and consumers in "Past Pleasures and Present Ideals: Women, Work and the Family, 1920-1940," University of Minnesota, 1976.

Index

About the Author

Lois Scharf is a lecturer in American history at John Carroll University. Her articles on women's history have appeared in scholarly journals. She is currently the director of National History Day.